Mathematical Ecology

Mathematical Ecology

edited by
Peter Allen (Brussels), Werner Ebeling (Berlin),
Manfred Peschel (Berlin), Peter Schuster (Vienna),
Yuri M. Svirezhev (Moscow)

Mathematical Ecology deals with mathematical models of evolution processes, in the biosphere as a unity of growth and structure-building, with spring-up of new species, their interaction and possible extinction, with the impacts of human activities on the environment and the corresponding consequences for the biosphere.

The whole field seems to be a certain amalgam of suitable system philosophy, in which real world phenomena are considered through an ecological pair of spectacles with the help of system methodology and mathematics.

All publications published herein are of interdisciplinary interest for ecology, biology, economy and technical engineering.

Dynamical Networks

Edited by

Werner Ebeling
Manfred Peschel

Akademie-Verlag Berlin 1989

Editors:

Prof. Dr. Werner Ebeling
Humboldt-Universität zu Berlin
Sektion Physik

Prof. Dr. Manfred Peschel
Akademie der Wissenschaften der DDR
Zentrum für wissenschaftlichen Gerätebau

Reproduction of the original author's manuscript.

ISBN 3-05-500666-6

Erschienen im Akademie-Verlag Berlin, Leipziger Straße 3—4, Berlin, DDR-1086

Lizenznummer: 202 · 100/417/89
Printed in the German Democratic Republic
Gesamtherstellung: VEB Druckerei „Thomas Müntzer", Langensalza, 5820
Lektor: Dr. Reinhard Höppner
LSV 1095
Bestellnummer: 763 977 6 (9203)

03600

Introductory Remarks

This volume "Dynamical Networks" deals with the mathematical, physical and systemanalytical approaches to the description and the optimization of dynamical networks.

The papers are concentrated on one hand on the generalisation of well-known concepts for neural networks, and on the other hand mainly on the analysis of the behaviour of neural network models and their applications in various fields.

There is a strong connection to biological and ecological problems, because the main aim of neural network models is a better understanding of the processing of our brain and to apply the recognized properties to new computer architecture.

We find dynamical networks in the immune system and in metabolic processes in animals and plants.

Trophic networks are of great importance for getting a better insight into the complex dynamical interactions within ecological systems.

Most of the papers of this volume were presented at the Wartburg conference "Dynamical Networks" March 1988 in Eisenach GDR and some of them were presented at a workshop of GIDDER "Evolution of Information" August 1987 in Berlin GDR.

Part I is devoted to the systemtheoretical approach to the modelling of the phenomena in dynamical networks with special attention on the properties of selforganization.

In Part II new concepts for neural networks are presented, some informations are given on the properties of the Hopfield model of neural networks.

In Part III it is shown that concepts of dynamical networks can be applied successfully to various fields especially the design of intelligent networks.

Part IV presents some papers on the very promising line of application of dynamical networks, namely for solving complex combinatorial problems.

Some insight is given into the properties of the socalled thermodynamic approach and it is shown that replicator networks based on Lotka-Volterra equations can lead to very effective algorithms for solving complex structuring problems.

Contents

Knowing how the brain works
is intrinsically interesting and
could be practically useful.
J.A. Anderson

SELFORGANIZATION AND INFORMATION-PROCESSING BY NETWORKS

Werner Ebeling 1)

1. Introduction

The technical information-processing systems surrounding us are man-made. On the other hand all biological species including humans which show in part high developed sensory and information-processing systems are made by natural evolution. Doubtless the top-product of natural evolution is the brain of mammals and especially of humans. The information-processing by brains is based on the selforganization of billions of neurons, which form a dynamical network. The developement of such highly complex systems appears to be the result of a very long historical process lasting 3-4 billions of years which led to all the forms of life on earth. What means life? There are many approaches to answer this difficult question. Let us elucidate the problem of finding a proper definition of life by a 'Gedankenexperiment': We imagine that we are travelling on a space ship through the interplanetary and interstellar spaces meeting there various forms of matter. Let us assume we would meet among them also systems which receive, store, treat and transmit information. Under what circumstances we would denote these systems as living beings. Certainly we would never accept automatic stations as living systems. In all cases we would ask wether these systems are the products of other intelligent living beings. In no case we would accept an artificial information processing system as 'living'. However probably we would not hesitate to apply the term 'living' in the case that we find somewhere a population of information-processing systems going back to a process of natural evolution. Certainly we would not insist on a close chemical or biological relation to life on earth. In this way way we propose the definition:

1) Sektion Physik der Humboldt-Universitaet Berlin, Invalidenstr. 42, Berlin, 1040

Living beings are natural information-processing systems originating from processes of selforganization and natural evolution. We see that selforganization, evolution and information are are indeed closely connected.

Evolution we understand here as in earlier work as unlimited sequences of selforganization steps /1,2/. Selforganization is defined as the spontaneous formation of order in open entropy-exporting systems. Biogenesis is the result of many little steps of selforganization. The exploration of many of these steps we owe to researchers like Oparin and Eigen. Many problems however are still open and a closed theory of biogenesis does not yet exist. The already existing parts of such a theory show however clearly that processes of selforganization played a central role /1-5/. Since the neuronal networks in living systems are still the most capable information-processing systems we know, we may conclude that the study of selforganization processes in networks may be useful also for the solution of many difficult problems of modern informatics.

2. The Physical Basis of Information Processing

The concept of information is not among the central concepts of physics, however entropy is one of them. Therefore it might be useful to start our consideration with a closer inspection of the relations between entropy and information /6,7/. In spite of the fact that information is not a term of physics all information processes are intimately connected with physical systems and physical processes. Also the foundation of modern informatics was strongly influenced by the developement of physics and we should mention in this connection names like Helmholtz, Maxwell, Boltzmann, Gibbs, Szilard, von Neumann. The process of information transfer between systems is always connected with the transfer of energy and entropy. However information is not identical with energy or entropy, it stands for another quality. From the physical point of view information denotes an exchange quantity which reduces the uncertainty of a system. We assume that the exchange of this quantity occurs between two systems denoted source and receiver (Fig.1).

Information is a binary relation between two systems and it is connected always with the flow of energy and entropy between these systems. There are two standard situations:

(i) The source causes the preparation of the receiver by means of a signal which leads to a transition between two states in the receiver system.

(ii) The receiver is an observer or a measuring instrument. The reception of a signal shows the transition of the source in a definite state.

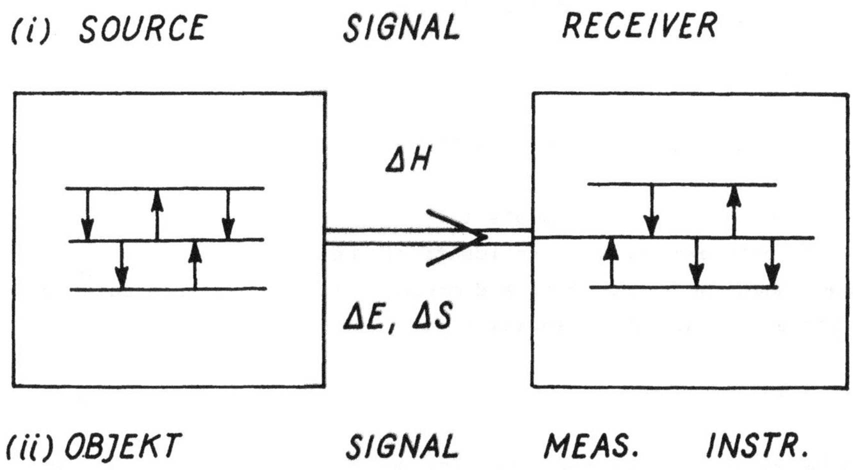

Fig. 1 Exchange of entropy and information between to systems

Preparation as well as measurement are irreversible acts and are connected with changes in entropy.
In this way information transfer is intimately connected with entropy transfer. The close connection between both term follows from the relation between Shannon-entropy and Boltzmann-Gibbs entropy. For the purpose of information theory we describe after Shannon the state of the system by a set of macroscopic state variables X (macroscopic state space). Assuming a probability distribution P(X) the Shannon entropy of the system is defined by

$$H = - \int dX \; P(X) \; \ln P(X) \tag{1}$$

Here the X is to be understood as a complete set of order parameters describing the macroscopic state relevant for the observation or information transfer process. On the other hand the Boltzmann-Shannon entropy refers to aspecial state space, the phase space of the microscopic coordinates and momenta (in the classical theory) or the Hilbert space of the quantum states (in the quantum theory). Let us for simplicity consider only the classical case of a N particle system with the phase points

$$x = \{q_1 \dots q_N, p_1 \dots p_N\}$$

and the normalized probability distributuion

$$P(x) = P(q_1 \dots q_N p_1 \dots p_N) \ .$$

Then the Gibbs-Boltzmann entropy is given by the well-known formula

$$S = - k_B \int dx \ P(x) \ ln \ P(x) \qquad (2)$$

where k_B is the Boltzmann constant.
Evidently both expressions are identical (up to the constant k_B) in the case that the macroscopic and microscopic descriptions coincide and further we have the inequality

$$H \leq k_B^{-1} S \ . \qquad (3)$$

It is based on the fact that the macroscopic description is always a reduced one. The finest possible description of the state of a system is the microscopic one.
Information exchange between two systems is always connected by changes of the Shannon entropy which are accompagnied by corresponding changes of the Boltzmann-Gibbs entropy. Due the basic inequality given above we find a corresponding inequality for the changes

$$\Delta H \leq k_B^{-1} \Delta S \qquad (4)$$

We shall give now an interpretation of this important relation.
Information transfer is always connected with entropy transfer however the opposite is not true, information transfer appears to be a special form of entropy transfer. There are other forms of entropy transfer as heat conduction which have nothing to do with information transfer.
According to our view, inside a body entropy has no form, it is just plaine entropy. However passing from one body to another it assumes a form and one of the possible forms is Shannon entropy, i.e. entropy possessing information character.
Due to the inequalities discussed above, information transfer is bound to the second law of thermodynamics. This law states that entropy be produced but never be destroyed. In the formulation of Prigogine this reads

$$dS = d_e S + d_i S \qquad (5)$$

Here d_eS denotes the exchange part of the entropy change and d_iS the production part which is always nonnegative according to the second law. In equilibrium systems entropy is maximal i.e. uncertainty is maximal and this excludes information transfer. Decrease of uncertainty is necessarily connected with deviations from equilibrium. Information processing requires nonequilibrium conditions and in general this is possible only under the condition of a permanent export of entropy to the surrounding. In this way information processing appears as a special form of selforganization of a system. Information processing is possible only in systems which are pumped with high-valued energy. This may be electrical energy in the case of present-day computers or food in the case of animals.

Let us summarize again: Information-processing is a special form of selforganization. If requires non-equilibrium conditions and pumping of the system with high-valued energy (what is equivalent to the export of entropy). Information-processing is connected with the transfer of a special form of entropy, called information entropy, from one system to another or with the change of other forms of entropy into information entropy. The second law refers only to the sum of all entropy forms as well as the first law refers to the sum of all energy forms only. So far the relation between thermodynamics and information theory is still unclear in spite of several new contributions to the discussion /8,9/. Even the old question of Maxwell's demon raises new deep discussions (see Lamprecht in /9/). Evidently the thermodynamics of information processing is still at the initial state of developement. At the same time all living systems and technical devices constitute systems in which thermodynamic and information processes play the decisive role. This underlines the urgency of the continuation of the discussion on this matter. The point of view, we have adopted here, is based on the following general picture:

(i) The first law expresses the conservation of the full energy which may assume various forms. In the process of transfer between systems energy assumes a definite form as heat or work. The value of a specific form of energy is measured by the entropy of the system.

(ii) The second law states that entropy can be produced in irreversible processes but never be destroyed. Since entropy is a measure of order (and of the value of energy) this leads in closed systems to maximal disorder (and minimal value of energy). The creation of order (and high valued energy) requires non-equilibrium conditions i.e. the export of entropy (through pumping with high-valued energy).

The second law refers to the total entropy of a system. In the process of exchange between systems entropy may assume several forms, one of them is information entropy.

(iii) The forms of entropy can have an information value if they are exchanged between information-processing systems. The quantity of information contained in a message is bound by the inequality (4). The quality of the information contained in a message is specific and cannot be measured by physical quantities. On the other hand some methods developed by the theory of selforganization (synergetics) are useful to determine the 'information content' (see Haken in /9/ and /10/). Our hypothesis is, that there exists an objective quantity which measures the information quality of entropy in the same way as entropy measures the work quality of energy. So far no method is to be seen, how to specify this quantity in clear terms. If however such a quantity 'information value of entropy' really exists, one would expect the existence of a law (similar to the second law of thermodynamics) which excludes that the information value of entropy can increase spontaneously in a system. Certainly all these questions need further investigation.

Let us still mention that J.S. Nicolis /11/ developed the very interesting new hypothesis that chaos in dynamical systems may provide the connection between information theory and physics. Nicolis states that information is a physical entity and should not be treated in the absence of its dynamical (hardware) substratum.

3. Selforganization of Dynamical Networks

In the following we define a dynamical network as a system of numbered nodes $i = 1, 2, 3, \ldots, n$ connected by binary edges (ij), ternary edges (ijk) etc.. The nodes and the edges are associated with time-dependent numbers (real or integer)

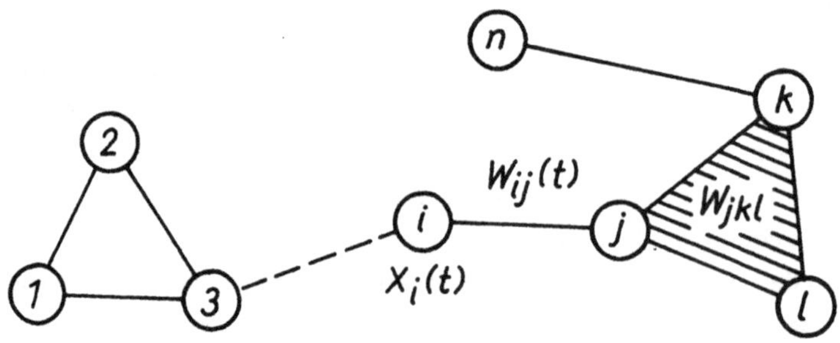

Fig.2 A dynamical network

The dynamical state of the network is characterized by time-dependent vectors and matrices

$$x(t) = \{x_i(t)\} \quad ; \quad w(t) = \{w_{ij}(t)\ , w_{ijk}(t) \ldots\}$$

A dynamics with fixed weights may be introduced by the map

$$x(t + \Delta t) = T\{x(t),\ w(t),\ \lambda,\ \Delta t\} \tag{6}$$

(where λ is a control parameter and Δt is discrete or real and positive). The map may be deterministic or stochastic. An example of a stochastic map is ($\xi(t)$ - stochastic Langevin force)

$$\dot{x} = f(x, w, \lambda) + \xi(t)$$

Introducing a time-dependent structure we need two maps for defining the dynamics.

$$x(t+\Delta t) = T\{x(t),\ w(t), \Delta t\}\ ; \quad w(t+\Delta t) = U\{w(t), x(t), \Delta t\} \tag{7}$$

We speak about adaptive networks, if a scalar function $U(x, w)$ exists which is optimized according to certain principles during the dynamics of the network. An example is the gradient system

$$\dot{w} = -c \operatorname{grad} U(w, x, \lambda) \tag{8}$$

optimizing U by changing the structure-matrix by steepest descent. We speek about learning networks if the system has to react on repeating stimuli (external fields, inputs etc.) and manages somehow to optimize the reaction or output of the system by its dynamics

Let us give now some examples of dynamical networks:

(i) mechanical networks /2/

$$m_i \ddot{q}_i + \rho_i \dot{q}_i + \partial_i U = \xi_i(t)$$

(q_i -coordinate of mass point i).

(ii) ideal reaction systems /1,3/.

$$\dot{x}_i = \sum_j a_{ij} x_j - \sum_{jk} b_{ijk} x_j x_k + c_i\ , \ (c_i \geq 0)$$

(x_i -concentration of component i).

(iii) ecological networks /12/.

$$\dot{x}_i = x_i \left(a_i - \sum_k b_{ik} x_k \right)$$

(X_i -population number (density) of species i).
The optimization of networks played an important role in evolution. For example the polypeptides (proteins) and the polynucleotides (DNA and RNA) may be considered as mechanical (quantum-mechanical) networks of atoms, the structure of which was optimized with respect to certain biological functions. The 'optimization' of chemical networks played a great role in the evolution of life from the primary soup as well as in the developement of the chemical milieu inside of biological cells. A further step in the biological evolution was the 'optimization' of the ecological communities with respect to the available space and the ressources /1/. The enormeous flexibility and adaptability of dynamical networks evidently is responsible for their great role in evolution. It is just this property which is responsable also for the ability of networks to process information.

4. Information-Processing by Dynamical Networks

As well known the natural information processing is based on the function of neural nets. Neurons are electrically excitable cells, which are able to receive, process and transmit electrical signals. The morphological structure of neurons is rather complex. These cells consist of a compact cell body containing the nucleus and the long dendrites which may be connected to neighbouring neurons through synapses. By these connections neurons may form very complex networks consisting of billions of connected nerve cells. The design of brains is not yet known inspite of the efforts of an army of researchers attacking this fundamental problem. However even the most primitive estimate proves that the genes cannot be act as blueprints of the brain. On a DNA-molecule consisting of about one billion nucleotides the storage of the brain structure is physically impossible. At each nucleotide site there can exist any of four bases, so that the information per nucleotide is 2 bits. An upper limit to the amount of information stored in the human genome is therefore of the order of 10 billion bits. The genome does at first appear to be severely limiting in the specification of neural circuitry. Assuming 100 billion neurons in the brain of mammals with each 10000 connections we get a total number of 10^{15} connections in the network. In order to programm the 10 to the power 15 connections in the brain we would need at least the same number of nucleotides in the DNA. The brain research has shown in the last time, that the connection structure of the brain developes (on the basis a few epigenetic rules and data stored on the DNA) by selforganization in the process of individual developement /14/.

What is the information-processing power of brains in comparision to modern computers. Let us assume for an estimate again that a information-processing brain consists of 100 billions of neurons each with about 10000 connections to other neurons. Let us further assume that through each connection about 1 bit per second may be transferred. Then our estimate gives the phantastic number of 10 to the power 15 operations per second, which the brain potentially could perform /15/. The most powerful computers which are available now are restricted to about one billion operations per second. A simple extrapolation based on the available data leads to the estimate that computers may reach the operation speed of the brain about the year 2020, if no new technical principles are introduced (Fig.3). However this must not be the last word. If computers could be developed, which imitate to some extent the basic working principle of the brain - selforganization of a network - the situation would change basically. In this way we see that the study of the selforganization of networks may have in future important implications for the design of new computer generations /16-18/. The first scientists to conceive the fundamentals of neural computing were Mc Culloch and Pitts (1943), Hebb (1949), Farley and Clark (1954), Rosenblatt (1958), Steinbuch (1961), Zypkin (1968) and Kohonen (1971). Since the beginning of the eighties we observe an explosion of papers on neural computing.

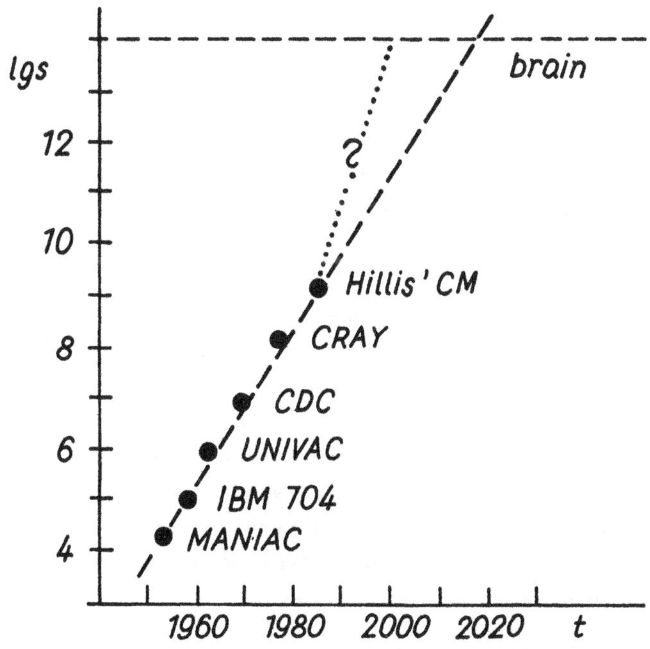

Fig.3 Operation speed of computers (s - operations per second) in comparision to the brain.

However very soon it became clear, that the nature of the information processing is completely different in the brain and in digital computers. No machine instructions or control codes work in the brain. Further brain circuits do not implement recursive computation and thus are not algorithmic. The brain is more similar to an analog computer. Further the memory of the brain is mainly associative opposite to the local storage in usual computers. In this sense we may say, that the brain is a kind of selforganizing and selfinstructing analog computer with associative memory, working on the basis of the nonlinear dynamics of complex networks.

In order to analyse the information processing in the brain in fact two main methods are being used:

(i) Systematical experimental studies of the functioning of real neurons in the brain.

(ii) Theoretical investigations on the basis of very simple network models.

We shall follow here only the second route. It has the advantage that simulations can be made relatively quickly but it suffers also from several severe limitations:

1) The consideration is restricted up to now to a rather small number of different neuron types. It is known that in reality a larger number of different kinds of neurons are cooperating.

2) The model dynamics of neurons is restricted so far to bistable systems with one degree of freedom (discrete or continuous). In reality a neuron appears to be a very complex system having many degrees of freedom and showing very complex behaviour.

3) The model connections are of simple additive or multiplicative type which is again an oversimplification of the real situation.

In spite of all these severe restrictions the model networks studied so far in the literature show already very interesting abilities with respect to information processing.

There are 3 classes of problems to which nonlinear networks were successfully applied:

(i) Hopfield-networks:

This class of networks consists of bistable neurons with simple far-reaching interactions of Hamiltonian type. The structure of this type of networks proposed in 1982 by Hopfield is related to physical spin-glasses (Fig.4). The network possesses only internal bistable nodes (spins). The dynamics is stochastic (Glauber type or Monte Carlo type) and is based on the existence of an Hamiltonian

$$H = -\frac{1}{2} \sum_{ij} w_{ij} x_i x_j \quad .$$

The dynamics is directed to minimize the Hamiltonian H.

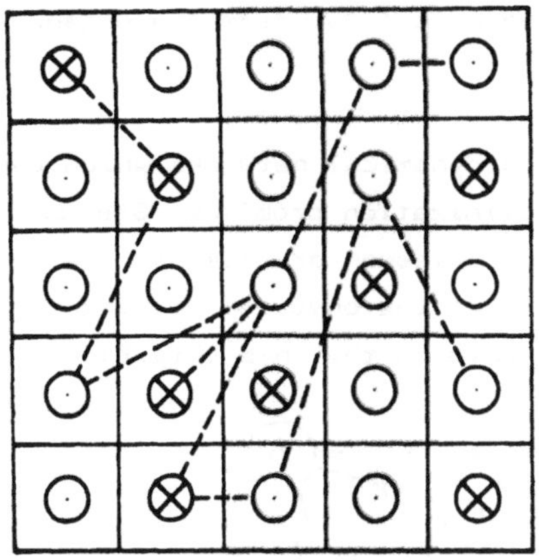

Fig.3 Hopfield-networks of spinglass-type

In order to store in the network m patterns

$$x^{(k)} = \{x_1^{(k)} \; \dots \; x_n^{(k)}\} \quad , \quad k = 1,2,\dots,m$$

the following choice of the memory matrix is required

$$w_{ij} = \sum_{k=1}^{m} x_i^{(k)} x_j^{(k)} \tag{9}$$

The Hopfield network is able to store and to recognize patterns. A given initial state relaxes after a short time to the nearest of the stored patterns. For the dynamics the stored patterns play the role of (stochastic) attractors. There exist many refinements of the Hopfield net among them a variant proposed by Englisch and Engel /19/ which uses appropriate external fields correlated to the stored patterns. We are presenting now a continuous variant of the Hopfield system which is based on the Langevin dynamics

$$\dot{x}_i = - \partial_i U(x_1 \dots x_n) + \xi_i(t) \tag{10}$$

with $\langle \xi_i(t) \rangle = 0 \;, \; \langle \xi_i(t) \, \xi_j(t') \rangle = \sqrt{2D} \, \delta(t-t')$

$$U = \sum_i \left(\frac{1}{4} x_i^4 - \frac{1}{2} x_i^2 \right) - \frac{1}{2} \sum_{ij} w_{ij} \, x_i \, x_j \, .$$

The stationary solution of the corresponding Fokker-Planck equation is /20/

$$P_o(x_1 \dots x_n) = Z^{-1} \exp \left(- U(x_1 \dots x_n) / D \right)$$

and the relaxation times may be calculated from the eigen values of a Schrödinger equation /20/.

(ii) Problem-solving networks:

Under this category we comprise dynamical networks which dynamics is designed to solve difficult optimization problems. Standard problems of this type are the travelling salesman problem and the optimal wiring problem. Let us assume that the physical problem has the size n i.e. we have n towns or n elements on the chip (Fig.5).

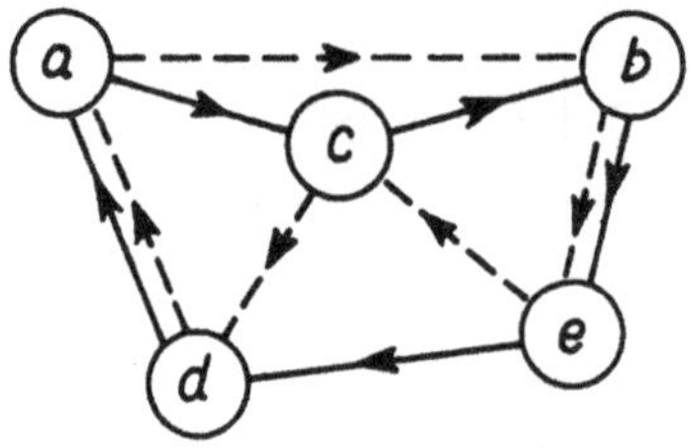

Fig.5 The TSP to find the shortest route which connects 5 towns

There are several possibilities for the design of problem-solving networks. In the pioneering work of Kirkpatrick in fact adaptive n-neuron networks were used. Voigt developed n-neuron networks of Volterra type which are non-adaptive in the sense defined above and solve the problem on the basis of the node dynamics /21/. A similar approach based on electrical networks with n nodes was proposed by Hopfield and Tank /22/. A stochastic variant of the Hopfield-Tank network was considered in /20/. Let us still mention the evolutionary approach developed by Boseniuk et al. /23/ which works with N competing adaptive networks each with n nodes ($N \ll n$). Muhlenbein et al. gave a systematical comparision of the different approaches and further developements /24/.

(iii) Learning networks:

Without doubt the study of learning neural networks belongs to the most fascinating topics in the field. The history as well as the state of art is reflected in several recent surveys /16-18,25/ as well as in other contributions to this volume /27-29/ . We restrict our consideration here to a special type of a learning dynamical network proposed by Sejnowski and Rosenberg /30/ called error propagation network (EPN). The schema of such a network is given in Fig.6 for the special case of one output line only. The internal (dynamical) nodes of an EPN have a layered structure. The dynamical coupling goes from the input layers to the output layers i.e. from left to right in Fig.5. The learning procedure (correction of the matrix w) goes in the opposite direction.

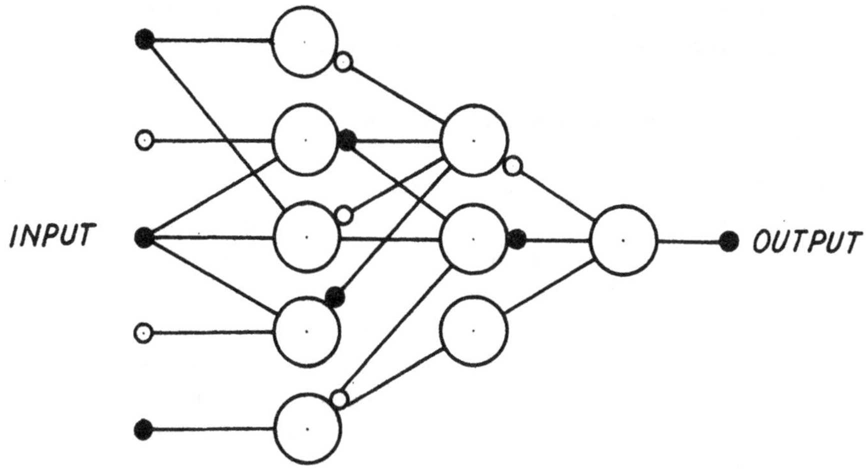

Fig.6 Schema of an error propagation network with one output (yes-no answers only)

Learning in the EPN works in the following way: A certain digital pattern is presented to the machine; the task is, to teach the machine to give certain wanted output pattern. In the simplest case, corresponding to Fig.6, the task is to classify the (digital) input pattern into two classes, the yes-class and the no-class. In general the output consists of O nodes (output lines) and allows in principle a classificcation of the input patterns into 2^{O} classes. if the actual output is x_i and the desirable output is x_i^* we define an error function at time t in the following way

$$E(t) = \frac{1}{2} \sum_i (x_i(t) - x_i^*)^2 \tag{11}$$

The sum is to be extended over the output states only. Let us describe the functioning of the machine first in a discrete time regime (Δt in equ. (7) is constant): After presenting a pattern on the input lines the first internal layer calculates for each node an activation function according to

$$a_i(t) = \sum_j w_{ij}(t)\, x_j(t) - \Theta_i \tag{12}$$

and corrects then the state of the node according to the rule

$$x_i(t + \Delta t) = f(a_i(t)) \quad ; \quad f(x) = (1 + e^{-x})^{-1} \tag{13}$$

Instead of the exponential Fermi-type function any other similar monotoneously increasing function f(a) may be used. This procedure is continued up to the output layer is reached. Then the error function is calculated and the weights are corrected according to the rule

$$w_{ij}(t+\Delta t) = w_{ij}(t) - \varepsilon \partial E(t) / \partial w_{ij} . \qquad (14)$$

Now the cycle is closed and the next may begin. One sees easily that the whole procedure will minimize the error. In other words the machine comes all the time nearer to the aim, to give correct outputs and in this way to fulfil the task.

In order to demonstrate, that such a schema really works, we have made several simulations for different types of problems /26/. We shall give here only the general results, more details will be given by Pöschel /28/. With one network which worked as decribed above the following problems were solved successfully:

1) Comparision and ordering of two 8-digit numbers. The schema is given in Fig.7.

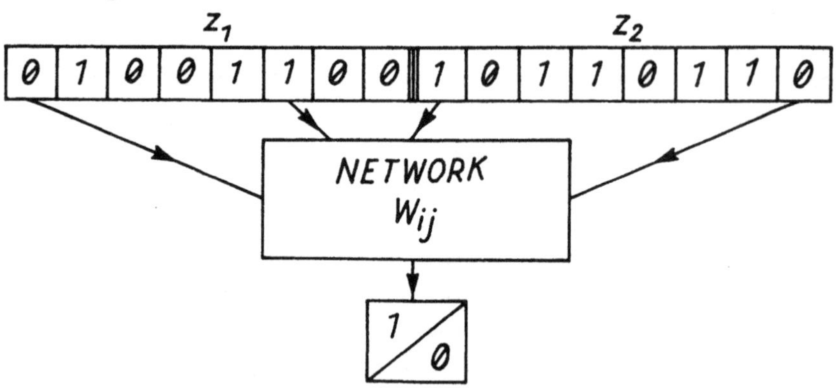

Fig.7 A network which learns to decide, whether z_2 is larger than z_1 or not.

The problem is posed to the input of the machine in the form of a 16-digit string. If the number on the left side is the smaller one, the machine should answer yes (1) if it is smaller or equal it should answer no (0). in the simulations carried out by Pöschel the machine learned the task in a few hundred iterations. In fact the machine has just to 'understand' that it is essential to 'look' at the first digits and to compare them. In spite of the fact that we present to the machine only a very small part of the possible variety of 2^{16} inputs, the machine learns to give the correct answer in nearly all cases. This shows that the EPN has the ability to some kind of abstraction. We may look into the interior of the machine during their learning. The observation can be made that the network changes the strength of the connections in such a way that the digits 1 and 9 are strongly coupled to the output, the digits 2 and 10 less strong etc.. The comparision of numbers is a problem where the networks finds a nearly trivial solution. We would like to mention however that the problem is not as trivial as it could seem to the reader who knows some mathematics and the solution before. Some test experiments with unprepared persons have shown that most persons are not able, after presenting a few hundred 16-digit strings together with the wanted yes/no answers, to find out the rule. Evidently it is not an easy task for persons to find out that the presented 16-digit strings consist of two 8-digit substrings which have to be compared.

2) The hidden XOR problem:

We present many 15-digit strings to the machine, two of them being relevant, say x_i and x_j . The task is, to present at the output yes (1) or no (0) corresponding to a XOR-table for the relevant inputs i.e. (11) requires the answer 0, (01) requires 0, (10) requires 1 and (00) requires 0. All the other inputs are to be ignored. The machine has to find out, what are the relevant digits and to determine the 4 correlations. The machine masters the task after about 100 learning cycles and reaches nearly 100% reliability. Again we may observe some kind of abst raction since among the 2^{15} input possibilities just a very small part had be presented to the machine.

3) Pattern recognition problems:

Several long strings were presented to the input and the wanted output consisted of definite substrings which may be contained (Fig.8). This type of problems is of relevance for the analysis of biomolecular sequences /5/.

Fig.8 recognition of substrings by the EPN

The machine is also well able to fulfil the task to find out substrings. Another problem which has studied is the recognition of letters /27/. Here the input consisted of 150 elements arranged in a 10 by 15 matrix. The machine was trained with 12 alphabets written by different authors. The wanted output was a 26-digit string with just one 1 marking the input letter. After about 2000 learning cycles the machine fulfilled the task to recognize a presented letter with 99% reliability. However letters written by authors unknown to the machine were recognized only with about 70% reliability. This shows that the EPN in the present version cannot compete with professional recognition methods.

A disadvantage of the Sejnowski-Rosenberg network is the fact that the connections between the nodes are of additive type (eq.(12)). Our proposal is therefore to use better a combination of linear and multiplicative combinations of type

$$a_i(t) = (1 - \alpha) \sum_j w_{ij} x_j + \alpha \prod_j x_j^{w_{ij}} - \theta_i \qquad (15)$$

In the sense of Peschel and Mende /13/ this would correspond to a transition from pure Volterra connections to Riccati connections or mixed forms respectively. Let us further mention that also an EPN with continuous time may be introduced based on a set of equations of type

$$\dot{x}_i = a_i^+ + \tau^{-1} x_i(1 - x_i^2)$$

$$w_{ij} = - \varepsilon \partial E / \partial w_{ij} \quad . \qquad (16)$$

Here a_i^+ denotes the input from the foregoing layer.

At the end of this section let as stress all of the examples presented here are not able to solve problems of optimization, classification, recognition etc. in a better way than other methods developed by specialists. We would like to underline however two facts which may be of interest:

(i) Nonlinear dynamical networks are quite universal. A sufficiently flexible network machine is well able to solve problems of different nature.

(ii) No special programming specific for the task is required. The dynamics of adaptive networks allows a special kind of 'self-organization' of the network which is appropriate to the given task. There is no need to underline that both these properties remind in a rudimentary way the functioning of brain. However a word of warning is to say here. All this is just a beginning and we are still far from a real understanding of the information-processing capabilities of dynamic networks.

5. Conclusions

The study of nonlinear dynamical networks is a new field of science which is interesting per se and with respect to many important applications. Under the necessary physical condition that the system is pumped with high-valued energy and that the appropriate couplings and nonlinearities are provided, networks are able to selforganization. The spectrum of static structures and dynamic behaviour is surprisingly rich. The highest form of selforganisation of networks is information processing, which is possible under special conditions as shown above. A deeper understanding of these processes should be the subject of further research in this field.

References

/1/ Ebeling, W. und R. Feistel: Physik der Selbstorganisation und Evolution. Akademie-verlag Berlin 1982 und 1986

/2/ Feistel, R. and W. Ebeling: Evolution of Complex Systems. Verl. d. Wiss., Berlin 1989

/3/ Eigen, M. and P. Schuster: The Hypercycle. Naturwiss. 64(1977)541; 65(1978)341

/4/ Schuster, P.: Dynamics of Molecular Evolution. Physica 22D(1986)100

/5/ Ebeling, W., Feistel, R. and H. Herzel: Dynamics and Complexity of Biomolecules. Physica Scripta 35(1987)761

/6/ Völz, H.: Information I u. II. Akademie-Verlag Berlin 1982 u.1983

/7/ Ebeling, W.: Chaos, Ordnung und Information. Urania-Verlag Leipzig 1989

/8/ Wolkenstein, M.W.: Entropie und Information. Nauka Moskva 1986 (in Russ.), Dt. Ubers. Akademie-Verlag Berlin 1989.

/9/ Lamprecht, I. and A.I. Zotin (Eds.): Thermodynamics and Regulation of Biological Processes. De Gruyter Berlin New York 1985

/10/ Haken, H.(Ed.): Complex Systems - Operational Approaches in Neurobiology, Physics, and Computers. Springer-Verlag Berlin-Heidelberg-New York 1985

/11/ Nicolis, J.S.: Chaotic Dynamics Applied to Information Processing Akademie-Verlag Berlin 1987

/12/ Ebeling, W., Peschel, M. (Eds.): Cooperation and Competition in Dynamical Systems. Akademie-Verlag Berlin 1985

/13/ Peschel, M. and W. Mende: The Predator-Prey Model: Do we Live in in a Volterra World? Akademie-Verlag Berlin 1986

/14/ Lumsden, C.J., Wilson, E.O.: Genes, Mind and Culture. Harvard University Press. Cambridge Mass. 1981

/15/ Hillis, W.D.: The Connection Machine. Sci. American 256,6(1987)86

/16/ Ebeling, W.: Physik komplexer nichtlinearer Netzwerke und neue Wege der Informationsverarbeitung. Sitzungsberichte der AdW der DDR. Akademie-Verlag Berlin 1987

/17/ Kohonen, T.: An Introduction to Neural Computing. Neural Networks 1(1988)3

/18/ Grossberg, S.: Nonlinear Neural Networks. Neural Networks 1(1988)17.

/19/ Englisch, H., Engel, A.: Contr. to this volume.
Engel, A., Englisch, H. and A. Schutte: Improved Retrieval in Neural Networks with External Fields. Preprint HUB Berlin 1988

/20/ Ebeling, W., Schimansky-Geier: Transition Phenomena in Multi-Dimensional Systems- Models of Evolution. In: Noise in Nonlinear Dynamical Systems (F. Moss, P. McClintock, eds.). Cambridge University University Press, Cambridge Mass. 1989
Press. Cambridge Mass. 1989

/21/ Voigt, H.-M.: Contr. to this volume.

/22/ Hopfield, J.J., Tank, D.W.: Computing RC-Networks. Biolog. Cybernetics 52(1985)141

/23/ Boseniuk, T.: Contr. to this volume.
Boseniuk, T., Ebeling, W., Engel, A.: Boltzmann and Darwin Strategies in Complex Optimization. Phys. Lett. 125(1987)307
Boseniuk, T., Ebeling, W.: Optimization of NP-Complete Problems by Boltzmann-Darwin Strategies Including Life-Cycles. Europhys. Lett. 6(1988)107; Evolution Strategies in Complex Optimization The TSP. Syst.Anal.Model.Simul. 5(1988)411

/24/ Mühlenbein, H.: Contr. to this volume.
Mühlenbein, H. et al.: Parallel Computing 4(1987)269
Schwefel, H.P.: Numerical Optimization of Computer Models. Wiley Chichester 1981

/25/ McClelland, J.L., Rumelhard, D.E. (Eds.):Parallel Distributed Processing. MIT Press Cambridge Mass. 1986

/26/ Ebeling, W., Boseniuk, T., Pöschel, T.: Simulation of Learning Networks. Proc. Parcella Berlin 1988

/27/ Körner, E.: Contr. to this volume.

/28/ Pöschel, T.: Contr. to this volume.

/29/ Van der Meer, M.: Contr. to this volume.

/30/ Sejnowski, T.J., Rosenberg, C.R.: Parallel Networks that Learn to Pronounce English Text. Complex Systems 1(1987)145

Simulation of Dynamical Networks with Generalized Exponentials

M.Peschel Academy of Sciences of GDR, Centre for Scientific Instruments
A.R.Druschke Borgsdorf b. Oranienburg
F.Breitenecker ,Institute for Technical Mathematics, Technical University, Vienna.
I.Santibáñez-Koref Academy of Sciences of GDR, Centre for Scientific Instruments

Abstract

A unified description is given for the MSD-system with its three different modes of autonomous motions. The chosen approach based on associative finite algebras is then generalized for a 4-dimensional unified description of a gyroscope.
This approach is used for local model approximations for any network of dynamical systems described by ordinary differential equations.
For simulation purposes recursion formulas of different numerical order are derived.

Key-words:finite algebras, hypercomplex numbers, MSD-system, networks, local models, simulation, recursion.

1.Introduction

Local models reflect the state-variable information at the reference point up to a certain order of derivatives of the state-variables after time t.
Every local model concept can be used as a simulation approach for any dynamical network which allows a description of its behaviour by a set of ordinary differential equations.
The specific of this paper is to check the feasibility of generalized exponential elements on an associative finite algebra as concepts for linear local models.
Two cases are considered in some detail in this paper, namely a unified description of the very well-known MSD-system and a generalisation of the kinetics of the Euler gyroscope.
Some features of these two examples which might be also contained in the general approach described here seem to be shared by both.

- In any case for a complete description of the dynamics of the corresponding physical system we need some finite algebras, each of which reflects exactly one behavioural mode.
- To every behavioural mode there corresponds in the respective Euclidian space a certain coordinate system which is responsible for a mode-orientated computation of the components of the tangential vector of the system-trajectory.
- The local model motion with fixed parameters of the local model can be interpreted as a uniform motion on a mode-specific hyperplane combined with an exponential expansion or contraction.

Using the generalized exponentials as local models for the simulation of Dynamical Networks they are Euler-like methods of first order, if we adapt the tangential vectors only. If we shift the measurement information from some state-variables to higher derivatives of others we can construct then higher order numerical simulation methods, but we have then to solve the difficulty to determine reference state-variable values for all excluded state-variables in our simulation model, which is always a first order recursion method.

2. The MSD-System as the basic module of a network of gyroscopes with parallel rotation axis.

To a certain degree all the following considerations are based on the exponential function.
The exponential function:

$$z(t)=e^{At}$$

obeys the law of natural growth

$$\frac{dz}{dt}=Az$$

with the general solution

$$z(t)=z(0)\cdot e^{At}$$

For the corresponding inhomogenous equation holds

$$\frac{dz}{dt}=Az+E(t)$$

Here *E(t)* is an arbitrary integrable excitation function.
The inhomogenous differential equation has the following general solution:

$$z(t)=e^{At}z(0)+\int_0^t e^{A(t-t')}E(t')dt'$$

For the calculations with the exponential function the following Taylor-series expansion is important:

$$e^{At}=\sum\frac{A^i t^i}{i!}$$

We introduce a variable u to provide the possibility for a two-dimensional generalisation of the exponential function.
For this purpose we put

$z=x+u\cdot y$

$A=a+u\cdot w$

z,A are now so-called hypercomplex numbers.
The sum and difference of these hypercomplex numbers is defined by the corresponding operations of two-dimensional vectors.
Problems arise for the multiplication.
By multiplying two linear forms in the usual way we leave the frame of the two-dimensional linear forms here. We need a reduction formula, which substitutes a suitable linear expression for u^2.
Generally the following reduction is possible:

$u^2=\alpha+\beta u$

By quadrate complementation we can see that only three different reduction formulas are of importance.

$u^2=-1$ complex numbers
$u^2=+1$ binary numbers
$u^2=0$ dual numbers

Then for the product of two hypercomplex numbers we get the following expression:

$$(x_1+uy_1)(x_2+uy_2)=(x_1x_2+u^2y_1y_2)+u(x_1y_2+x_2y_1)$$

For the computation of the quotient of two hypercomplex numbers we apply the notion of a conjugate number.
For

$$z=x+uy$$

the so-called conjugate number $\bar{z}$ is introduced by:

$$\bar{z} = x - uy$$

With z and $\bar{z}$ we can define a norm:

$$N(z) = z \cdot \bar{z} = x \cdot x - u^2 \cdot y \cdot y$$

Obviously for $u^2=1$ and $u^2=0$ we meet nonvanishing numbers $z \neq 0$ with

$$N(z) = 0$$

Therefore it can occur, that the corresponding multiplication has zero-divisors.
With the normfunctions $N(z)$ the division can be reduced on multiplication.
Division:

$$\frac{(x_1 + uy_1)}{(x_2 + uy_2)} = \frac{(x_1 + uy_1)(x_2 - uy_2)}{N(z_2)}$$

Therefore all arithmetic operations can be performed, although divisions only then, when the nominator is not a number with vanishing norm.
These arithmetic operations are commutative and associative
Based on these arithmetics we now discuss the two-dimensional exponential differential equation.

$$\frac{dz}{dt} = Az + E, \quad E = E_x(t) + u \cdot E_y(t)$$

with all variables and parameters now being hypercomplex numbers.
If we express this exponential differential equation in real components, we get:

$$\frac{dx}{dt} = ax + u^2 wy + Ex(t)$$

$$\frac{dy}{dt} = ay + wxs + Ey(t)$$

By differentiation and assuming $E=0$ we achieve at once the following expression:

$$\frac{d^2x}{dt^2} = 2a\frac{dx}{dt} + (u^2w^2 - a^2)x$$

The same differential equation is obtained for the state variable $y(t)$.
This is obviously the differential equation of the very well-known MSD-system with the corresponding autonomous differential equation:

$$\frac{d^2x}{dt^2} + D_{ae}\frac{dx}{dt} + Cx = 0$$

Here is D_{ae} the Newton friction and C the elasticity constant of the spring.
By comparison with the above derived expression we obtain:

$$-D_{ae} = 2a$$

$$-C = u^2w^2 - a^2$$

$$R = \left(\frac{D_{ae}}{2}\right)^2 - C$$

is the so called resolvent of the MSD-system.
We recognize from this comparison the following interesting facts:
- Oscillating mode corresponds to $u^2=-1$
- Nonoscillating mode corresponds to $u^2=+1$
- Aperiodic limit case corresponds to $u^2= 0$

We shall now interpret the autonomous MSD-motion as a special gyroscope motion.
For this purpose we consider the following two kinds of "polar"-coordinate transformations:

$$x = r\cos_u(\phi)$$

$$y = r\sin_u(\phi)$$

with

for $u^2= 1$	for $u^2=-1$	for $u^2=0$
$\cos_u(\phi) = \cosh(\phi)$	$\cos_u(\phi) = \cos(\phi)$	$\cos_u(\phi) = 1$
$\sin_u(\phi) = \sinh(\phi)$	$\sin_u(\phi) = \sin(\phi)$	$\sin_u(\phi) = 0$

The corresponding differentials will then be transformed as follows:

$$\frac{dx}{dt} = ax + u^2 wy$$

$$\frac{dy}{dt} = ay + wx$$

But here is

$$a = \frac{d\theta}{dt}$$

with

$$r = e^\theta \text{and } w = \frac{d\phi}{dt}$$

We shall now interpret these relations for the case *a=const., w=const.*
According to the above performed computations it is clear, that with constant parameters *a* and *w* the derived equations coincide with the differential equation description for the MSD-system.
On the other hand from the polar coordinate description we obtain the following transparent geometrical interpretation for the corresponding autonomous motions.
For $u^2=-1$ we obtain a uniform motion circle (for example the unit circle) with the angle velocity *w*. The radius of this circle depends on whether the sign of *a* either uniformly extends (for *a*>0) or contracts (for *a*<0).
For *a*=0 the motion is reduced on a uniform motion on a circle,for *w*=0 the motion will become a uniform radial expansion.
Obviously in this case the motion of a nonexcited MSD-systems is that of a gyroscope with a constant rotation impulse orthogonal on the coordinate plane.
For $u^2=1$ the unit circle:

$$x^2 + y^2 = 1$$

will be substituted by the unit hyperbola

$$x^2 - y^2 = 1$$

Now with a constant velocity we run along one branch of this hyperbola uniformly, whereas, depending on the sign of *a*, this reference motion will be combined with a uniform expansion or contraction.
For $u^2=0$ we meet a uniform reference motion now on a straight line:

$$x^2 = 1$$

We now make use of the above derived results for the simulation of arbitrary motions at first only on a two-dimensional phase plane.

3. MSD-simulation of 2-nd order systems

An arbitrary plane kinetics may be described by the two state variables x(t) and y(t).
We are interested in expressing this kinetics in trigonometric or hyperbolic polar coordinates.
In 1. we obtained the following relations between the corresponding differentials in cartesian and polar coordinates

$$\frac{dx}{dt} = \frac{d\theta}{dt}x + u^2\frac{d\phi}{dt}y$$

$$\frac{dy}{dt} = \frac{d\theta}{dt}y + \frac{d\phi}{dt}x$$

In the sense of a local model we can in every point of time describe the real kinetics by a local MSD-system preserving tangent values if we admit that the parameters of this MSD-system:

$$a = \frac{d\theta}{dt} \text{ and } w = \frac{d\phi}{dt}$$

must be readjusted time after time.

Therefore the real kinetics can be interpreted as the kinetics of a plane gyroscope which nonuniformly expands or contracts and which uses as reference the unit circle, the unit hyperbola or a straight line. Also the reference motions on these curves will now no longer be uniform motions.
The nonuniformities in *a(t)* and *w(t)* now result from the nonlinear internal interaction, but adding an excitation function *E(t)* to the MSD-system already leads to welldetermined nonuniform motions.
If we solve the relations between the differentials after *a* and *w* we get:

$$a = \frac{\left(x\frac{dx}{dt} - u^2 y \frac{dy}{dt}\right)}{\left(x \cdot x - u^2 y \cdot x\right)} \text{ and } w = \frac{\left(x\frac{dy}{dt} - y\frac{dx}{dt}\right)}{\left(x \cdot x - u^2 y \cdot y\right)}$$

4. The universality of networks of coupled MSD-systems

Based on the above given informations we shall here show that arbitrary dynamical systems can be described as networks built up from coupled plane gyroscopes.
This does not mean that an arbitrary given physical kinetics is a network of plane gyroscopes, we only want to show, that the behaviour of such a global physical system can be described by a network of MSD-systems for the purpose of numerical computations in the sense of simulation.
The original system is assumed to admit a description in the form of a set of ordinary differential equations.

$$\frac{dx_i}{dt} = f_i(\ldots) \quad i = 1, 2, \ldots, n$$

In these functions the arguments can be the state variables, excitation from the environment, also the time t can be represented explicitly in the right-hand sides of these equation.

<u>Circle Dynamics Simulation</u>
For n even we make a partition of all state variables into pairs in an arbitrary manner, for n odd we add the time t as an additional state-variable.
Now we simulate every couple of state variables *x* and *y* as following two first order differential equations:

$$\frac{dx}{dt} = f(\ldots), \quad \frac{dy}{dt} = g(\ldots)$$

Here we put $u^2 = -1$ and work with corresponding differential equations for the parameters of an oscillation MSD-system:

$$\frac{d\theta}{dt} = \frac{xf + yg}{r^2}$$

$$\frac{d\phi}{dt} = \frac{(xg - yf)}{r^2}$$

with

$$r^2 = x \cdot x + y \cdot y$$

The general solution of the corresponding exponential differential equation as pointed out above is:

$$z(t) = z(0) \cdot e^{At}$$

If we rewrite this equation incrementally we get the following recursion of first order

$$z' = z \cdot e^{AD}$$

Here we have *z'=z(t+D), z=z(t)* and *D* is a time step-width.
After hypercomplex multiplication we get the following recursion scheme:

$$x' = e^{\frac{d\theta}{dt}D}\left(x\cos\left(\frac{d\phi}{dt}D\right) - y\sin\left(\frac{d\phi}{dt}D\right)\right)$$

$$y' = e^{\frac{d\theta}{dt}D}\left(y\cos\left(\frac{d\phi}{dt}D\right) + x\sin\left(\frac{d\phi}{dt}D\right)\right)$$

For the derivatives we have of course here to substitute the above given expressions for

$$\frac{d\theta}{dt} \text{ and } \frac{d\phi}{dt}$$

Because we meet here only an adaptation up to first order derivatives the numerical quality of the corresponding simulation method is only of order 1.

<u>Generalized Circle Dynamics</u>
We completely repeat the considerations above but using the more flexible reduction approach:

$$u^2 = \alpha + u\beta$$

The corresponding exponential differential equation

$$\frac{dz}{dt} = Az$$

has now the following real counterpart

$$\frac{dx}{dt} = G_{11}x + G_{12}y$$

$$\frac{dy}{dt} = G_{21}x + G_{22}y$$

Here G_{ij} are now arbitrary real numbers.
We obtain now the following relations

$$G_{11} = a, \quad G_{12} = \alpha w, \quad G_{21} = w, \quad G_{22} = a + \beta w$$

The identification of the local model now needs an adjustment up to the second order of both state variables.
From

$$\frac{dx}{dt}, \frac{d^2x}{dt^2} \text{ and } \frac{dy}{dt}, \frac{d^2y}{dt^2}$$

we now compute in the reference point of time t the values of G_{ij}.
From these values we can compute uniquely a, w, α and β thus fixing the corresponding generalized function needed for the recursion

$$z' = z \cdot e^{AD}$$

The numerical quality of this simulation is already of order 2.

<u>A third-order MSD simulation method</u>
Now we develop for every state-variable separately a corresponding MSD simulation scheme. The state variable x under consideration follows the differential equation

$$\frac{dx}{dt} = f(\ldots)$$

We again start from general MSD-systems differential equation

$$\frac{dz}{dt} = Az$$

with $A=a+uw$, $z=x+uy$.
But now we cannot assume that we are able to measure $x(t)$ as well as $y(t)$.
Now we assume that we can measure only $x(t)$ and the corresponding derivatives up to the necessary order.
For the parameter adjustion in this case we choose the following approach:

1. If already holds

$$\frac{dz}{dt} = A_1 z$$

for a real value A_1, then we have

$$\frac{dx}{dt}=A_1, \quad \frac{d^2x}{dt^2}=A_1\frac{dx}{dt}$$

that means the matrix

$$\begin{pmatrix} \frac{dx}{dt} & x \\ \frac{d^2x}{dt^2} & \frac{dx}{dt} \end{pmatrix}$$

is degenerated.
In this case we have to iterate with:

$$x'=x\cdot e^{A_1 D}$$

(Natural Recursion see /3/).

2. In any case it must hold

$$\frac{d^2z}{dt^2}=A_1\frac{dz}{dt}+A_2z$$

with real parameters A_1 and A_2, because $x(t)$ and $y(t)$ as solutions of a local MSD-system obey in any case a certain linear 2-nd order differential equation with constant coefficients.
We estimate the real parameters A_1 and A_2 according to the following two equations:

$$\frac{d^2x}{dt^2}=A_1\frac{dx}{dt}+A_2x$$

$$\frac{d^3x}{dt^3}=A_1\frac{d^2x}{dt^2}+A_2\frac{dx}{dt}$$

Because the matrix of this linear system of equations after we escaped case 1 is a regular one, the parameters A_1 and A_2 can be uniquely determined.
Because for determining this systems of equations we need derivatives up to the third order the resulting numerical integration method obviously is of order 3.
Because $A_1=-D_{ae}$ and $A_2=-C$ of a corresponding MSD-system now u^2 (the mode), a and w can be uniquely determined.

3. Recursion formula for the simulation

$$x'=e^{aD}\left(x\cdot\cos_u(wD)+u^2\cdot y\cdot\sin_u(wD)\right)$$
$$y'=e^{aD}\left(y\cdot\cos_u(wD)+x\cdot\sin_u(wD)\right)$$

To offer a simulation according these recursion formulas we need the actual value of the adjoining state variable $y(t)$ which cannot be measured directly.
We determine the actual value of the state-variable $y(t)$ from the relation

$$\frac{dx}{dt}=ax+u^2wy$$

and we obtain the expression

$$y=\frac{\left(\frac{dx}{dt}-ax\right)}{u^2w}$$

5. Simulation approach with the 3-dimensional gyroscope

In generalising the 2-nd order MSD-sytems we get many different generalized exponential functions as a 4-dimensional MSD-system reflecting a 3-dimensional generalized gyroscope.
One of these generalisations is of special interest for us, because it seems to be well related to the 2-nd order MSD-system.
For this purpose we consider the following 4-dimensional exponential differential equation:

$$\frac{dz}{dt} = zA$$

Here we put

$$z = x_0 + u_1 x + u_2 y + u_3 z$$

$$A = a + u_1 w_1 + u_2 w_2 + u_3 w_3$$

With u_1, u_2 and u_3 being free variables with the help of which the above given exponential differential equation corresponds to a system of 4 linear differential equation with constant parameters.

For this relation we need quadratic reduction formulas for the free variables u_1, u_2 and u_3.

Here we base on the following reductions:

$$u_1^2 = +1/-1/0$$

$$u_2^2 = +1/-1/0$$

$$u_3^2 = +1/-1/0$$

$$\Omega_1 \Omega_2 u_2 u_1 = \Omega u_3$$

$$\Omega_3 \Omega_2 u_3 u_2 = \Omega u_1$$

$$\Omega_1 \Omega_3 u_1 u_3 = \Omega u_2$$

$$u_1 u_2 = \Omega_3 u_3, \quad u_2 u_3 = \Omega_1 u_1, \quad u_3 u_1 = \Omega_2 u_2$$

From the associative law, which in any case should be fulfilled for the multiplication we obtain

$$\Omega_1 u_1^2 = \Omega_2 u_2^2 = \Omega_3 u_3^2 = \Omega$$

This means the Ω_i are determined, if we know the reductions of u_1^2, u_2^2 and u_3^2 and the sign of Ω.

For Ω we admit

$$\Omega = +1/-1/0$$

If we demand this for

$$A = a + wv$$

with an arbitrary 3-dimensional direction

$$v = v_1 u_1 + v_2 u_2 + v_3 u_3$$

the overall behaviour should be reduced to that of a 2-dimensional MSD-system oriented in the direction v, we get the restriction

$$\Omega = -\Omega_1 \Omega_2 \Omega_3$$

With this restriction we have thus constructed a 4-dim. system with 27 modes of behaviour according to the basic reductions of the u_i^2. One of these modes corresponds to the kinetics of the Euler gyroscope, namely for $u_1^2 = u_2^2 = u_3^2 = -1$. We arrive with Quaternion algebra as the corresponding system of hypercomplex numbers.

6. The general identification and simulation scheme on finite algebras.

We characterize in general terms an approach for using, generalized exponentials as an identification and simulation tool.

A finite associative (but not necessarily commutative) algebra may be given with hypercomplex numbers of the form

$$z = x_0 + x_1 u_1 + x_2 u_2 + \ldots + x_n u_n$$

The multiplication stays within these linear forms if we base it on the following quadratic reduction formulas

$$u_i u_j = \sum G_{ij}^k u_k$$

The structure constants cannot be chosen absolutely freely, because the associative law should hold

$$(u_i u_j) u_k = u_i (u_j u_k)$$

On this associative finite algebra we consider the differential equation for the corresponding exponential element

$$\frac{dz}{dt} = Az$$

with A being a parameter and an element of the finite algebra

$$A = a + w_1 u_1 + w_2 u_2 + \ldots + w_n u_n$$

We interpret a as an expansion (or contraction) parameter and the other vector

$$w_1 u_1 + w_2 u_2 + \ldots + w_n u_n$$

as a generalized angle impulse vector.
In any case the differential equation is a substitute for a corresponding real linear differential equation of the order (n+1) with constant parameters.
In any case we can formally write the solution in the following form

$$z(t) = Z(0) \cdot e^{At}$$

where we define the generalized exponential function e^{At} by the following Taylor-series

$$e^{At} = \sum \frac{A_i t^i}{i!}$$

Here we meet no difficulties resulting from noncommutative multiplication laws.
In any case we can at the same time compute the corresponding exponential function from the following considerations:
It must hold

$$e^{At} = g_0(t) + g_1(t) u_1 + g_2(t) u_2 + \ldots + g_n(t) u_n$$

From the exponential differential equation we obtain a special linear system of differential equations with constant parameters for the coordinate functions $g_i(t)$.
We will now use these generalized exponentials as local models for dynamical systems.
Simulation scheme for the case of complete state-variable information.
We take any system of ordinary differential equation of (n+1) first order equations

$$\frac{dx_0}{dt} = f_0(\ldots)$$

$$\frac{dx_i}{dt} = f_i(\ldots) \text{ for } i = 1, 2, \ldots, n$$

We will now use as first order simulation scheme the above constructed generalized exponential function (This is a generalisation of the formerly considered circle dynamics).
We assume that we can measure

$$\frac{dz}{dt}$$

and z for all state variables. We then compute in the ring of hypercomplex numbers the quotient

$$A = \frac{dz}{dt} z^{-1}$$

passing first a zero divisor test.
We use the information A in a recursion scheme for simulation constructed on the knowledge of the coordinate function $g_i(t)$.
In the case where we met a zero divisor we expect a degeneration and hope that we now can work within a lower order finite algebra.
Simulation for the case, where we have measurement only for $x_0(t)$ and its derivatives up to a certain order.

In this case we take into account, that holds

$$A_{\bullet}^{(n+1)} = A_n A^n + A_{(n-1)} A^{(n-1)} + \ldots + A_0$$

May be we meet here a degeneration, because the minimum polynom for A has a smaller order then (n+1).
In the degenerated cases we can apply corresponding lower order recursion formulas for the identification.
If we apply this relation to z and taking into account the property

$$A^p z = \frac{d^p}{dt^p} z$$

and assuming nondegeneracy we determine a linear system of order (2n+1) containing the derivatives of $x_0(t)$ up to that order for the determination of the unknown parameters A_i, i=0,...,n+1.
From the characteristic equation for A we have to determine then the mode, that means the suitable finite algebra and the corresponding parameters $a, w_1, w_2, \ldots, w_n$ of A because we need these parameters for the determination of actual values of all help state variables x_i, i=1,2,...,n.
These help state-variables have to be determined from a system containing on the left hand side n suitable chosen derivatives of x_0(t) and on the right hand side x_i(t), i=1,2,...,n being a linear equation system for the help state variables.

7. References

/1/ Deuring,M.:Algebren. Ergebnisse der Mathematik und ihrer Grenzgebiete, Berlin, Springer-Verlag 1935.
/2/Saizew,G.A.:Algebraische Probleme der mathematischen und theoretischen Physik. Studien zur Algebra und ihre Anwendungen. Akademie-Verlag, Berlin, 1979.
/3/Peschel,M.;Mende,W.;Breitenecker,F.:Anwendungen der diskreten Theorie ratengekopelter Systeme in der Reglungstechnik. msr. Berlin, 30(1987), 7.
/4/Peschel,M.;Voigt,H.M.;Mende,W.;Breitenecker,F.:Modellbildungsrahmen von Zeitreihen als Grundlage für die Simulation dynamischer Systeme. msr. Berlin, 31(1988), 3.
/5/Peschel,M.;Voigt,H.M.;Mende,W.;Breitenecker,F.:System-Engineering Methodology for Simulation and Control of Dynamical Networks. System Analysis and Simulation part I, Volume 46 of Mathematical Research, Akademie-Verlag Berlin, 1988, p.232-236.

THEORY AND APPLICATIONS OF S-SYSTEMS

Eberhard O. Voit [1)]

Introduction

In the analysis of natural and modern technological systems, methods of linear mathematics are often not able to capture all important aspects in sufficient detail. All natural systems saturate, oscillations are usually stable, and synergistic effects are the rule rather than the exception. All these phenomena are intrinsically nonlinear and difficult to represent or even mimic with the means of linear mathematics. Nevertheless, the first attempt to understand a complex system is often linearization about an appropriate operating point and the analysis of the linearized system. The obvious reason is the practical superiority of linear over nonlinear formulations. A variety of theorems and conditions help to determine solvability and actually to compute solutions; the evaluation of steady states, their stability, and of the sensitivity of the system to changes in input variables and parameter values is so well understood that it is part of any standard analysis and implemented in several software packages. In contrast, nonlinear systems analysis suffers from a lack of such powerful yet straightforward methodology. No analogue to the Laplace transform exists and the derivation of analytical solutions is a sophisticated art and even then limited to but very special cases. One fundamental difference between linear and nonlinear functions and differential equations is that linear representations are completely determined by a set of parameter values, whereas nonlinear representations additionally differ in structure. Consequently, it is *a priori* impossible to compare and classify arbitrary nonlinear functions. Even nonlinear functions producing almost indistinguishable graphs can show no obvious similarity (cf. Savageau, 1980; Voit, 1989) and it seems futile to decide which of two nonlinear functions would more appropriately serve a given purpose. What is needed is a nonlinear theory that is based on a language powerful enough to compare any two nonlinearities in an objective fashion and to make them amenable to standardized analyses. Ideally, such a theory would rival the linear theory in power and methodology but apply to the incomparably richer domain of nonlinear functions. While we are still far from this goal, some recent research has addressed at least the question of comparability and classification, and we are now able to represent almost any nonlinear differentiable function and ordinary differential equation within the same finite mathematical structure. Such a unifying structure can be considered a nonlinear canonical form in which all differentiable nonlinearities are special cases and, indeed, only differ in a set of parameter values, as is the case in linear analysis. This homogeneity in representation offers a spectrum of academic and practical advantages.

1) Department of Biometry, Medical University of South Carolina, Charleston, SC 29425-2503 USA

In recent years, two formalisms have emerged that may provide a basis for a general nonlinear theory in the above sense. One is the Power-Law Formalism with its associated S-system equations, the other is based on the differential equations of Lotka and Volterra. In the following, I shall demonstrate some of the features of S-systems and refer the reader interested in Lotka-Volterra systems to the comprehensive treatises by Ebeling and Mende (1985) and by Peschel and Mende (1986) and to Voit and Savageau (1986).

The inappropriateness of linear formulations and the mathematical intractability of rational functions have motivated the development of the Power-Law Formalism. Its concept derives from the observation that many nonlinearities in nature show linear characteristics when plotted in logarithmic coordinates. Consequently, the Power-Law Formalism is based upon linear approximation in logarithmic space. It only requires that the system constituents be positive and that the functions describing the processes within the system be differentiable. Biological systems represented by continuous variables almost always satisfy these requirements. To describe the dynamics of a system we formulate the change in each component X_i as the difference of all influences that increase X_i or affect its production and all those that diminish X_i or influence its degradation. Symbolically, the change in X_i is thus represented as

$$\dot{X}_i = F_i^+(X_1,\ldots,X_n) - F_i^-(X_1,\ldots,X_n)$$

where $X_1, \ldots, X_n$ are the system components and $\dot{X}_i = dX_i/dt$; F_i^+ and F_i^- are logarithmically differentiable functions of all system components and describe synthesis and degradation of X_i. F_i^+ and F_i^- are then nonlinearly approximated by first expressing their logarithms as functions of the logarithms of their arguments, second, developing a Taylor series, third, retaining only the constant and linear terms of these expansions, and finally, translating the truncated Taylor expansions back into the Cartesian space (Savageau, 1969, 1976). The result is a nonlinear local representation for F_i^+ and F_i^-, each in the form of a product of power-law functions:

$$F_i^+ \sim \alpha_i \prod_{j=1}^{n} X_j^{g_{ij}} \qquad F_i^- \sim \beta_i \prod_{j=1}^{n} X_j^{h_{ij}}$$

The system defining equations are thus

$$\dot{X}_i = \alpha_i \prod_{j=1}^{n} X_j^{g_{ij}} - \beta_i \prod_{j=1}^{n} X_j^{h_{ij}}$$

and this structure is called an S-system to indicate its applicability to saturable and synergistic systems.

S-systems were originally developed as modelling tools for organizationally complex biological systems; nevertheless, it is now known that differential equations can be *recast* exactly into the S-system form and, therefore, that S-systems provide a very general framework for a vast spectrum of nonlinearities. During the development of S-system analysis, methods and applications have been reviewed several times (Savageau, 1972, 1976, 1985; Voit and Savageau, 1982; Savageau and Voit, 1987; Voit, 1988c). Thus, I shall not try to capture all aspects of S-systems but rather demonstrate with one recent example each the modelling and the recasting aspects.

Modelling with S-systems: Dynamics of Self-Thinning Plant Stands

When plants grow in a dense community they have to compete for nutrients and space. It has long been known that this competition limits the size of the plants and that, in turn, the increase in average size is accompanied by a decrease in the number of plants as a result of competition-based mortality, a phenomenon referred to as self-thinning. These observations can be formulated in a simple mathematical relationship that states that the maximum average size, S, in an even-aged pure stand is a power-law function of the number of plants, N:

$$S = a\,N^{-b} \qquad (1)$$

where a and b are positive parameters that reflect properties of the particular plant stand and the measure of size used. Observed plant stands usually start with quantities of S and N below this relationship, gradually approach it and, over some period of time, number and size relate to each other as predicted by (1). In stands of perennial plants such as trees, self-thinning will in time be supplanted by non-competition mortality agents such as insects and disease. In such stands, the survivors are physiologically unable to make full use of the increased growing space with the result that plants remain smaller than predicted by the size-limiting relationship (1). For a wide variety of plant species the parameter b has a value close to 3/2, when biomass is used as the measure of size, and the relationship (1) is then referred to as the 3/2 power rule.

The Power-Law Formalism allows us to describe the relationships between average size and number of plants with a mathematical model in S-system form that (i) yields insight in the dynamics of even-aged, pure stands, (ii) generates the power-law relationship between sizes and numbers of plants as well as the observed modes of approaching or leaving this relationship, (iii) can be justified biologically and mathematically, (iv) can be related to established representations of growth and population dynamics, and (v) requires only a minimum of restricting assumptions.

When we consider the number of plants, X_1, and the average plant size, X_2, as the two significant variables of the self-thinning process, the canonical most general S-system description is

$$
\begin{aligned}
\dot{X}_1 &= \alpha_1 X_1^{g_{11}} X_2^{g_{12}} - \beta_1 X_1^{h_{11}} X_2^{h_{12}} \\
\dot{X}_2 &= \alpha_2 X_1^{g_{21}} X_2^{g_{22}} - \beta_2 X_1^{h_{21}} X_2^{h_{22}}
\end{aligned}
\qquad (2)
$$

It is immediately evident that the change in either variable is intimately connected with the current status of both, size and number.

This two-variable representation obviously is a simplification since the growth dynamics of a plant population depends on a multitude of influences. These influences could be included in the S-system representation at the cost of additional variables and equations of the same S-system structure. However, in many cases this is not necessary. All processes occurring much faster than macroscopic growth, such as biomolecular reactions, and all processes on much slower time scales, such as evolutionary changes, are implicitly incorporated in S-system (2): The fast processes can be considered to be in a quasi steady state and the slow processes can be assumed to be constant during the time period of individual growth. As a consequence, the system behavior is essentially determined just by a few temporary dominant processes and, using the Power-Law Formalism as the modelling tool, these few equations have S-system form (Savageau, 1979).

The S-system (2) contains 12 parameters that determine its dynamics. Some of the parameters are mainly responsible for the mode of growth in size and decline in numbers, others reflect the steady-state values and the time scale. Without loss of generality, some of the latter parameters can be eliminated by selecting appropriate units for X_1 and X_2 and for time. More precisely, if we express the units of the two variables in terms of their steady-state values, then we obtain as constraints among the parameters $\alpha_1 = \beta_1$, $\alpha_2 = \beta_2$, and subsequently both variables have steady-state values of 1. Furthermore, we can select an appropriate time unit which allows us to specify one of the α or β-values. For instance we can set $\alpha_2=1$. The choice of convenient units reduces the number of free parameters by three.

The general two-variable S-system (2) can exhibit a variety of behaviors including different types of oscillations and unstable systems that grow without bound or die out. Many of these behaviors are not physically realizable or not consistent with observations made in the self-thinning process. For instance, in even-aged stands the number of plants cannot increase. Such observations impose valuable constraints on the set of admissible parameter combinations and provide an example for how biological facts can be translated directly into properties of S-system models.

The following observations can be translated into constraints:

(i) The average size increases monotonically.

(ii) The number of plants decreases monotonically, since we are concerned with a pure stand of even-aged plants.

(iii) The system is stable, with the average size reaching a maximum and the number of plants reaching the carrying capacity of the site.

(iv) The relationship between average size and number of plants approaches the power-law relationship (1).

(v) For an initial period following establishment there is no self thinning and the averag increases while the number remains constant.

As an example for how such conditions can be employed to constrain the set of possible parameter values, I shall discuss the first condition. The remaining conditions are analyzed elsewhere (Voit, 1988a).

The monotonic increase in plant size corresponds mathematically to $\dot{X}_2>0$. To derive parameter combinations that fulfill this condition, we study first under which non-steady-state conditions $\dot{X}_2$ is equal to 0. Then we exclude such parameter combinations and assure that X_2 is always greater than 0.

The condition $\dot{X}_2=0$ is equivalent with the equation

$$\alpha_2 X_1^{g_{21}} X_2^{g_{22}} = \beta_2 X_1^{h_{21}} X_2^{h_{22}} \quad (3)$$

which, upon taking logarithms and noting that $\alpha_2 = \beta_2$, reduces to the linear equation in $\ln(X_1)$ and $\ln(X_2)$

$$(g_{21}-h_{21}) \ln(X_1) + (g_{22}-h_{22}) \ln(X_2) = 0 \quad (4)$$

As a consequence of the scaling of variables, the steady-state values of X_1 and X_2 are both equal to 1, and since we are concerned with a decrease in number and a concomitant increase in size, $\ln(X_1)$ approaches the steady-state value of 0 from above and $\ln(X_2)$ from below. Hence, we have for all time points $\ln(X_1)>0$ and $\ln(X_2)<0$, and $\dot{X}_2$ can only be equal to zero if $g_{21}\geq h_{21}$ and $g_{22}\geq h_{22}$ or if $g_{21}\leq h_{21}$ and $g_{22}\leq h_{22}$. Not only is this possible but, independent of the particular parameter values, both combinations will actually lead to $\dot{X}_2=0$ and hence, at different times, to an increase and to a decrease in X_2, when the initial conditions of the system are chosen appropriately. For instance, when we assume $g_{21}=1$, $h_{21}=1.1$, $g_{22}=1$, and $h_{22}=2$ and start with 1.1 as the initial value of X_1 and with 0.99 as the initial value of X_2 then we find $\dot{X}_2<0$ for small t and $\dot{X}_2>0$ for large t. This would have the following biological interpretation: When a stand initially consisted of few large plants then their size would temporarily decrease, which is nonsensical. The above conditions lead to $\dot{X}_2=0$

and have to be excluded, yielding the admissible parameter combinations $g_{21} \geq h_{21}$, $g_{22} \leq h_{22}$ and $g_{21} \leq h_{21}, g_{22} \geq h_{22}$. The latter combination corresponds to $\dot{X}_2 \leq 0$ and, hence, the conditions for monotonic growth so far are $g_{21} \geq h_{21}$, $g_{22} \leq h_{22}$, and equality must not hold in both relations simultaneously. However, these conditions are still not sufficient. When $g_{21} > h_{21}$ and X_2 is initially close to its steady-state value, then a sufficiently large initial value for X_1 leads to X_2 overshooting its steady-state value temporarily. The biological interpretation would be: When the stand initially consists of plants with almost maximal size, then they grow, their growth exceeds its possible limit, and subsequently they "shrink" back to the limiting size. This behavior has to be excluded, and we conclude that monotonic growth translates into the conditions

$$g_{21} = h_{21}$$

$$\tag{5}$$

$$g_{22} < h_{22}.$$

Similar arguments hold for condition (ii); condition (iii) is analyzed with straightforward S-system methodology (Savageau, 1976); conditions (iv) and (v) are discussed in detail in Voit (1988a). Incorporation of all constraints yields the general admissible S-system

$$\dot{X}_1 = b^{-1} X_2^{g_{12}} (X_1^{g_{11}} - X_1^{h_{11}})$$

$$\tag{6}$$

$$\dot{X}_2 = X_1^{g_{21}} (X_2^{g_{22}} - X_2^{h_{22}})$$

satisfying conditions (5), the constraints $g_{11} < h_{11}$, $g_{12} = h_{12}$, resulting from condition (ii), and

$$g_{12} = h_{22} + b^{-1}(g_{11} - g_{21} - 1) - 1$$

$$\tag{7}$$

$$h_{11} = g_{11} + b(h_{22} - g_{22})$$

resulting from conditions (iii) - (v).

In comparison with the general two-variable S-system (2), the constraints reduce the number of parameters from twelve to four plus the known parameter b of the relationship (1). These four parameters represent the actually observed modes of the growth process and the decline in numbers over time, as well as the coupling between the two processes.

Analytical Solution. Due to the constraints imposed upon the parameter values of the system, the S-system (6) possesses as one particular solution the size-limiting relationship (1), if the initial values satisfy this relationship. The question now arises whether analytical solutions of X_2 as a function of X_1 can be obtained for other initial conditions.

The method of choice is to try to deduce an analytical (trajectorial) solution $X_2(X_1)$ by solving the differential equation in X_1. This step generally leads to rather complicated integrals (cf. Voit and Savageau, 1984), but in numerically convenient cases these integrals can be solved.

For instance, for $b = 0.5$, $\alpha_2 = 1$, $g_{11} = 0$, $g_{21} = -1$, $g_{22} = 0$, and $h_{22} = 4$, the constraints developed above require $\alpha_1 = 2$, $\beta_1 = 2$, $\beta_2 = 1$, $g_{12} = 3$, and $h_{11} = 2$, and we obtain upon separation of variables the trajectorial solution

$$X_2 = (1 - \gamma(1 - X_1^{-2}))^{1/4} \tag{8}$$

where γ is a constant reflecting the initial conditions. For $\gamma = 1$, we obtain directly the size-limiting relationship, for $\gamma<1$, the system starts above, for $\gamma>1$ below the limiting relationship. In the latter, relevant case X_2 is only defined as long as $X_1 \leq (\gamma/(\gamma-1))^{1/2}$ with the slope of $X_2(X_1)$ approaching $-\infty$, which reflects the observation that there is rapid plant growth but almost no decline in number for stands of small plants or for stands initiated with few plants.

For this numerical example the parameter values were chosen in a way that a trajectorial solution could be obtained analytically. Usually, we will not be able to derive a solution like Eqn. (8). Nevertheless, any admissible S-system produces the observed types of trajectories, even if one cannot identify their explicit functional form.

Deviation from the Size-Limiting Relationship. After having approached and followed the size-limiting relationship for some while, plants usually reach a stage of development where the growth response does not reflect the growing space made available by continued mortality, and as a consequence, mean size is less than predicted by the self-thinning rule. The plants are still growing, though slowly, and self-thinning proceeds more slowly, giving way to other causes of mortality. Mathematical models of the self-thinning process have not accounted for this deviation from the size-limiting relationship.

In the S-system model (6) the observed deviation is readily generated by changing a few or even just one parameter. For instance, if we decrease the parameter h_{11}, the early parts of the trajectories (representing large numbers of small plants) very much resemble the trajectories in the previous model, whereas with increasing age all trajectories flatten out and approach a horizontal tangent in a plot of X_2 versus X_1, which corresponds to a decline in numbers and almost no further growth, as observed.

Interpretation in Terms of Growth Laws. Savageau (1980) demonstrated that a wide variety of well-known growth laws can be formulated exactly as S-systems. Although many influences affect growth, the exact S-system representation of these laws usually requires only one or two equations, the first of which describes a measure of growth, such as total weight, the second a transformation of the time scale or another process affecting growth that cannot be further specified. The growth of plants in our S-system model with size limitation can easily be interpreted within Savageau's framework of growth functions. When we consider the average size of a plant, X_2, as only insignificantly influenced by the number of plants, X_1, we can specify $g_{21}=0$. The equation for X_2 then does not contain X_1 and describes a variety of famous growth laws. For $g_{22}=0$ and $h_{22}=1$, the equation is equivalent to the so-called limited or decreasing exponential growth; with $g_{22}=1$ and $h_{22}=2$ we generate the logistic growth law; $g_{22}<1$ and $h_{22}=1$ corresponds to the growth law of von Bertalanffy (1957); $g_{22}=2/3$, $h_{22}=2$ is a representation of Aikman and Watkinson's (1980) basic model for plant populations. Unlimited growth, like linear or exponential growth, can be represented with one-variable S-systems but these are characterized by $g_{22} \geq h_{22}$, which we had to exclude from the set of admissible parameter combinations (cf. Eqn. (5)). This is consistent with our requirement of size limitation. When the change in the average size does depend on the number of plants in the stand, the S-system representation (6) yields a multitude of growth functions without a particular name.

Naito (1983) in his analysis used for both, the increase in size and the decline in number, the growth model of Richards (1959). Our "recasting" techniques, discussed in the next section, show immediately, that his model is an uncoupled special case of the S-system (5). Models of this form satisfy the constraints derived from the requirements of monotonicity and stability and they also reproduce the size-limiting relationship (1), but since these special cases do not satisfy the constraint (5), they do not describe correctly the self-thinning process below the limiting trajectory.

Conclusion. In this section, I have shown with the example of self-thinning plant stands how a biological phenomenon can be represented and analyzed in S-system form. Assuming only that average size and density are the significant variables, the phenomenon was formulated as a general two-variable S-system. Then a number of biological facts about self-thinning stands were translated into the S-system language, which led to constraints on the set of admissible parameter values in the general S-system model. These constraints reduced the number of parameters from twelve to four.

The resulting S-system model combines maximal generality with simplicity in structure. Previous growth models were readily demonstrated to be special cases of the S-system model, but direct comparison with the conditions for an admissible system also revealed why these models fail to represent correctly stands in which competition is not yet or not any more the primary reason of mortality.

Because of its generality and flexibility, the S-system representation is particularly suited for analysis and simulation. In contrast to most *ad hoc* models, major parts of such analyses reduce to paper and pencil methods that address the characteristic feature of the dynamical system, and a variety of recipes is available for extending the S-system model with additional variables or processes (e.g. Savageau, 1976; Voit and Savageau, 1982; Voit, 1988b). Furthermore, the particular mathematical structure of the S-system has permitted the implementation of S-system methods in the interactive computer program ESSYNS. This program very efficiently solves and analyzes S-systems and thus facilitates the fast and convenient simulation of different plant stands and the analysis of model extensions, such as the inclusion of non-competition mortality, different ages, or fluctuations in the environment.

This concludes our demonstration of the modelling aspect of S-systems, and we shall now study an example for the recasting of a nonlinear function in the S-system form.

Recasting: A Class of Probability Distributions in S-system Form

Representation of the Distribution. In 1980, Johnson, Tietjen and Beckman introduced a "super-family" of symmetric probability distributions. It includes as special cases the exponential power distribution and, hence, the uniform, normal and Laplace distributions. Moreover, it also includes an infinite number of distributions with arbitrary mean and variance, and kurtosis in the range (1.8,∞). It is useful for Monte Carlo simulations and for the investigation of nonnormality. The four-parameter distribution, to which I will refer as "JTB", is based on the incomplete gamma function:

$$f(t) = \frac{A}{2\sigma\Gamma(\alpha)} \int_{y(t)}^{\infty} w^{\alpha-\tau-1} e^{-w} dw \ , \qquad (9)$$

where $\alpha,\tau,\sigma > 0$, $-\infty < \mu < \infty$, $y(t) = [A(t-\mu)/\sigma]^{1/\tau}$ and $A = [\Gamma(\alpha+2\tau)/3\Gamma(\alpha)]^{1/2}$.

To obtain the S-system form, we first differentiate (9) with respect to y

$$\frac{df(t)}{dy} = -\frac{A}{2\sigma\Gamma(\alpha)} y^{\alpha-\tau-1} e^{-y} ,$$

then we differentiate y with respect to t

$$\frac{dy}{dt} = \frac{A}{\tau\sigma} y^{1-\tau} ,$$

and define $z(t) = \exp[-y(t)]$, which yields

$$\frac{df(t)}{dt} = -\frac{A^2}{2\sigma^2\tau\Gamma(\alpha)} y^{\alpha-2\tau} z$$

$$\frac{dz}{dt} = -\frac{A}{\tau\sigma} y^{1-\tau} z$$

(cf. Rust and Voit, 1988). Since f(t), y(t), and z(t) are positive-valued, we can directly rename X_1 = f(t), X_2 = y(t), X_3 = z(t) and obtain the S-system

$$\begin{aligned}
\dot{X}_1 &= -\frac{A^2}{2\sigma^2\tau\Gamma(\alpha)} X_2^{\alpha-2\tau} X_3 \\
\dot{X}_2 &= \frac{A}{\sigma\tau} X_2^{1-\tau} \\
\dot{X}_3 &= -\frac{A}{\sigma\tau} X_2^{1-\tau} X_3
\end{aligned} \tag{10}$$

Savageau (1982) has described a "suprasystem of probability distributions" in S-system form. He showed that a variety of distributions can be represented as an S-system with just one or two equations. Employing recently developed recasting techniques for S-systems (Savageau and Voit, 1987), one can rewrite Savageau's suprasystem as a *Half-system* with three equations, which is an S-system that contains only one product of power functions in each equation. The super-family JTB is thus a special case of this Half-system (cf. also *Riccati systems* in Peschel and Mende, 1986).

In order to generate the cumulative of the JTB distribution, we add X_4 as the cumulative, which corresponds to expanding system (10) by the equation

$$\dot{X}_4 = X_1 \tag{11}$$

Speed and Accuracy of Solution in S-system Form. As a first example, we specify $\mu = 0, \sigma = 1, \alpha = 1.5, \tau = .5$ which corresponds to the standard normal distribution. While these particular specifications enormously simplify the direct evaluation of equation (9), one should note that the speed and accuracy of solution in S-system from is not much influenced by whether we select such a prominent special case or an uncommon combination of parameter values as in our second example. Since for $t_0 = 0$ the second variable is zero, which implies inferior computational efficiency, we select $t_0 = 1$ and solve the positive branch of the distribution in two runs, one from 1 in the positive direction, and one from 1 toward 0. The "complete" solution from 1 to

5, with data of the density and the cumulative reported at every interval of 0.05, requires about 7 seconds on an IBM AT with numeric coprocessor; the solution toward 0 requires about 14 seconds. Comparisons of the results at $t = 2, 3, 4, 5$ with direct evaluation of the original integral in JTB, using the chi-square points from the program RTAIL (Rust, 1986), and with tables of the normal density in Abramowitz and Stegun (1972) show that the accuracy at all points is better than 10^{-14}. If we are interested only in the density and cumulative at one point, say $t=2$, the solution is obtained in less than half a second when we specify a local error tolerance of 10^{-3}.

As a second example, we select $\mu = 0, \sigma = 1, \alpha = 7.75, \tau = .25$, representing a distribution without a specific name. The S-system analysis requires the following steps.

1. For the positive branch of the distribution, define the S-system (10), (11); for the negative branch, exchange t with -t and multiply the right-hand sides in (10) with -1 since the S-system variables are defined to be positive (Savageau, 1982).

2. Compute the constants in (10) with sufficient accuracy.

3. Specify initial conditions. Evaluate f(1), y(1), z(1) and specify $X_4(1) = 1$. The exact value of $X_4(1)$ is unknown, but since X_4 does not appear on the right-hand sides of the system, different initial conditions produce solutions of $X_4(t)$ that are merely shifted linearly for all t. Hence, we can solve the system from an erroneous initial guess, e.g. $X_4(1) = 1$, and obtain the asymptote $X_4(t \rightarrow \infty) = 1 + c$. $X_4(t) - c$ then is the correct cumulative for all values of t (Rust and Voit, 1988).

4. Solve the system for $(-\infty, -1]$, $[-1, 0)$, $(0,1]$, and $[1,\infty)$.

While the actual numerical solution of the S-system requires only a few seconds, direct evaluations of the integral in JTB with sufficient accuracy are time consuming. For convenient parameter values of α and τ the incomplete gamma function reduces to tabulated χ^2 cumulatives, and for tabulated percentiles and within the accuracy of the table, the results can be obtained by multiplication. For arbitrary α, τ and t, the necessary χ^2 cumulatives are usually not tabulated. If $2(\alpha-\tau)$ is a positive integer, the degrees of freedom are integral and one can find results by interpolation or with the program RTAIL (Rust, 1986). In other cases, the density at one point must be evaluated with other numerical methods. In any event, it should be emphasized that in the S-system approach the JTB density has to be evaluated at only one point to provide an initial value for X_1; then all other values of the p.d.f. and the c.d.f. follow within a few seconds, as exemplified in Table 1. In contrast, "direct" evaluation of the JTB density in its original form requires the computation of incomplete gamma functions at every required value of the independent variable.

TABLE 1

Accuracy and Computation Time of S-system Solution to the JTB-Distribution with $\alpha = 7.75$ and $\tau = 0.25$

Local Error Tolerance	Accuracy* at t = 1.5	1.8	2.0	2.5	Solution Time† for [-2.5,2.5]
10^{-4}	$<10^{-4}$	$<10^{-4}$	$<10^{-4}$	$<10^{-4}$	6 sec
10^{-8}	$<10^{-9}$	$<10^{-9}$	$<10^{-9}$	$<10^{-9}$	10 sec
10^{-16}	$<10^{-14}$	$<10^{-14}$	$<10^{-14}$	$<10^{-14}$	28 sec

* Difference between S-system solution and independent evaluation of JTB, using RTAIL. See Text for details.

† Solution reported for [-2.5, -2.4, -2.3, ···, 2.4, 2.5]. If only one specific P-value or cumulative is desired, the solution time reduces to a fraction of the values given. For instance, with a local error tolerance of 10^{-16} the solution at t = -2 is obtained in 5.4 seconds with an accuracy of $1.1 \cdot 10^{-15}$; with a tolerance of 10^{-4}, the solution at t = 1.5 is computed in 0.33 seconds.

Cumulatives and Quantiles. The problem of obtaining quantiles could be approached on a trial and error basis, i.e., one could specify t, calculate $X_4(t)$, compare it with the desired tail area, and iterate the process with improved guesses on t. However, the S-system representation provides a more efficient and accurate method: The quantile question can be reformulated as the problem of expressing the (formally) independent variable t as a function of the cumulative X_4. This is done by applying the chain rule. It is first necessary to make the independent variable t explicit, which requires the additional S-system variable $X_5 = t$ with its associated equation

$$\dot{X}_5 = 1 \qquad (12)$$

We can now express equations (10) and (11) as functions of the cumulative X_4, which is achieved by dividing (10) and (12) by equation (11) with the result

$$\frac{dX_1}{dX_4} = -\frac{A^2}{2\sigma^2\tau\Gamma(\alpha)} X_1^{-1} X_2^{\alpha-2\tau} X_3$$
$$\frac{dX_2}{dX_4} = \frac{A}{\sigma\tau} X_1^{-1} X_2^{1-\tau}$$
$$\frac{dX_3}{dX_4} = \frac{-A}{\sigma\tau} X_1^{-1} X_2^{1-\tau} X_3 \qquad (13)$$
$$\frac{dX_5}{dX_4} = X_1^{-1}$$

System (13) can be solved with initial conditions set at $X_4 = 0.50$ and incremented up to the quantile Q of interest, achieving the primary goal of finding $X_5(Q)$. Of course, the values of the JTB density X_1 and of the other variables are also available.

Conclusion. The approach to evaluating probability density functions based on the solution of differential equations in S-system form is novel and needs to be justified. The resulting S-system equations are highly nonlinear and, except for some special cases (Voit & Savageau, 1984), have no analytical solutions and thus have to be solved numerically. This might seem a very restrictive limitation. However, the intrinsic complexity of some probability distributions requires evaluation per computer, no matter which representation is chosen. This need for numerical tools implies that mathematical beauty is no longer the only criterion for the selection among competing representations. Rather, for numerical evaluations it becomes more important which representations allow for the most efficient and most accurate computational method. Of course, explicit compact formulas often provide insight and intuitive meaning. For instance, noncentral probability distributions are usually expressed in terms of infinite sums which permit one to draw some conclusions on their qualitative behavior. However, the numerical evaluation of these representations is often rather involved and has to be performed for every argument of interest. Even worse are the cumulative distributions, that are usually expressed in terms of infinite series, improper integrals, or special functions, which are computationally so complicated that accurate evaluations of the cumulatives and their tail areas do not always exist. Although S-system representations may not provide much immediate insight they are far superior to the mathematically more appealing series formulations when computational efficiency and accuracy are the primary criteria of quality. The S-system generates central and noncentral distributions (see above and Rust and Voit, 1988) for the whole range of the independent variable; cumulatives are provided with little extra effort and quantiles are readily calculated from the inverted S-system; the evaluation of power follows naturally from the simultaneous S-system representation of a central distribution and its noncentral counterpart. While current approaches to calculate these features are comparatively fragmentary and cumbersome, the S-system approach has proven rather general and very fast. Of course, the actual computation time depends on the given problem and, in contrast to direct evaluations, on the distance between the initial point and the points desired for evaluation. Thus, there are certainly specific problems in which the explicit formula is based on rapidly converging power series or continued fraction expansions which make a single evaluation faster than with the method proposed here. However, other formulas are notoriously difficult to compute with high accuracy, and if such a distribution has to be evaluated at several points, the advantages of our method become more and more pronounced. This is particularly true for the evaluation of cumulatives, for which explicit formulas are sometimes only defined as integrals of integrals, as is the case in the JTB distribution. The speed of evaluation based on the S-system form is not compromised with accuracy. On the contrary, the results are so precise that it is difficult to find published values to compare them with (e.g. see Table 1). Thus, the computational advantages of the S-system representation clearly outperform direct implementation of the commonly known procedures.

Discussion

We have discussed two aspects of S-systems, the representation of biological networks and the recasting of nonlinearities. The first provides a powerful modelling tool, the latter a general canonical form for the classification and analysis of functions and differential equations. Even though these aspects may seem to be unrelated, their combination opens new ways of analyzing complex phenomena. While this area of S-system research is just beginning to emerge, two immediate applications are visible. First, recasting allows the optimization of functional forms in the analysis of data. For instance, if the problem under investigation involves growth, it is not *a priori* evident which of the many known growth functions is most appropriate, and usually the choice of any one function is arbitrary. Instead, if one represents the growth process with an S-system that includes all growth functions as special cases (cf. Savageau, 1980; Voit, 1989), no *a priori* choice needs to be made and an unbiased parameter estimation procedure will yield which function indeed is best. Analogous considerations apply to other S-system classes of functions, e.g., probability laws (cf. Savageau, 1982; Voit and Anton, 1985). A second example for the simultaneous application of S-system modelling and recasting is the incorporation of non-S-system submodels into S-system master models, upon recasting. The advantage of this strategy is that the resulting master model is completely in S-system form and thus permits the application of the established S-system methodologies and of the highly efficient interactive computer program ESSYNS that was designed specifically to analyze S-systems. The technique of recasting submodels has recently been used to analyze alternative models for endemic infections (Voit, 1988b, 1989).

References

[1] Abramowitz M, Stegun I.A.: Handbook of Mathematical Functions, 9th printing, Dover Publications, New York, (1972).

[2] Aikman, D.P., and Watkinson, A.R.: A model for growth and self-thinning in even-aged monocultures of plants. Ann. Bot. 45 (1980), 419-427.

[3] von Bertalanffy, L.: Quantitative laws in metabolism and growth. Q. Rev. Biol. 32 (1957), 218-231.
[4] Ebeling, W. and M. Peschel (Eds.): Lotka-Volterra-Approach to Cooperation and Competition in Dynamic Systems, Akademie-Verlag, Berlin (1985).
[5] Johnson M.E., Tietjen, G.L., and Beckman, R.J.: A new family of probability distributions with applications to Monte Carlo studies. Journal of the American Statistical Association 75 (1980), 276-279.
[6] Naito, K.: An analysis of forest stand growth based on the Richards function. J. Jap. For. Soc. 65 (1983), 399-407.
[7] Peschel, M. and W. Mende: The Predator-Prey Model: Do We Live in a Volterra World? Akademie-Verlag, Berlin (1986).
[8] Richards, F.J.: A flexible growth function for empirical use. J. Exp. Bot. 10 (1959), 290-300.
[9] Rust, P.F.: Programming common distributions for precise P-values. Computational Statistics & Data Analysis, 4 (1986), 205-209.
[10] Rust, P.F. and E.O. Voit: Statistical densities, cumulatives, quantiles and power obtained by S-system differential equations (1988; submitted).
[11] Savageau, M.A.: Biochemical Systems Analysis, II. The steady-state solutions for an n-pool system using a power-law approximation. J. Theor. Biol. 25 (1969), 370-379.
[12] Savageau, M.A.: Concepts relating the behavior of biochemical systems to their underlying molecular properties. Arch. Biochem. Biophys 145 (1971), 612-621.
[13] Savageau, M.A.: The behavior of intact biochemical control systems. Curr. Top. Cell Reg. 6 (1972), 63-130.
[14] Savageau, M.A.: Optimal design of feedback control by inhibition: dynamic considerations. J. Mol. Evol. 5 (1975), 199-222.
[15] Savageau, M.A: Biochemical Systems Analysis: A Study of Function and Design in Molecular Biology. Addison-Wesley, Reading, Mass. (1976).
[16] Savageau, M.A.: Growth of complex systems can be related to the properties of their underlying determinants. Proc. Nat. Acad. Sci. 76 (1979), 5413-5417.
[17] Savageau, M.A.: Growth Equations: A general equation and a survey of special cases. Math. Biosci. 48 (1980), 267-278.
[18] Savageau M.A.: A suprasystem of probability distributions. Biometrical Journal, 24 (1982), 323-330.
[19] Savageau, M.A.: Mathematics of organizationally complex systems. Biomed. Biochim. Acta 44 (1985), 839-844.
[20] Savageau, M.A. and E.O. Voit: Recasting nonlinear differential equations as S-systems. A canonical nonlinear form. Mathem. Biosci. 87 (1987), 83-115.
[21] Voit, E.O.: Dynamics of self-thinning plant stands. Ann. Bot. 61: (1988a; in press).
[22] Voit, E.O.: Recasting nonlinear models as S-systems. Mathl. Comput. Modelling 11 (1988b), 140-145, .
[23] Voit, E.O.: New nonlinear methodologies for modeling molecular and cellular systems. Proc. of the 1st IFAC Symp. on Modelling and Control in Biomedical Systems, Venice, Italy, 1988(c).
[24] Voit, E.O.: S-system modelling of endemic infections. (1989; submitted).
[25] Voit, E.O. and H.J. Anton: Derivation of the frequency distributions of cycle durations from continuous labeling curves. J. Theor. Biol. 112 (1985), 575-588.
[26] Voit, E.O. and M.A. Savageau: Power-law approach to modeling biological systems, III. Methods of analysis. J. Ferment. Technol. 60 (1982), 233-241.
[27] Voit, E.O. and M.A. Savageau: Analytical solutions to a generalized growth equation. J. Math. Anal. Appl. 103 (1984), 380-386.
[28] Voit, E.O. and M.A. Savageau: Equivalence between S-systems and Volterra-systems. Math. Biosci. 78 (1986), 47-55.

An Information Theoretic Approach to Computer Vision

P. Bergmann, W. Paul and L. Thiele - University of Saarbrücken, West Germany

Abstract: Man tries to understand the real world by making theories. Two theories are competing, if they describe the same phenomena. The principle of Occam's Razor says that among competing theories the simpler one is to be preferred over the more complicated one. In the spirit of Kolmogorov and Solomonoff [K,S] a theory *is nothing but* a set of descriptions for observations. The theory is nontrivial if the descriptions are shorter than the observations. Formally observations are sequences of zeros and ones and descriptions are computer programs. In this paper we try to give evidence that with present technology systems can be constructed, which build such theories *in reasonable time*.

1. Introduction. This paper contains speculations about how to build artificial intelligent systems. We start with some observations about freshly made natural intelligent systems (babies).

1.1 babies are born with a brain. This brain is presumed to have computing power which is very large compared to that of traditional AI-systems.

1.2 in spite of all the computing power of their brain babies behave for many months not very intelligently. Suppose babies *do* compute during that time. What are they computing ? And has this extended startup phase something to do with the fact that eventually humans become smarter than traditional AI-systems, which have to be smart right away.

1.3 babies have a basic drive to understand and control the part of the world which they can observe. While lying in their cradle they learn to focus their eyes at things, particularly their hands. They learn (apparently by trial and error) how to control their hands, for example in order to hit at objects which are suspended within reach of their hands.

Suppose we attach a camera and a robot arm to a sufficiently powerful computer system. Is there a way to program the system *in a uniform way*, such that the following happens: the system learns to focus the camera and to control the robot arm. It starts to play with objects which are placed within reach of the robot arm and it eventually discovers, that when it lets an object fall, then in time t it falls down by a distance proportional to t^2.

Such a system might not be completely beyond reach. In this paper we will sketch a system for the particular AI problem of computer vision which has the following properties.

1.1a it benefits from large computing power

1.2a it spends considerable amounts of time with exponential search, particularly after a cold start.

1.3a it is driven by *one single principle* : it searches for short descriptions of large sets of input data.

We will argue that such a system will by itself find the concepts :

straight line
rectangle
parallelogram
neighborhood

and will identify these concepts as useful. It will describe figure 1 as

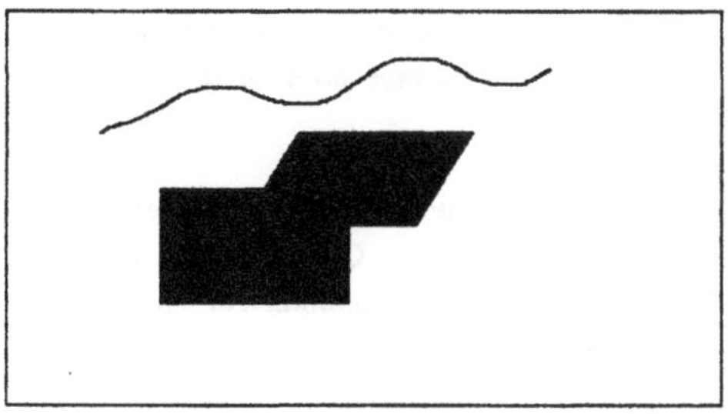

Fig . 1

a white rectangle, on top of it a black rectangle, a parallelogram and a line (not a straight one).

2. Information theoretic view of pattern recognition. Let P and Q be two dimensional patterns. In this section we will propose a very general definition of what it means to *recognice pattern* P *in pattern* Q.

As a first example consider figures 2 a to 2 e. A human will clearly recognize the A of figure 2a in figures 2b and 2d, probably in figure 2c and probably not in figure 2e. Observe that definitions based on Hamming distance will suggest that in fugure 2b the A is as absent as it can possibly be.

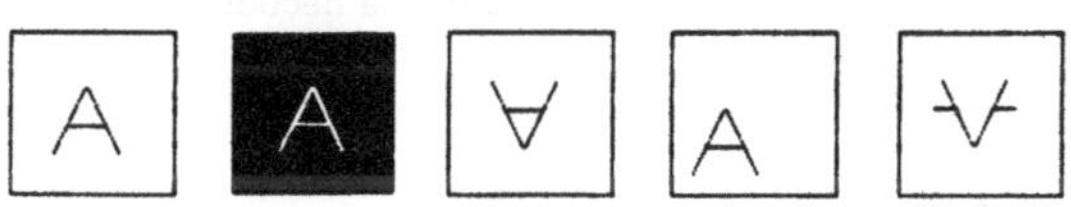

Fig. 2a - 2e

As a second example consider figures 3a to 3c. A human will recognize the camel in figure 3a in figure 3b but probably not in figure 3c, because the animal behind the palm tree migh as well be a cow.

Fig. 3a

Fig. 3b

Fig. 3c

Our definition will be based on the concept of ***relative Kolmogorov complexity*** [K,S]. Fix a universal programming language L. The relative Kolmogorov complexity $K_L(P \mid Q)$ of pattern P given pattern Q relative to language L is the length (measured in bits) of the shortest program p in L which started on input Q produces output P and halts. Let ε be the empty pattern. Then $K_L(P) := K_L(P \mid \varepsilon)$ is called the Kolmogorov complexity of P relative to L.

If L' is a second universal language and s is the length of an interpreter written in language L for programs in L', then $K_L(P \mid Q) \leq K_{L'}(P \mid Q) + s$. In the usual applications of Kolmogorov complexity one is only interested in the asymptotic growth of the complexity of infinite sequences of patterns. In this case by the argument above the choice of language L contributes only an additive constant and is therefore of little consequence. Therefore the subscript L is usually dropped. We are here interested in complexities of particular fixed patterns like the ones in figures 2 and 3. Hence for us the choice of L *is* important. For the remainder of the paper it suffices to assume L to be a reasonable language somewhere between PASCAL and assembler language.

Now suppose $K(P \mid Q) = K(P)$. Then pattern Q is of no help whatsoever in reproducing pattern P. Hence this is a good formalization of the intuitive concept: Q does not in any sense contain P. This formalization was used in several proofs of lower bounds for the runtime of Turing machines[P,PSS].

If on the other hand $K(P \mid Q)$ is much smaller than K(P) then Q contains much information about P. Pattern P can be reproduced from pattern Q by a program which is much shorter than any program which has to produce P from scratch. It is tempting to use this as a formalization of the concept: P can be recognized in Q. But there are several drawbacks. First the function $K(\ \mid\ )$ is not computable. Thus for the purpose of constructions of any kind this would be of very limited use. Second no requirements are made on the computational requirements of the short program which produces P from Q. This program might have a very large runtime. Third there might be a short and fast program which would reproduce P from Q but in a sense the program is so far out that one would hardly try it. Take as an example a portrait of 1000 x 1000 pixels of a well know person. Align the pixels linearly row by row. Roll up the resulting bit string of 1 million bits. For most purposes the well known person cannot be recognized in the resulting round picture, although the decoding procedure is simple enough, *if you know it.*

This suggests the following "subjective" definition: pattern P can be recognized in pattern Q by system S if S knows a short and fast program p, which produces P from Q and which is much shorter than any program known to S, which produces P from scratch.

The reader is asked to check this definition against the examples in figures 2 and 3. It also covers the example in figure 4 which we recognize as a camel, although a whole hind leg is missing. The procedure to complete the camel is simply: copy the hind leg which is there and put it in the proper place.

Fig. 4

3. How to formally define a camel or a good set of programs which reproduce a prototypical camel from patterns Q is something we don't know how to do. Thus if we want to build a camel recognizer, then our only hope is to build a system which by itself produces the definition of the camel and the procedures for reconstructing same camel by itself.

We proceed to sketch a system which makes successive observations of the world (for our purposes an NxN array of black and white pixels), tries to identify *interesting* patterns in it, and in case it succeeds remembers that pattern. The system will find a pattern P interesting if it can find a program p, which is fast, has much less bits than P and which reproduces P. Pattern P is remembered by storing program p.

There should be three basic mechanisms for generating candidate programs p.

3.1 systematically enumerating all programs which have at most c instructions, where c is some small magic constant (like 7).

3.2 mutation of programs which are already stored: changing constants, deleting instructions, adding instructions or replacing instructions by one or few other instructions.

3.3 combination of programs: concatenation, replacing instructions by other programs.

If a system like that is confronted with something which is unlike anything it has seen before (like after a cold start), then it will have to rely heavily on 3.1 . During the systematic enumeration of candidate programs little progress can be observed superficially. Also progress comes like ideas: even immediately before the idea is there, there is no hint that it will come.

Programs p must be stored by the system in a nontrivial data structure. The underlying programming language L can be designed such that is has few types of instructions, thus the combinatorial explosion in 3.1 can be kept moderate. But the number of programs p which are remembered will become very large. This is bad for the runtime of the system if mechanisms 3.2 or 3.3 are used. Also if in a new pattern P a subpattern P' is found, which was previously successfully combined (by mechanism 3.3 say) to another pattern P", then chances are, that this combination will be successful again. Think of P as a face, P' as a pair of eyes and P" a nose. Therefore it would make sense to store programs as nodes of a weighted graph: if program p' was successfully combined to program p", then there should be an edge between p' and p". This weight should vary in time and represent the rate at which this combination was successfully applied.

One can try to teach a system like that by confronting it with an appropriately chosen sequence of patterns. A new pattern P can be taught in reasonable time, if the system can derive from the programs it has stored a good description for P with a reasonable number of tries, i.e. by modifiying existing programs in 5 or 7 places but not in 100 places. As long as progress can be made in small steps like that the system can continue to learn. Thus we begin to study the question:

4. How much progress is possible in small steps ?

This question turns out to be amenable to theoretical study. Suppose an all white pixel array A is presented to the system. Then by enumeration of all very short programs the system will find the program p_1:

```
j := j0;
for i = α to β do
A[i,j] := 0 od
```

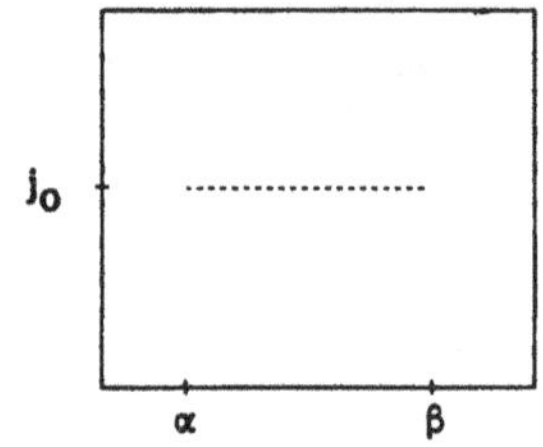

Fig. 5a

(see figure 5 a). This program is very fast and has a length of $\log \alpha + \log \beta + O(1)$ bits. It describes a pattern (a white horizontal line) of $\beta - \alpha + 1$ bits. Thus if $\beta - \alpha$ is large enough, this pattern will be classified as interesting and the program above (or a better one) for it will be stored.

By adding instructions to program p_1 one gets program p_2:

```
j := j0;
for j = γ to δ do
for i = α to β do
A[i,j] := 0 od od
```

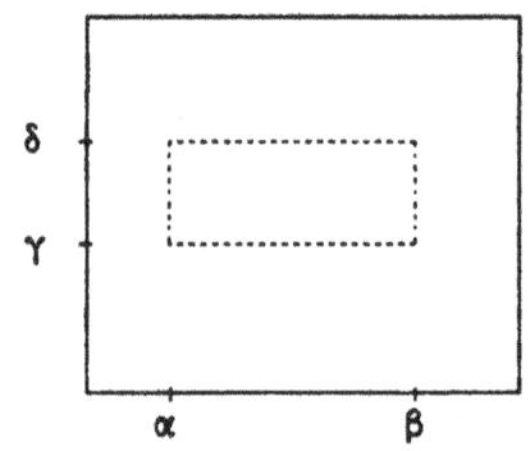

Fig. 5b

(see figure 5 b), which describes a white rectangle. The first instruction in p_2 can be deleted. This turns produces the even shorter program p_3:

```
for j = α to β do
for i = γ to δ do
A[i,j] := 0 od od.
```

Variation of the constants will produce in the case $\alpha = \gamma = 1$, $\beta = \delta = N$ an all white background.

Next if we present to the system figure 5 c we ge by variation of the constants in p_3 a program p_4 which produces the black rectangle. Concatenating a program for white background with this program produces figure 5 c.

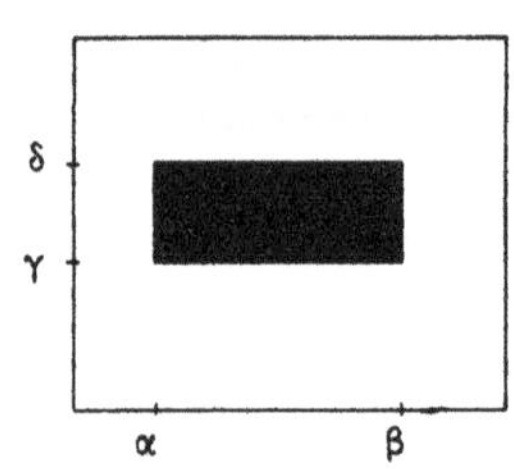

Fig. 5c

By a somewhat greater mutation of program p_4 we get p_5:

for $j = \gamma$ to δ do
for $i = \alpha$ to β do
$k := i + j - \gamma$;
$A[k,j] := 1$ od od

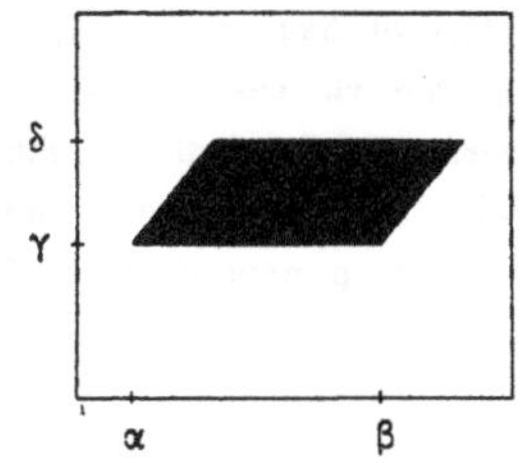

Fig 5d

which produces the parallelogram in figure 5d Except for the crooked line the system can now reproduce figure 1 by concatenation of programs it knows. Consider figure 6a . It has a white background and a single black dot P_0, which can be described by program p_6:

$i := x_0$;
$j := y_0$;
$A[i,j] := 1$.

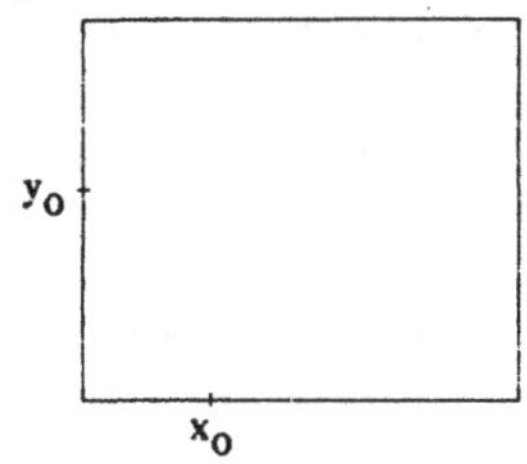

Fig. 6a

Two black dots like in figure 6b can be described by concatenating two copies of p_6 and chanching constants in the second copy. One gets program p_7:

$i := x_0$;
$j := y_0$;
$A[i,j] := 1$;
$i := x_1$;
$j := y_1$;
$A[i,j] := 1$.

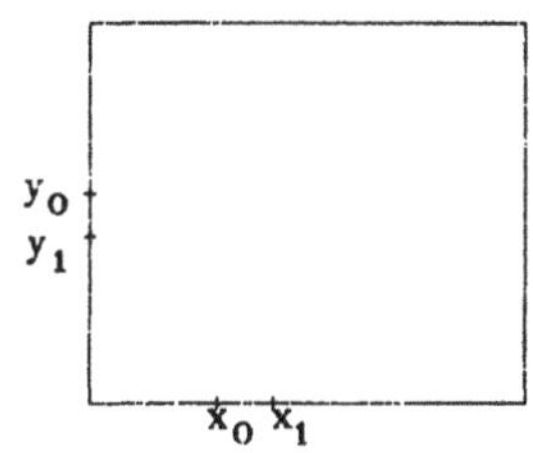

Fig. 6b

This program has length $\log x_0 + \log y_0 + \log x_1 + \log y_1 + O(1)$. This would be fine if the two dots were in generai position. But the dots in figure 6b are not. Indeed changing only two instructions in p_7 produces p_8:

$i := x_0$;
$j := y_0$;
$A[i,j] := 1$;
$i := i + x_1 - x_0$;
$j := j + y_1 - y_0$;
$A[i,j] := 1$.

This program is shorter than p_7 if $\log (x_1-x_0) + \log (y_1-y_0) < \log x_1 + \log y_1$. Repeating the same process k-2 more times produces a description of a crooked line of k points. This description reflects human intuition.

5. Plans for experimantal work. Installation of a system of the kind described above is planned for 1988 as a subproject of the I.I.I. (Innovative Informations Infrastrukturen) project. This is a joint project of the University of Saarbrücken and Siemens. In this projects hundreds of Siemens PC's are hooked together via the network CANTUS, which was developped at the computing center of the University of Saarbrücken. Further processing power will be available on DATIS-P, a massively parallel computer under construction in Saarbrücken as a project of SFB (Sonderforschungsbereich) 124 sponsored by the DFG.

6. References

[K] Kolmogrov, A. N.: Three approaches to the quantitative definition of information problems in information transmission vol. 1 No. 1 pp. 1-7, 1965.

[P] Paul W.: Kolmogorov complexitiy and lower bounds, Fundamentals of computation theory 79, Band 2, pp. 325-334, 1979

[PSS] Paul W. Seiferas J. I. Simon J.: An information-theoretic approach to time boungs for on-line computation, Journal of computer and system sciences Vol. 23, No. 2, 10/81, pp 108 - 126, 1981

[S] Solomonoff R. J.: A formal theory of inducture inference Part 1 & 2 Information and Control Vol. 7, pp. 1-22, 224-254, 1964.

PROPERTIES OF NETWORKS WITH CHAOTIC NEURONS

M. Peschel, H.-M. Voigt
Academy of Sciences of the GDR
Centre for Scientific Instrumentation (ZWG)

H. Herzel
Humboldt University
Department of Physics

Abstract

Some neuronal nets concepts are proposed taking into account different kinds of sensorial functions of the individual neurons as well as a possible chaotic mapping as an autonomous dynamic activity of the neuron cells.

Under some reasonable demands for the coaction of the different input channels of a neuronal cell Lotka-Volterra like interaction structures are met resembling some local model concepts from system simulation experiences.

Despite of their different representations the proposed neuronal networks usually show quick transition to equilibrium states which could play the same role as in the well-known Hopfield model.

Keywords

Sensorial transition, local model, chaotic mapping, neuron, network

1. Introduction

Our main aim in this paper is to take into account in the behavioural model of a neuronal network the sensorial function of a neuron.

From psychological and neurophysiological experiences some different concepts for the sensorial functions of a cell were established, e.g. the Weber-Fechner law and the Stevens power law.

With some reasonable demands on the behaviour of an individual neuronal cell as a module of a neuronal network we get new quasi normal form descriptions of deterministic neuronal networks.

Accidentally these normal forms are very similar to some first-order simulation schemes for arbitrary dynamical systems [3,6] making use of two types of local models, the so-called **Direct Recursion** [2] and **Natural Recursion** [4,5].

We are convinced that besides a quasi deterministic interaction structure linking the neurons of a network every individual neuron should possess an autonomous activity which we describe with the help of a chaotic mapping.

Without such an own dynamic activity the proposed neuronal networks would not be able to lead to a quasi-logical behaviour with a quick transition to equilibrium states because in such a case the neuronal networks would be given by simulation schemes for any dynamic behaviour.

2. Demands on the Individual Neurons

2.1 Every neuron cell, not only the so-called sensorial neurons, should possess its own sensorial apparatus. With the help of this sensorial function it performs information transformation according to a suitable nonlinear characteristics.

The purpose of this transformation is to have a large aperture, to beware the neuron of to much energy, or to have a high signal sensitivity for example in the case of sensorial pain.

We differ between the following three forms of the nonlinear transformation

a) $E \cdot G = \ln\left(\frac{R}{R_0}\right)$ Weber-Fechner Law

b) $E \cdot G = \left(\frac{R}{R_0}\right)^k - 1$ Stevens Power Law

c) $E = EI \frac{1 - \exp(-a \cdot U)}{1 + EI \cdot \exp(-a \cdot U)}$

with

$U = \frac{R}{R_0} - 1$ Logistic Saturation Law.

In these transformations the variables have the following significance:

E	synaptic excitation
G	proportional factor, inverse of amplification
R	stimulus intensity
R_0	stimulus sensorial threshold
EI	asymptotic excitation value .

2.2 A cell has at its entries not only the property of information transformation (respective reduction) but also the ability of interpretation of the received transformed information.

That means besides the above mentioned nonlinear transformations every channel has at a membrane the ability to realize the corresponding inverse transformations

a) $\frac{c}{c_s} = \exp(E \cdot G)$ **Nernst Law**

b) $\frac{c}{c_s} = (1 + E \cdot G)^{\frac{1}{k}}$

c) $\frac{c}{c_s} = 1 + \frac{1}{a} \cdot \ln\left(\frac{1+E}{1-\frac{E}{E_l}}\right).$

Here the excitation E is given by an electrical activity, a potential difference being transformed into a concentration ratio c/c_s of an exchanged ions flow at the membrane.

Therefore in every synaptic channel of any neuron leading to the nucleus of the cell we should meet an ion flow quantitatively represented by the above given expressions. An ion flow carries at the same time an electrical charge, that means represents an electrical signal.

2.3 The problem arises, what is the coaction law for the combination of the signals of the different channels leading to the cell nucleus, responsible for the generation of the overall excitation law of the considered cell.

As a feasible coaction law we demand a conjunction realized by multiplication of the signals represented by the ratios c_i/c_{is} on the different channels.

This conjunction multiplied with the cells own activity x_i generates then the cell activity in the next moment, i.e. after a characteristic tact *DS* of the cell.

We differ here between the slow tact *DS* ,characteristic for the information processing properties of the cells, and the quick tact *DQ*, characteristic for the cells own dynamic activities. *DQ* should be at least one order larger then *DS*.

Therefore we get for the slow tact behaviour of the neuronal network the following three possible concepts following consequently all our demands

a) $x'_i = x_i \exp\left(\sum_j G_{ij} x_j\right)$

b) $x'_i = \prod (1 + |G_{ij}| \cdot x_j)^{\frac{\operatorname{sgn}(G_{ij})}{k}}$

c) $$x'_i = \prod \left(1 + |G_{ij}| \cdot \ln\left(\frac{1 + x_j}{1 - x_j} \right) \right)^{\mathrm{sgn}(G_{ij})}$$

with $EI = 1$.

It turns out that all three derived deterministic neuronal nets concepts are general simulation schemes for arbitrary dynamical networks.

That means especially that we cannot expect a stable tendency to approach one of the possible equilibrium states of these networks. Before we introduce additional the cells own chaotic activity let us study the connection to simulation models for using simple local models.

3. Local Models for Simulation Purposes

In describing approximately the behaviour of time series of arbitrary dynamical systems in short period of time we can apply a huge multifold of very different local models. Here we need only the most simple of them.

3.1 Local Models with Direct Recursion

For a given differential equation

$$\frac{dx}{dt} = y$$

we use as a first order integration scheme (local linear)

$$x' = x\left(1 + D \cdot \left| \frac{y}{x} \right| \right)^{\mathrm{sgn}\left(\frac{y}{x}\right)}.$$

For positive right hand side y and positive x this scheme corresponds to Euler method of first order integration. In [1] we have shown that every autonomous dynamical system given by a set of ordinary differential equations can be transformed into the famous Lotka-Volterra equation

$$\frac{dx_i}{dt} = x_i \sum G_{ij} x_j \quad , \quad i = 1, 2, \ldots, n.$$

In the non-autonomous case we would get

$$\frac{dx_i}{dt} = x_i \left(\sum G_{ij} x_j + \sum H_{is} y_s \right).$$

If we apply the above defined local model concept to the case of autonomous Lotka-Volterra equations we get the following simulation scheme

$$x'_i = x_i \prod \left(1 + |G_{ij}| x_j\right)^{sgn(G_{ij})}.$$

Here the simulation tact *DS* is included into the system parameters G_{ij}. Obviously this simulation scheme is a special case of the above derived neuron network b).

3.2 Local Models with Natural Recursion

The method of natural recursion integrates the simple differential equation

$$\frac{dx}{dt} = y$$

with the following scheme (local exponential function)

$$x' = x \cdot \exp\left(D \cdot \frac{y}{x}\right).$$

If we apply this integrator to the autonomous Lotka-Volterra equation we get

$$x'_i = x_i \exp\left(\sum G_{ij} x_j\right)$$

where the simulation tact *DS* is included into the system parameters G_{ij}.

This first order simulation scheme for an arbitrary dynamical system obviously coincides completely with the proposed neural network a).

In the case of neuronal networks we are interested to establish for the neuronal network itself an equilibrium state approached quickly during the autonomous dynamical behaviour. To get the equilibrium approaching property in one autonomous layer we combine now the dynamical interaction activities of the network above derived with individual chaotic mappings of all neurons of the network.

4. Chaotic Mappings of a Single Neuron

We demand that every single neuron has an own dynamical activity which is quasi-chaotic and should expose a huge set of different frequencies between the highest frequency corresponding to the quick tact *DQ* of the neuron and lower frequencies reaching the frequencies of possible periodic motions corresponding to the Lotka-Volterra dynamical interaction model.

As a model for a rather flexible chaotic mapping of the individual neuron we propose a generalization of the May-Feigenbaum mapping, the so-called EVOLON chaotic mapping

$$x' = R \cdot N \cdot x^k \cdot (1 - x^w)^l.$$

Here for the amplification R holds

$$0 < R \leq 1.$$

N is a normalization factor chosen in such a way that the maximum value of the mapping is equal to R

$$N = \frac{(1+\varkappa)^{l+\frac{k}{w}}}{\varkappa^{\frac{k}{w}}}$$

with

$$\varkappa = \frac{k}{l \cdot w}.$$

If we substitute in every row of the neuronal network instead of the factor x_i the value of this chaotic mapping, we can observe what we wanted to see:
Under very different conditions of parameter sets G_{ij}, initial values and parameters k_i, w_i, and l_i of the corresponding chaotic mappings, we find a rather quick transition to an equilibrium state.

This is a necessary condition which a neuronal network should fulfil if the set of its equilibrium states should be used as models pattern entrained into the network e.g. for pattern recognition purposes.

But at the same time we observe a certain handicap or restriction. A neuron without signals in the synaptic channels should show a tendency to approach with its quick tact DQ very quickly a low value of its activity x corresponding to the logical value zero. This property holds for sufficiently small values of $\varkappa$ (k small or/and l respectively w high).

The EVOLON chaos becomes under this condition a rather inhomogeneous chaos with a tendency to hinder the deterministic dynamic interaction to reach an equilibrium point.

Obviously under these conditions a reasonable work of the neuronal network can be established only with a certain compromise between both tendencies.

The chaos must be inhomogeneous enough to allow for the non-activated neuron to approach the logical zero state, but it should not be to inhomogeneous that at the same time we meet a quick and reliable transition to one of the possible equilibrium states of the network.

References

[1] Peschel, M. & W. Mende: Predator-Prey-Models: Do We Live in a Volterra World ? Akademie-Verlag Berlin & Springer-Verlag Wien 1986

[2] Peschel, M., W. Mende & F. Breitenecker: Anwendung der diskreten Theorie ratengekoppelter Systeme in der Regelungstechnik. msr, Berlin, 30(1987)7

[3] Peschel, M., H.-M. Voigt, W. Mende & F. Breitenecker: Modellbildungsrahmen für Zeitreihen als Grundlage für die Simulation dynamischer Systeme. msr, Berlin, 31(1988)3

[4] Voigt, H.-M.: Evolution und Optimierung. Dissertation B (Habilitation). Academy of Sciences of the GDR 1986

[5] Voigt, H.-M.: Optimization by Selection Pressure Controlled Replicator Networks. Systems Analysis, Modelling and Simulation (to appear)

[6] Peschel, M., H.-M. Voigt, W. Mende & F. Breitenecker: Systems-Engineering Methodology for Simulation and Control of Dynamical Networks. Proc. Int. Symp. on Systems Analysis and Simulation. Mathematical Research 46, Akademie-Verlag, Berlin 1988, 232-236

[7] Voigt, H.-M. & I. Santibanez-Koref: Solving Assignment Problems by Selection Pressure Controlled Replicator Networks. Proc. Int. Symp. on Systems Analysis and Simulation. Mathematical Research 46, Akademie-Verlag, Berlin 1988, 274-277

LEARNING RULES AND LEARNING TIMES IN NEURAL NETWORKS

Manfred Opper [1)]

Abstract

The performance of learning rules for neural networks is discussed. For learning of random patterns, mean field methods are used to calculate learning times for ADALINE and PERCEPTRON rules .

1.Introduction

Neural network models have become increasingly popular in statistical physics. They allow to store a set of bit patterns as attractors in a system of interacting neurons and to memorize them by presenting incomplete or distorted input versions . Neural networks have therefore been considered as simple models of associative memory [1].

Networks of spin -glass type are modelled by N two state neurons $S_i \in \{-1,+1\}$, $i=1,\dots,N$. The neurons are connected by couplings J_{ij}; $i,j=1,\dots,N$; $J_{ii}=0$. The information on the stored patterns is encoded in the matrix of these 'synapses'. Each neuron is assumed to feel the internal field

$$h_i(t) = \sum_j J_{ij} S_j(t)$$

and changes its state according to the threshold operation

$$S_i(t+1) = \mathrm{sign}(h_i(t)) \qquad (1)$$

An important problem is how to store or 'learn' sets of patterns in a network . One assumes a second type of dynamics which takes place in a learning phase of the network prior to pattern retrieval. Here the couplings J_{ij} are dynamical quantities rather than the neurons . In this paper I shall discuss different types of 'learning rules' which have been recently applied to learning in neural networks [2-4].

The statistical physics of disordered materials has proven to be very useful in understanding generic features of pattern recognition in networks of the type (1) . Large Networks storing extensively many random patterns could be treated by mean-field methods developped for spin-glass models [5] . As will be shown the same methods apply to the performance of learning algorithms for large networks.

---

1) Institut für theoretische Physik der Justus Liebig Universität Giessen,
D- 6300 Giessen, Heinrich Buff Ring 16, BRD.

2. Learning rules

We study algorithms which allow to adapt a network to a given set of patterns by a proper adjustment of the J_{ij}'s during the network's training phase. To store a set of P patterns $\underline{S}^{\nu} = (S_1^{\nu}, \ldots, S_N^{\nu})$, $\nu=1,\ldots,P$ in the network the couplings J_{ij} must be chosen such that the patterns become stable attractors of the dynamics (1) i.e. a set of inequalities

$$S_i^{\nu} \cdot h_i^{\nu} \geq c_i > 0 \quad ; \quad h_i^{\nu} = \sum_j J_{ij} \cdot S_j^{\nu} \qquad (2)$$

must be fulfilled for every neuron i and pattern ν. We also require that a pattern provided with not too much noise should be properly memorized. A pattern should therefore be stable against a large number of spin flips. It has been argued [4] that if the magnitudes of the internal fields for all patterns are large compared to the absolute values of the couplings good stability is achieved. One can thus use the ratio

$$\Delta_i = c_i / \sqrt{\sum_j J_{ij}^2} \qquad (3)$$

as a local measure of stability.

If the concept of neural networks should lead to technical applications there is a necessity to have simple algorithms which solve the problem of pattern storage most efficient. A requirement which helps to perform the storage in *parallel* for all neurons is that learning rules should be local: At a given neuron i the change of the synaptical strengths J_{ij} due to a pattern ν depends only on the states S_i^{ν} and S_j^{ν} of the connected neurons and possibly on the neuron's internal field h_i^{ν}. Thus most learning rules are based on a generalized Hebbian [6] type of rule: Whenever a pattern ν is presented to the network a term $\delta J_{ij} \sim S_i^{\nu} S_j^{\nu}$ is added to the synaptical couplings. This choice is not only motivated from biological considerations of real neurons but can also be implemented in artificial optical neural networks. The model with coupling matrix

$$J_{ij} = N^{-1} \sum_{\nu} S_i^{\nu} S_j^{\nu} \qquad (4)$$

is the famous Hopfield model [1,7]. If extensively many, $P = \alpha N$, random patterns are stored in this network the inequalities (2) are not strictly fulfilled. However the attractors of the dynamics (1) lie very close to the stored patterns as long as $\alpha < 0.14$ in the limit

$N \to \infty$. For higher storage capacities α or correlated patterns the network fails to memorize the patterns or relaxes into unwanted mixture states [7].

3.ADALINE learning algorithm

Different storing prescriptions have been discussed which allow to overcome certain of the limitations of the Hopfield model . It has been shown that the memory can be prevented from an overload by a mechanism which allows to forget old patterns when new ones are added [8]. On the other hand there have been attempts to stabilize the patterns exactly and enable to store also correlated ones. In the so called Pseudo-Inverse [9,10] approach one requires that the inequalities (2) should be fulfilled with the special choice

$$S_i^\nu \cdot h_i^\nu = 1 \tag{5}$$

for each neuron and pattern. As we shall see later this system of linear equalities for the couplings J_{ij} is not the most general solution to the storing problem.
A local algorithm [3] which converges asymptotically to a solution of (5) is defined by a change δJ_{ij} of the couplings

$$\delta J_{ij} = N^{-1} (1 - S_i^\nu \cdot h_i^\nu) S_i^\nu S_j^\nu \tag{6}$$

whenever a pattern is added to network. This is of the type of a Hebbian rule provided with a weight factor depending on neuron and pattern. For finitely many patterns and large N this procedure again would do the job. If however P is of order N new patterns will destroy the stability of the previously stored ones. Therefore the procedure (5) has to be repeated sequentially for the whole set of patterns again and again. A variant of this algorithm uses the *entire* set of patterns in parallel to update the couplings: At each discrete time step $t = 0,1,2,3,4,\ldots$ they are changed according to

$$J_{ij}(t+1) = J_{ij}(t) + \gamma N^{-1} \sum_\nu (1 - S_i^\nu \cdot h_i^\nu(t)) \, S_i^\nu S_j^\nu \tag{7}$$

$$J_{ii} = 0$$

The parameter γ must be chosen small enough to ensure convergence. Since a similar learning procedue has been used for the ADAptive LINear Element network of Widroff and Hoff in the 60's the algorithm (7) is called ADALINE learning rule (see e. g. [10]). The dynamical system (7) is linear in the couplings $J_{ij}(t)$ and can thus be treated by linear algebra. We define local error of learning for each neuron i,

$$E_i^\mu(t) = 1 - S_i^\mu h_i^\mu(t) \quad , \quad \mu = 1,\dots,P \tag{8}$$

which tells how good pattern μ fulfills condition (5) at this specific neuron. Omitting the argument i in the following one easily derives the linear homogenous equations

$$\underline{E}(t+1) = (\underline{I} - \gamma \underline{B}) \underline{E}(t) \tag{9}$$

with $$B^{\mu\nu} = S_i^\mu S_i^\nu \sum_{j=1} S_j^\mu S_j^\nu \quad , \quad \underline{E} = (E_i^1,\dots,E_i^1)$$

To investigate some typical behaviour of the algorithm for $P,N \to \infty$ one can study its performance for statistical ensembles of patterns ,the simplest choice being that the bits S_i^ν are set +1 or -1 with equal probabilities , independently for each i and ν . In this case the matrix $\underline{B}$ has (correlated) random elements and the components of $\underline{E}$ are random numbers too. The law of large numbers tells us that their are additive functions of the E^ν 's which do not depend on the special realization of the random process in the limit $N,P \to \infty$ .Such quantity is e.g. the total squared error

$$H(t) = (NP)^{-1} \sum_{i\mu} (E_i^\mu(t) E_i^\mu(t)) \quad , \quad t = 0,1,2,3,\dots \tag{10}$$

which is a measure of whether and of how fast the algorithm converges. The statistical fluctuations of H(t) for fixed t vanish in the limit of a large system and H(t) becomes selfaveraging i.e. its actual value coincides with its average with probability one. Therefore we have to calculate $\overline{H}(t)$, the error averaged over the ensemble of random patterns. Solving eq. (9) for nonrandom initial conditions $E_i^\mu(0)$ we obtain

$$\overline{H(t)} = P^{-1} \overline{(\underline{E}^T(t) * \underline{E}(t))} = P^{-1} (\underline{E}^T(0) * \overline{(\underline{I} - \gamma \underline{B})^{2t}} * \underline{E}(0)) \quad ; \tag{11}$$

where T denotes the transpose of a P-vector and the bar denotes the average. We have also used the fact that the average will not depend on the index i. To carry out this average we shall first map the problem onto a model of statistical mechanics with a certain kind of disorder . After using the identity

$$(\underline{\underline{I}}-\gamma\underline{\underline{B}})^t = \int d\lambda\, \lambda^t\, \delta(\underline{\underline{D}}(\lambda)) = \pi^{-1} \lim_{\varepsilon\to 0} \operatorname{Im} \int d\lambda\, \lambda^t\, \underline{\underline{D}}^{-1}(\lambda - i\varepsilon) \tag{12}$$

with $$\underline{\underline{D}}(\lambda) = (\lambda-1)\underline{\underline{I}} + \gamma\underline{\underline{B}}$$

we can apply the Gaussian transformation

$$(D^{-1})^{\mu\nu} = -\frac{\partial^2}{\partial\varepsilon^\mu \partial\varepsilon^\nu} \ln Z[\underline{\varepsilon}]\Big/_{\underline{\varepsilon}=0} \tag{13}$$

where $$Z[\underline{\varepsilon}] = \int \prod_\nu dx^\nu \exp[-i(\underline{x}^T \underline{\underline{D}}\,\underline{x}) + i^{1/2}(\underline{\varepsilon}\,\underline{x})]$$

to express H(t) by the partition function Z of a Gaussian model at imaginary temperature. The random matrix elements $D_{\mu\nu}$ describe a type of quenched disorder. For the present model it can be shown that the averaging over the disorder commutes with the logarithm so that no replica - trick [11] is necessary. Since the interactions $D_{\mu\nu}$ of this auxiliary model are of infinite range a mean field treatment becomes exact for large N and P. The calculation is straightforward and resembles the procedures which are used to study the stable states of the networks themselves [5]. Details will be given elsewhere [12].
Assuming that initially the network was empty ,i.e. $E^\mu 0) = 1$ for all μ , one finally arrives at

$$\overline{H(t)} = \int_{\lambda_1}^{\lambda_2} d\lambda\, \lambda^{2t}\, \rho(\lambda) \tag{14}$$

where

$$\rho(\lambda) = (2\pi\alpha\gamma)^{-1}(1-\lambda)^{-1}\sqrt{(\lambda-\lambda_1)(\lambda_2-\lambda)} + (\alpha-1)/\alpha \cdot \Theta(\alpha-1)\cdot\delta(1-\lambda)$$

and $$\lambda_{1,2} = 1-\gamma(1\pm\sqrt{\alpha})^2$$

$\delta(x)$ and $\Theta(x)$ denote the Dirac function and the one step function respectively. This result shows that for $\alpha < 1$ one can always find a parameter γ such that $\overline{H(t)}$ will decay to 0. Fig.1 gives an example for our result (14) compared with a single simulation on a network of $N = 100$ and $P = 20$.
For $t\to\infty$ $\overline{H(t)}$ decays exponentially and one can optimize γ such that the the relaxati-

on time τ of $H(t)^{1/2}$, which defines a learning time for the algorithm will be a minimum for given α. One finds

$$\gamma_{opt} = (1+\alpha)^{-1} \qquad (15)$$

$$\tau_{opt} = \left(-\ln\left(\frac{2\sqrt{\alpha}}{1+\alpha}\right)\right)^{-1}$$

For $\alpha \to 1$ τ diverges like $(1-\alpha)^{-2}$. It can also be shown that then the magnitude $(\sum J_{ij}^2)^{1/2}$ of the coupling strengths diverges like $(1-\alpha)^{-1/2}$, thus the stabilities Δ_i vanish and the basins of attraction shrink to zero. These divergencies are due to the fact that the system of linear equations (5) becomes overdetermined for P>N. Therefore the failure of the algorithm for α >1 is not restricted to the case of random patterns but holds in general .

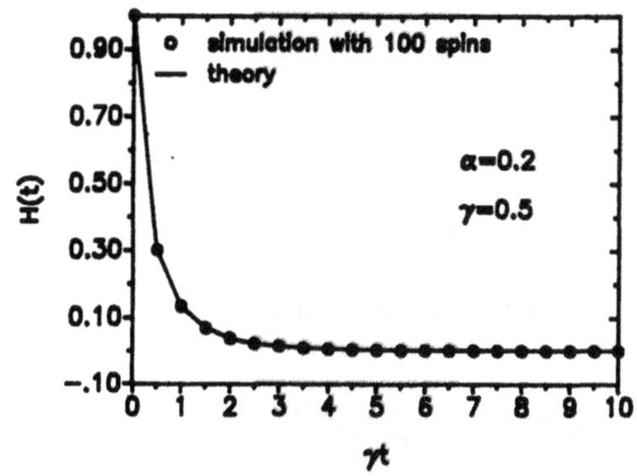

Fig.1 : Decay of quadratic error H(t).

3.PERCEPTRON learning algorithms

We shall now discuss a class of learning algorithms which are in a sense most general for networks of the type (1). They have been invented in the 60' s for learning in PERCEPTRONS (see e.g. [13]), a class of two layered feed forward networks . It has been proven that whenever a set of patterns can be stored by a network of type (1) such algorithm will find a solution for the matrix of couplings J_{ij} in a finite number of learning steps.
The aim of the learning rule is again to fulfill the set of inequalities (2) with given thresholds c_i. The patterns have to be presented repeatedly to the network .However the coupling strengths are *only* changed when the inequalities (2) are violated i.e. when $S_i^\nu \cdot h_i^\nu < c_i$ for the presented pattern. Then a contribution

$$\delta J_{ij} = N^{-1} S_i^\nu S_j^\nu \qquad (16)$$

is added . In a variant of the algorithm [4] also the stability ratios Δ_i are optimized . In this variant the sequence of presented patterns is not arbitrary but for each neuron i one must chose the pattern $\nu(i)$ which is stabilized worst i.e. the one with minimal $S_i^\nu \cdot h_i^\nu$. It can then be shown that in the limit $c_i \to \infty$, Δ_i reaches its maximal possible value. Numerical simulations with random patterns show that practically for $c_i \approx 10$ optimal stability is reached with good accuracy for finite $\alpha = P/N$.

Using a little trick we can calculate the asymptotic (large c_i) learning time for this algorithm. Since the learning rule is local all steps can be performed independently and in parallel for each neuron. Thus the total average learning time equals the average learning time for a single neuron. Defining $t_\nu(i)$ as the number of time steps pattern ν has led to an update of the coupling strengths J_{ij} at neuron i the total number of learning steps for this neuron is $T(i) = \sum_\nu t_\nu(i)$. By definition (16) also the couplings after learning are expressed by the t' s One has

$$J_{ij}(T) = N^{-1} \sum_\nu t_\nu(i) S_i^\nu S_j^\nu \tag{17}$$

Omitting the argument i in the following the conditions (2) become

$$f_\mu \equiv \sum_\nu B^{\mu\nu} x_\nu \geq 1 \qquad \text{with } x_\nu = t_\nu / c \tag{18}$$

and the stability Δ is expressed through the quadratic form

$$H \equiv N\Delta^{-2} = \sum_{\mu\nu} x_\mu B^{\mu\nu} x_\nu = \sum_{\mu\nu} f_\mu (B^{-1})^{\mu\nu} f_\nu \quad , \tag{19}$$

where $B^{\mu\nu}$ was defined in (9).

Assuming that for large but finite c , Δ is close to its maximal value ,we can calculate the t_ν's by simply minimizing the quadratic form H under the linear boundary conditions (18) . Carrying out the variation we have to distinguish between two possibilities for a pattern . Either it fulfills $f_\mu = 1$ or $f_\mu < 1$. Clearly this grouping of patterns varies from neuron to neuron. For the second group the necessary condition for an extremum is

$$0 = \frac{\partial H}{\partial f_\mu} = \sum_\nu (B^{-1})^{\mu\nu} f_\nu = x_\mu \tag{20}$$

i.e.for all μ either $\sum B_{\mu\nu} x_\nu = 1$ or $x_\mu = 0$ .Inserting this result into (19) yields

$$\lim_{c\to\infty} \quad N^{-1} c^{-1} T = N^{-1} \min H = (\max \Delta)^{-2} \tag{21}$$

We have thus expressed the asymptotic learning time by static quantities of the network after learning. Note that this result holds independently of the set of patterns and of N, the size of the network. For large networks $N\to\infty$ and $P = \alpha N$ random patterns the maximum stability Δ has been recently calculated by E. Gardner [14]. We shall use a related approach [15] which also allows for a determination of the entire distribution of the x_μ's. We define a partition function

$$Z = \int \prod_\mu (dx_\mu \Theta(f_\mu - 1)) \exp[-\beta H - \beta \lambda x_1] \tag{22}$$

with a temperature like parameter β^{-1}. For $\beta\to\infty$ only the point in phase space contributes which minimizes H under the boundary conditions $f_\mu = 1$. We can therefore calculate the value of x_1 for an arbitrarary pattern 1 by a logarithmic derivative of Z. Averaging x_1 over the ensemble of random patterns yields for the average of T.

$$\lim_{c\to\infty} N^{-1} c^{-1} \overline{T} = \alpha \overline{x}_1 = -\alpha N^{-1} \lim_{\beta\to\infty} \frac{\partial}{\partial\lambda} \beta^{-1} \overline{\ln Z}_{/\lambda=0} \tag{23}$$

Similarly the entire distribution of x_1 can be calculated from the average of $\ln Z$. (22) is again a model with quenched disorder and can be solved in the limit $N\to\infty$ by means of the replica trick. As one result we recover E.Gardner's solution for the maximum stability Δ

$$\int_{-\Delta}^{\infty} Dt(t+\Delta)^2 = \alpha^{-1} \quad , \quad Dt = e^{-t^2/2} dt/(2\pi)^{1/2} \tag{24}$$

Using (22) we can compare our prediction with numerical simulations. Fig 2. shows an excellent agreement between (21) and learning times averaged over 50 realizations of random patterns in networks of N=100 and P< 120. For larger P finite size effects become stronger which could in principle be treated by calculating the fluctuations around the mean field solutions. For $\alpha\to 2$ T diverges like $(2-\alpha)^{-2}$ and the network becomes overloaded. The result $\alpha = 2$ for the critical storage capacity however is restricted to completely random patterns. As has been shown e.g. for patterns with an average 'magnetization' m_0 in the limit $m_0\to 1$ (the patterns are almost identical) the storage capacity itself can become arbitrary large [14].

Preliminary numerical studies show that the result (21) is also an excellent approximations for the number of updates in the standard perceptron algorithm at large thresholds c.

Finally we have calculated the probability distribution w(x)dx, that an arbitrary x_μ has values between x and x+dx . For large P,N this also equals the distribution of **all** x_μ's for a given realisation of the random patterns at one neuron . As the main result we find that there is a nonzero fraction $P_0(\alpha)$

$$P_0(\alpha) = \int_{-\Delta}^{\infty} Dt \tag{25}$$

of patterns with $x_\mu = 0$. These patterns do not have to perform **any** learning steps at at a particular neuron. If these patterns could be selected in an early stage of the algorithm there would be a chance to speed up the algorithm remarkably. For the remaining patterns the condition $f_\mu=1$ is by (18) a linear system in the unknown x_μ' s (without an explicit dependence on the threshold c) and could therefore be solved by fast algorithms in times not diverging with c. This problem is presently under consideration.

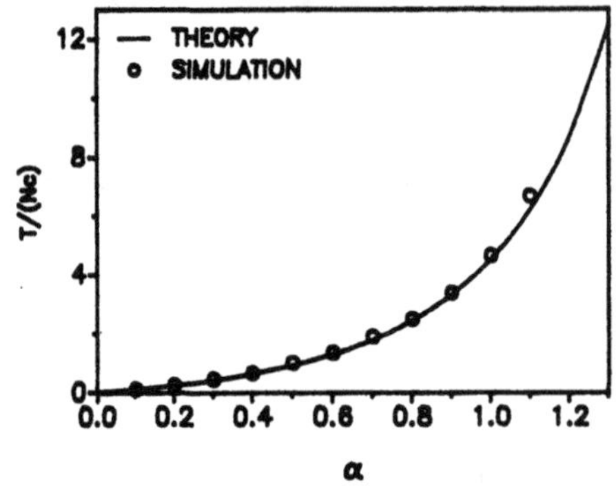

Fig.2 : Number of learning steps for PERCEPTRON algorithm.

4. **Conclusions** The statistical mechanics of disordered systems applies well to the dynamics of learning rules for large neural networks. Our results have been derived for completely random patterns. It would be interesting to see how the performance of the algorithms varies with the complexity of the patterns. For instance hierarchically correlated patterns might be more realistic candidates for a memory.

References

[1] Hopfield, J.J., Proc. Natl. Acad. Sci. U.S.A. 79 (1982), 2554.

[2] Bruce, A. D., Canning, A., Forrest, B., Gardner, E., and Wallace, D. J., in Proceedings of the Conference on Neural Networks for Computing, Utah, 1986.

[3] Diederich, S. and Opper, M., Phys. Rev. Lett. 58 (1987), 949.

[4] Krauth, W. and Mezard, M., J. Phys. A 20 (1987), L745.

[5] Amit, D.J., Gutfreund, H., and Sompolinsky, H., Phys. Rev. Lett. 55 (1985), 428.

[6] Hebb, D., *The Organization of Behaviour* (Wiley, New York) (1949).

[7] Kinzel, W., Z. Physik B 60 (1987), 205.

[8] van Hemmen, L., Europhys. Lett. (1988), 603.

[9] Personnaz, L., Guyon, I. and Dreyfus, G., Phys. Rev. A 34 (1986), 4217.

[10] Kohonen, T., *Self Organization and Associative Memory* (Springer, New York) (1988).

[11] Edwards, S. F. and Anderson, P. W., J. Phys. F 5 (1975), 965.

[12] Opper, M. and Diederich, S. in preparation.

[13] Block, H. D., Rev. Mod. Phys. 34 (1962), 123.

[14] Gardner, E., J. Phys. A 21 (1988), 257.

[15] Opper, M., to be published in Rap. Comm. Phys. Rev. A 38 (1988).

STORAGE AND RETRIEVAL DYNAMICS OF TEMPORAL SEQUENCES IN A NEURAL NETWORK

J.L.van Hemmen
Sonderforschungsbereich123
Universität Heidelberg
Im Neuenheimer Feld 294
D-6900 Heidelberg

ABSTRACT

In this paper three closely related issues are reviewed.

1. Derivation of exact deterministic equations which describe the evolution of temporal sequences with delay stabilization and a stochastic heat bath dynamics. The analysis includes the case of *extensively* many patterns outside a finite cycle. Both parallel and sequential updating are treated. The equations display limit cycle oscillations with a broad diversity of wave forms. For exponential delay it is shown how an increase of the transition amplitude leads to local chaos.

2. Complex temporal associations. These deal with situations where an ambiguity occurs in the succession of states: Depending on its history, the system has to choose one out of several equivalent possibilities. It is shown how simple interactions between three (or more) neurons and multiple time delays allow a satisfactory performance. No short-term synaptic plasticity is needed.

3. The Hebb rule, a local learning prescription. Taking advantage of the *broad* distribution of delays present in the natural retrieval dynamics, we incorporate these delays in the learning session as well. In so doing, we obtain a mathematical implementation of the Hebb rule which includes as special cases both the original Hopfield model, handling static objects, and the usual cycle generating mechanisms. However, due to the fact that the distribution of delays is broad, the procedure is surprisingly robust and faithful.

In all three issues, the unifying theoretical concept is the notion of sublattice in conjunction with the corresponding sublattice magnetization.

1. INTRODUCTION

Temporal associations, such as reciting a poem, counting, and the control of rhythmic movements, are integral parts of the repertoire of our nervous system. Though an extensive formalism has been developed to explain the associative recollection of a memory, until recently no analytic theory was available to describe the neurodynamics which is involved in temporal associations. In this paper such a theory is sketched [1], it is shown under what conditions regular sequences are present, and how a transition to local chaos can occur. We also deal with *complex* temporal associations [2] where, depending on its history, the system has to choose one out of several equivalent possibilities. Finally, we turn to a mathematical implementation [3] of the Hebb rule, a mainstay of the theory of learning [4], and indicate how it naturally accounts for a representation of both static and dynamic objects.

To describe collective effects in a neural network, we take the neurons as formal entities with only two states, active and quiescent, which are represented most conveniently by Ising spins, $S_i = \pm 1$. Here i ranges between 1 and N, the size of the network. At neuron i, the sum of the incoming signals gives rise to a postsynaptic potential or local field $h_i(t)$, where t denotes time, and the simplest possible dynamics is

$$h_i(t) = \sum_j J_{ij}\, S_j(t) \Rightarrow S_i(t + \Delta t) = \mathrm{sgn}[h_i(t)]. \tag{1}$$

Updating in (1) is either parallel (all spins are updated at the same time) or sequential (each time a single spin is updated). To take care of the noise present in the network one can introduce the notion of temperature and replace the dynamics (1) by a *stochastic* dynamics of the Glauber type [5] at inverse temperature β. At zero temperature ($\beta = \infty$), one recovers (1). We will return to this issue in Sec. 3.

According to Hebb [4], the data are to be stored in the J_{ij}. How this is done for both static and dynamic objects, using the very same dynamics as during a retrieval session, will be explained in Sec. 7.

By now the collective behavior of neural nets with symmetric couplings is rather well understood [6 − 10]. The basic idea is to introduce an energy function or Hamiltonian

$$H_N = -\frac{1}{2}\sum_{i,j} J_{ij}\, S_i\, S_j$$

with suitable symmetric couplings $J_{ij} = J_{ji}$ and realize that sequential (Glauber or Monte Carlo) dynamics is equivalent to the system performing a *downhill* motion in the (free-)energy landscape associated with H_N. However, this type of dynamics does not allow a temporal sequence. To wit, a downhill motion ends up in a (free-) energy minimum and the system stays there. We, therefore, have to look for another mechanism.

2. TEMPORAL SEQUENCES

Transitions between patterns require a certain amount of asymmetry. To this end, the synaptic efficacies are imagined to consist of two parts, *viz.* a symmetric part, $T_{ij}^{(1)} = \sum_{\mu=1}^{q} \xi_{i\mu}\, \xi_{j\mu}$, which is chosen so as to stabilize [6] a set of q binary random patterns $\{\xi_{i\mu}\ ;\ 1 \le i \le N\}$ with $1 \le \mu \le q$, and an asymmetric part, $T_{ij}^{(2)} = \sum_{\mu=1}^{p} \xi_{i\mu+1}\, \xi_{j\mu}\ ,\ p \le q$, which is expected (see below) to induce transitions between the patterns. We have a *cycle* if $p + 1 \equiv 1$ (mod p), which we assume from now on.

The above setup can be simplified. First, p is taken to be finite. (Nobody has ever recited a poem of a length comparable to the total amount of data stored). The case of extensively many patterns outside the cycle ($p < q = \alpha N$ with $\alpha > 0$) will be treated at the end of this paper. For finite q we can also assume $p = q$, since, as we will see shortly, the patterns outside the cycle do not play any active role.

If we take $J_{ij} = J_{ij}^{(1)} + \epsilon\, J_{ij}^{(2)}$ with $J_{ij}^{(\alpha)} = N^{-1}\, T_{ij}^{(\alpha)}, \alpha = 1, 2$, then [6] nothing will happen for small ϵ whereas for larger values of ϵ the sequence nearly instantaneously gets mixed completely. The reason is that $J_{ij}^{(2)}$ wants to induce yet another transition, $\mu \to \mu + 1$, *as soon as* μ appears. A solution to this problem was found by Kleinfeld [11] and by Sompolinsky and Kanter [12]. They introduced a *delay* which stabilizes the system in each state μ before it makes the transition to $\mu + 1$. If

$$\bar{S}_j(t) = \int_0^\infty ds\, w(s)\, S_j(t - s) \tag{2}$$

is the delay term which samples the past up to time t with positive weight w, then the postsynaptic potential (local field) experienced by neuron i is assumed to be given by

$$h_i(t) = \sum_j J_{ij}^{(1)} S_j(t) + \epsilon \sum_j J_{ij}^{(2)} \bar{S}_j(t). \tag{3}$$

The weight or memory kernel w is normalized to one. Typical weight functions, which all have a natural decay time τ, are $w(t) = \delta(t-\tau)$ for δ-function delay, $w(t) = \tau^{-1}$ if $0 \le t \le \tau$ and vanishing elsewhere for step function delay, and $w(t) = \tau^{-1}\exp(-t/\tau)$ for exponential delay. We will see in Sec. 7 that, from a physiological point of view, exponential and δ-function delay are the most natural ones.

Using the overlaps $m_\mu(t) = N^{-1}\sum_i \xi_{i\mu} S_i(t)$, we can write

$$h_i(t) = \sum_\mu \xi_{i\mu}\, m_\mu(t) + \epsilon \sum_\mu \xi_{i\mu+1}\, \overline{m}_\mu(t). \tag{4}$$

If a system operating at zero temperature ($T = 0$) has made a transition $\nu - 1 \to \nu$ at time $t = 0$, then we expect it to make another transition $\nu \to \nu + 1$ only after a time of the order τ and *provided* $\epsilon > 1$. Indeed, under these conditions stable cycles were shown to exist [11, 12], mainly through numerical simulations on small samples. The basic idea is most easily understood by considering δ-function delay with the parallel dynamics (1). Suppose that the system makes the transition $\nu - 1 \to \nu$ at $t = 0$ so that, directly afterwards, $h_i(t) = (1+\epsilon)\xi_{i\nu}$ and the asymmetric term stabilizes the pattern ν. As time proceeds, the delay term $m_\mu(t-\tau)$ still samples $\nu - 1$ until $t = \tau$. Then $h_i(\tau) = \xi_{i\nu} + \epsilon\xi_{i\nu+1}$ and the system makes the transition $\nu \to \nu + 1$, *provided* $\epsilon > 1$. And so on. In passing we note that for δ-function delay the symmetric "stabilizing" term $J_{ij}^{(1)}$ apparently is not needed. A more careful consideration shows that (a) this is indeed the case, (b) not all delays function with a transition term $J_{ij}^{(2)}$ only, and (c) even the δ-function case may profit from a stabilizing term, though this depends on the tasks the system has to perform. Details will be published elsewhere [1].

3. DYNAMICS OF A FINITE CYCLE

The equations of motion in the N-dimensional phase space ($N \to \infty$) are generated by either a sequential or a parallel dynamics of the Glauber type at zero or finite temperature. We now indicate how to reduce these equations, which are not amenable to an analytic treatment, to a finite system of nonlinear (ordinary differential) equations with delay. This reduction is *exact*. It allows a detailed investigation of rather surprising results on the behaviour of the solutions as a function of time and the role of temperature.

We start by taking $J_{ij}^{(1)} = N^{-1}\, Q^{(1)}(\underset{\sim}{\xi}_i; \underset{\sim}{\xi}_j) = J_{ji}^{(1)}$ and $J_{ij}^{(2)} = N^{-1}\, Q^{(2)}(\underset{\sim}{\xi}_i; \underset{\sim}{\xi}_j) \neq J_{ji}^{(2)}$ where $\underset{\sim}{\xi}_i = \{\xi_{i\mu}; 1 \le \mu \le q\}$ is the local information available to neuron i and $Q(\mathbf{x};\mathbf{y})$ is some synaptic kernel defined on $\mathbb{R}^q \times \mathbb{R}^q$. The case studied until now has $J_{ij}^{(\alpha)} = \phi(T_{ij}^{(\alpha)})$, $\alpha = 1, 2$, with $\phi(x) = x$ and is therefore called linear. However, $\phi(x) = \operatorname{sgn}(x)$ for both α (*double clipping*) will be shown to work equally well. It is highly relevant to hardware realizations.

Given q binary random patterns, there are 2^q different positions available to the random vectors $\underset{\sim}{\xi}_i$, *viz.* the 2^q corners $\mathbf{x}$ of the q-dimensional hypercube $C^q = [-1, 1]^q$. Each corner $\mathbf{x}$ has a probability $p(\mathbf{x})$. Introducing [5] the sublattices $I(\mathbf{x}) = \{i\,;\, \underset{\sim}{\xi}_i = \mathbf{x}\}$ and sublattice magnetizations

$$m(\mathbf{x};t) = |I(\mathbf{x})|^{-1} \sum_{i \in I(\mathbf{x})} S_i(t) \tag{5}$$

one easily verifies that the local field at i is

$$h_i(t) = \sum_{\mathbf{y}\in C^q} \{Q^{(1)}(\underset{\sim}{\xi}_i;\mathbf{y})\, m(\mathbf{y};t) + \epsilon\, Q^{(2)}(\underset{\sim}{\xi}_i;\mathbf{y})\, \overline{m}(\mathbf{y};t)\} p_N(\mathbf{y})$$

where $p_N(\mathbf{y}) = N^{-1}|I(\mathbf{y})|$ converges to $p(\mathbf{y})$ with probability one as $N \to \infty$. For unbiased patterns, $p(\mathbf{y}) = 2^{-q}$. For nonrandom patterns, one simply *requires* that $p_N(\mathbf{y})$ converge to a limit $p(\mathbf{y})$. (The modification for biased patterns is straightforward and, therefore, not given here.) Finally we note that if i belongs to $I(\mathbf{x})$, then $h_i(t)$ only depends on $\mathbf{x}$ since $\underset{\sim}{\xi}_i = \mathbf{x}$ for all i in $I(\mathbf{x})$. In the bulk limit $h_i(t)$ therefore converges to

$$h(\mathbf{x};t) = \sum_{\mathbf{y}\in C^q} \{Q^{(1)}(\mathbf{x};\mathbf{y})\, m(\mathbf{y};t) + \epsilon\, Q^{(2)}(\mathbf{x};\mathbf{y})\, \overline{m}(\mathbf{y};t)\} p(\mathbf{y}), \tag{6}$$

whatever i in $I(\mathbf{x})$.

The effect of temperature, *i.e.*, a heat bath, is simulated by requiring that the probability of flipping a spin ($\Delta S_i \neq 0$) be given by $[1+\exp(-\beta h_i(t)\Delta S_i)]^{-1}$. At zero temperature ($\beta = \infty$), this prescription reduces to (1). Updating may be either sequential or parallel.

Suppose a parallel updating is performed after each elementary time step Δt. We then find in the limit $N \to \infty$ that for all i in $I(\mathbf{x})$ the thermal average of $S_i(t+\Delta t)$ is $\tanh[\beta h(\mathbf{x};t)]$. The size $|I(\mathbf{x})|$ grows with N so that by (5),(6), and by the (strong) law of large numbers the dynamics converges to

$$m(\mathbf{x}; t+\Delta t) = \tanh[\beta h(\mathbf{x};t)]. \tag{7}$$

This is a recursion relation, which has to be iterated.

If we use sequential updating, only one spin per elementary time step Δt is updated. To obtain an extensive change as N becomes large one has to rescale time so that $\Delta t \propto N^{-1}$; for details, see Refs. 1 and 13. One then finds a set of 2^q coupled nonlinear ordinary differential equations,

$$\dot{m}(\mathbf{x};t) = -\Gamma\{m(\mathbf{x};t) - \tanh[\beta h(\mathbf{x};t)]\}, \tag{8}$$

where $\dot{m}$ denotes differentiation of m with respect to time and Γ is the mean attempt rate per (rescaled) unit time. Both (7) and (8) are exact, whatever the neural activity level and the synaptic kernels Q.

Because of the delay which is contained in $h(\mathbf{x};t)$, Eq. (8) represents a so-called *functional differential equation.* Explicit solutions are not known, but (8) can be solved numerically. The outcomes are presented most conveniently in terms of the overlaps $m_\mu(t)$. Plainly,

$$m_\mu(t) = \sum_{\mathbf{x}\in C^q} p(\mathbf{x})\, x_\mu\, m(\mathbf{x};t) \equiv < x_\mu\, m(\mathbf{x};t) > . \tag{9}$$

In the case of the linear model, and only here, we can reduce (8) to a set of q equations for the overlaps themselves,

$$\dot{m}_\mu(t) = -\Gamma\{m_\mu(t) - < x_\mu \tanh[\beta \sum_\nu x_\nu(m_\nu(t) + \epsilon \overline{m}_{\nu-1}(t))] >\}. \tag{10}$$

One easily verifies that for patterns ν not involved in the cycle we can put $m_\nu(t) = 0$.

Before proceeding we would like to point out [1] an interesting consequence of (8) and (9). At low temperatures, *i.e.*, in the limit $\beta \to \infty$, one may replace $\tanh[\beta h(\mathbf{x};t)]$ by $\mathrm{sgn}[h(\mathbf{x};t)]$. Since $h(\mathbf{x};t)$ is a continuous function of t, the sign function is piecewise constant (1 or -1). Hence the solution $m(\mathbf{x};t)$ of Eq. (8) is locally of the form $a + b\exp(-\Gamma t)$ where a and b are suitable constants. Because of (9), each $m_\mu(t)$ is a linear combination of the $m(\mathbf{x};t)$ and, thus, of the very same form. This is illustrated by Fig. 1.

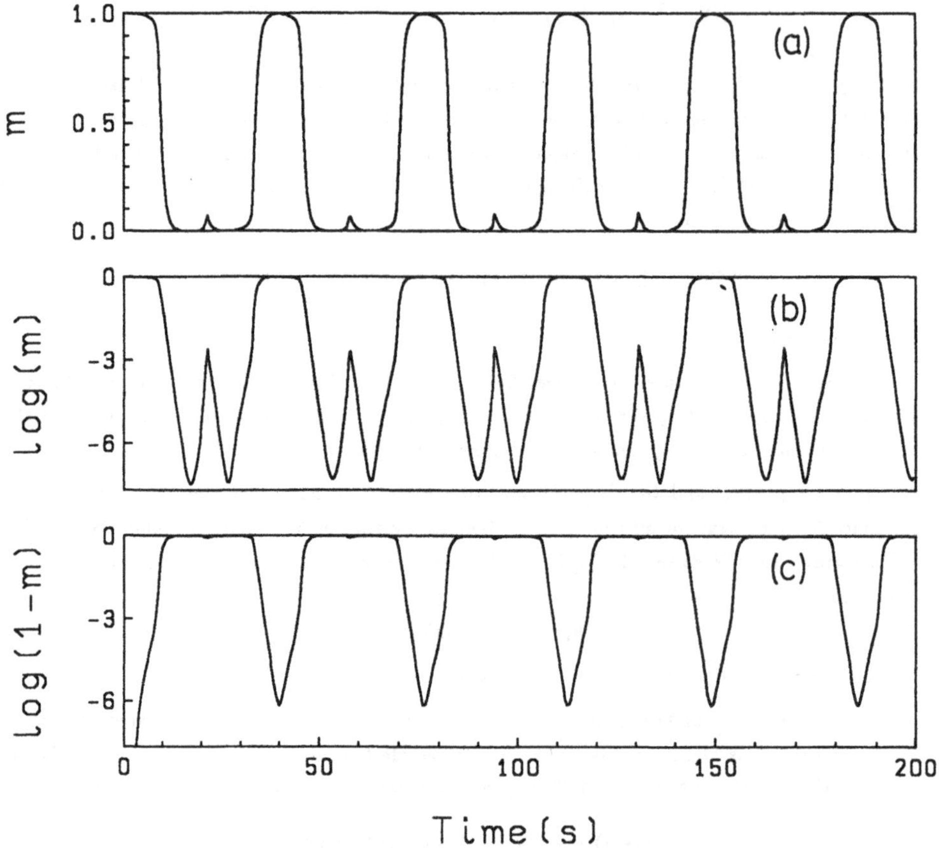

Fig. 1. Overlap $m_1(t)$ with the first pattern of a cycle consisting of three as a function of time: a. $m_1(t)$ itself, b. $ln[m_1(t)]$, c. $ln[1 - m_1(t)]$. We have taken exponential delay with $\tau = 3$ and $\Gamma = 1$. The initial condition is $m_1(0) = 1$; $\epsilon = 0.8$, and $\beta = 7$. The general considerations of Sec. 3 indicate that for sequential dynamics and at low temperatures the overlap is locally of the form $m_1(t) = a + b\exp(-t)$. a suggests that $m_1(t)$ alternately approaches 0 and 1 at an exponential rate. This is indeed brought out by the *down* going straight lines in b and c. Note that the transition $2 \to 3$ is clearly visible as an extra "hump" in b.

4. RESULTS

We now turn to the results. First, whatever the updating, double clipping works as well as the linear model. This is exemplified by Figs. 2 and 3a and b. In our numerical work, the patterns were taken to be unbiased.

Second, for $\epsilon > 1$ cycles may run at temperatures far above the critical temperature of the static model ($\epsilon = 0$), which is 1. See Fig. 3c. This implies that at *high* temperatures the picture of $\epsilon\, J_{ij}^{(2)}$ pushing the system through a free-energy landscape created by $J_{ij}^{(1)}$ is incorrect.

Third, for $\epsilon < 1$ thermal noise ($T > 0$) allows the persistence of (pure) cycles, which, as we have seen, cannot exist at zero temperature. See Fig. 4 for a typical phase diagram in the (β,ϵ) plane. As the inverse temperature β increases, we first have a continuous transition where the cycle appears out of the completely symmetric solution $m_\mu(t) = m$, $1 \le \mu \le q$; at high temperatures the latter is stabilized by $\epsilon > 0$. As β increases further, there is a first-order, discontinuous, transition when the cycle gets stuck in one of the free-energy valleys which it visits during its journey in phase space [14].

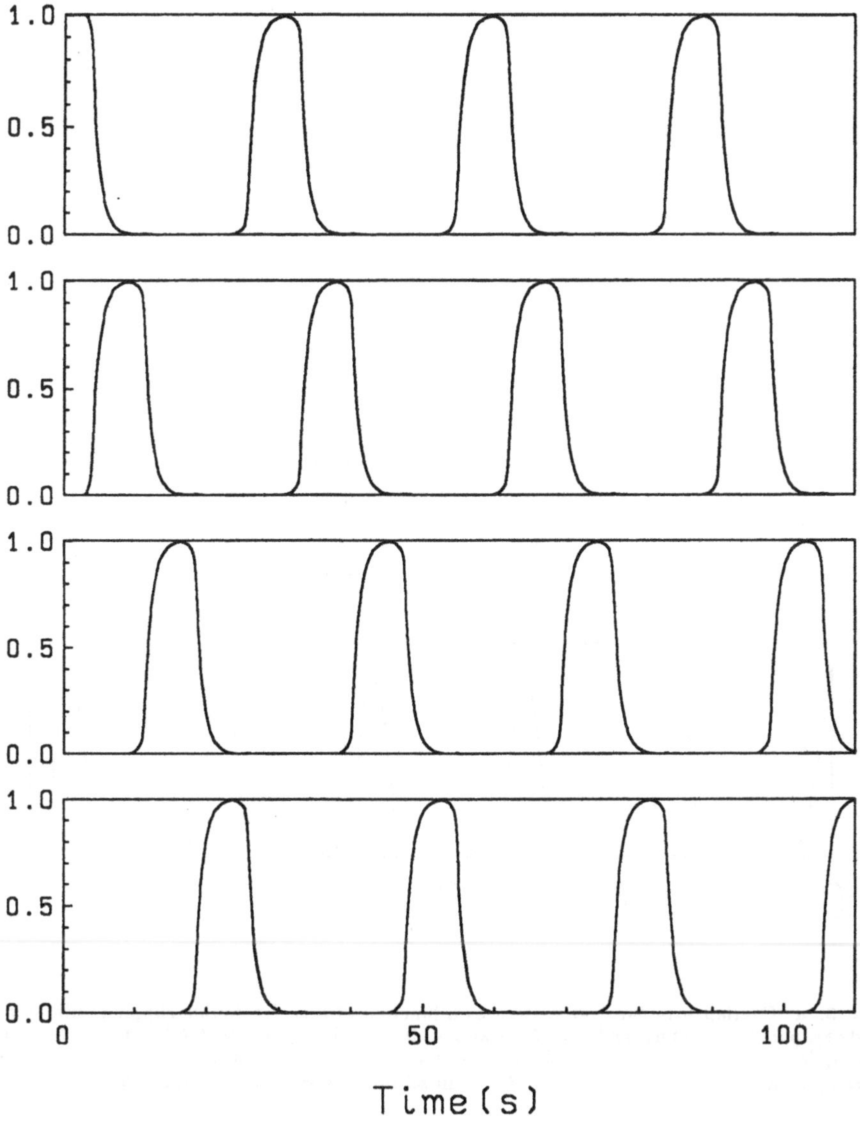

Fig. 2. The overlaps $m_\mu(t)$, $1 \leq \mu \leq 4$, for a cycle of 4 patterns as a function of t. Here we have taken δ-function delay. The other parameters are as in Fig. 1. Note how the pulse "propagates" from the top to the bottom of the figure, i.e., from 1 to 4.

At low temperatures, the picture of $J_{ij}^{(1)}$ creating a (free-)energy landscape where $\epsilon\, J_{ij}^{(2)}$ simply induces transitions between the valleys is reasonably adequate. For instance, in the original Hopfield model [6] m-symmetric states ($m \leq q$) are stable at low temperatures if m is *odd* [7]. Taking now $q = 4$, say, and starting with the 3-symmetric state (1,2,3) one finds a so-called 3-symmetric cycle $(1,2,3) \to (2,3,4) \to \ldots$ if ϵ in $\epsilon\, J_{ij}^{(2)}$ is large enough. A generous increase of temperature, however, will destroy the symmetric cycle and leave one with the pure $1 \to 2 \to 3 \to 4 \to 1$, in a way which is surprisingly similar to the statics [7].

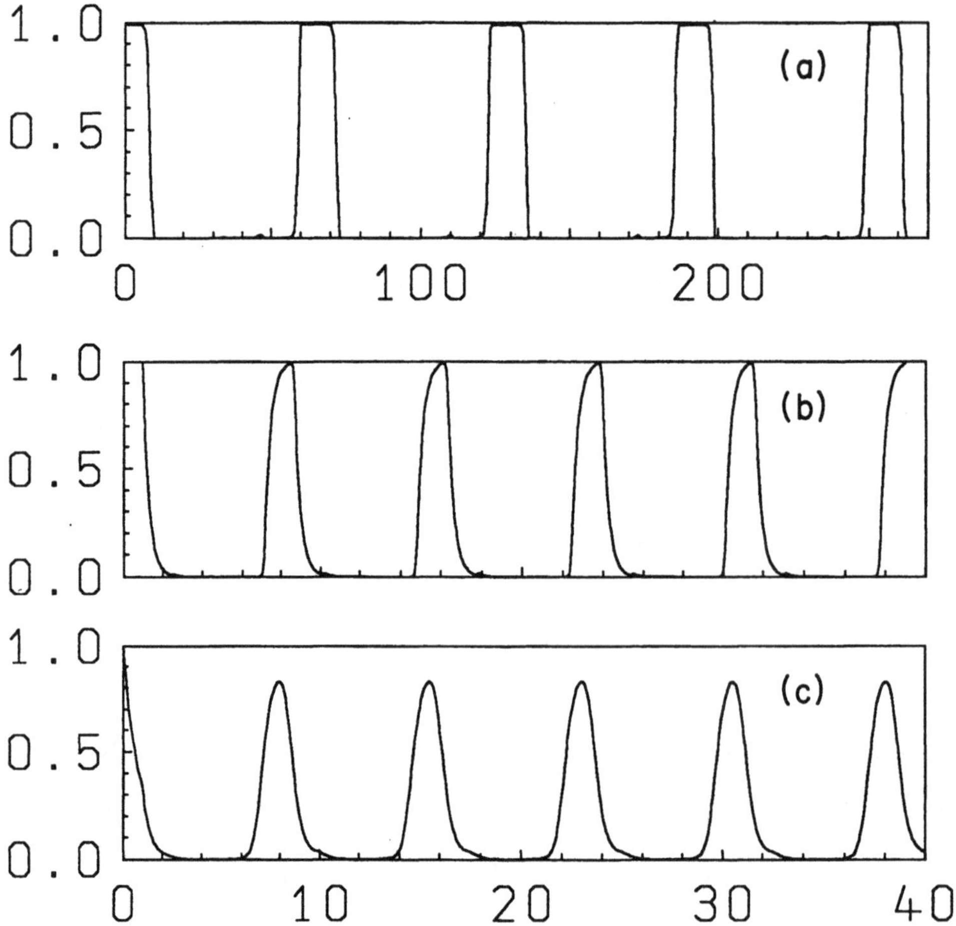

Fig. 3. **a.** Overlap with the first pattern as a function of time for double clipping with step-function delay, parallel updating, and $\tau = 15$ iterations. **b.** Double clipping with δ-function delay and sequential updating. Here $\tau = 1$ and $\Gamma = 3$. As in **a**, $\beta = 5$. **c.** The *linear* model with the same delay and updating as in **b**, but with $\beta = 0.7 < \beta_c^{Hopfield}$. In all three cases, $\epsilon = 1.5$ and $q = 5$.

Finally, we turn to the rather fascinating behavior of the cycles as we increase ϵ. Whatever $\epsilon > 1$, δ-function and step-function delay always allow pure cycles. Exponential delay, however, gives rise to a rather different behavior. In itself a very natural choice [15], it samples the remote past much better than the previous two memory kernels.

Let us fix the temperature T and increase $\epsilon \geq 1$. At low T we start with pure cycles but, as ϵ increases, the system apparently wants to perform a transition to a *fully symmetric* state. This reminds us of the malfunctioning of the model without delay and is consistent with the exponential distribution sampling the remote past. For odd q, the q-symmetric state is stable and invariant, for $\epsilon \geq \epsilon_c$ it is globally attracting, so wherever the system starts, it finally ends up here. The threshold ϵ_c depends on T. At $T = 0$, we have $\epsilon_c \approx 1.8$.

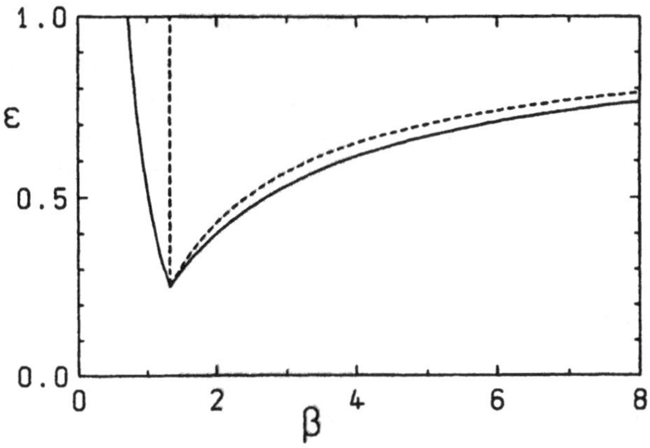

Fig. 4. Exact dynamical phase diagram for a cycle of length $q = 2$ with sequential updating, δ-function delay (solid curve) or exponential delay (dashed curve); $\tau = 1$, $\Gamma = 3$, and the initial condition is $m_1(0) = 1$. The lowest point $(\beta, \epsilon) = (1 + \gamma^{-1}, (1 + \gamma)^{-1})$ with $\gamma = \Gamma\tau$ is apparently universal. In the V-shaped region starting here a pure cycle exists.

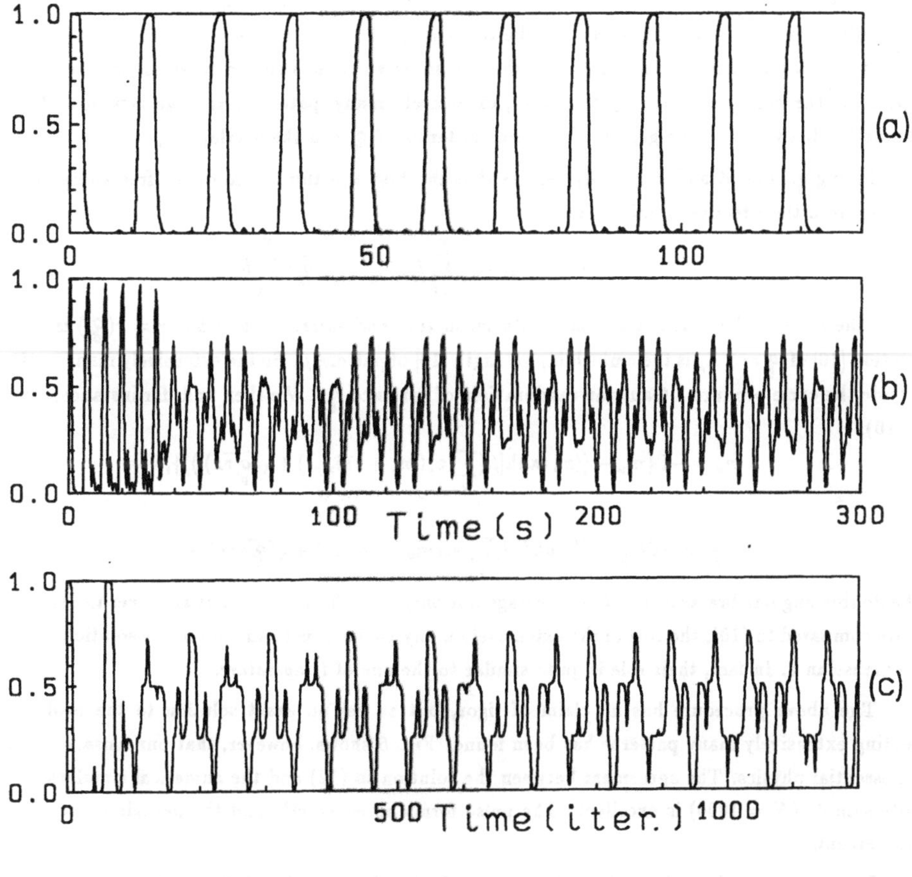

Fig. 5. Overlap with the first pattern as a function of time for exponential delay with $q = 4$ and $\beta = 5$. We have sequential dynamics in a and b and parallel dynamics in c. The pure cycle in a has $\epsilon = 1$. In b and c a globally attracting solution is shown for $\epsilon = 1.7375$. Note the transients.

For even q, a new type of solution appears since at low temperatures the q-symmetric state is not stable. In the case of $q = 4$ and $T = 0.1$, a "3-symmetric" cycle is globally attracting for $\epsilon > 1.73$ and, with it, apparently chaotic behaviour appears. For instance, at $\epsilon = 1.7375$ the orbit looks very chaotic; see Fig. 5b. Indeed, locally it is, though a closer examination reveals that there exists something like a global period, much longer than the one of the pure cycle at $\epsilon = 1$. As shown in Fig. 5c, parallel dynamics does not allow any periodicity. In both cases, however, a sensitive dependence upon the initial conditions [16] could not be found yet. For the moment we tentatively suggest that for $\epsilon > \epsilon_c$ the system is quasiperiodic with three different frequencies. The feature that is new is the local complexity as a function of β and ϵ.

5. EXTENSIVELY MANY PATTERNS

We now turn to the question how to describe a regular and finite cycle of length p in the presence of $q = \alpha N$ patterns outside the cycle. The intuitive idea is that the system spends most of its time in a specific valley (ergodic component), where it can be described by equilibrium thermodynamics. We make therefore a slight detour and turn to the computation of the free energy [7, 10] for the model without any transition term ($\epsilon = 0$). As in the ordinary Hopfield case [7], we single out the finitely many patterns which are involved in the cycle (to be labeled by μ) and average over the rest. Whatever the nonlinearity in Q, the expression for the free energy [10] then consists of three parts. The first refers to the μ-patterns we concentrate on, the second only depends on the order parameter $\mathfrak{q}$ which represents the noise generated by the other, extensively many, patterns, and the last describes the interaction between the two groups of patterns in terms of $\mathfrak{q}$ and the overlaps m_μ.

Fixing $\mathfrak{q}$, one straightforwardly verifies that the first and third term of the free energy can be derived from the effective Hamiltonian

$$H_{eff} = -\frac{1}{2}N \sum_{\mu} \Lambda_\mu (N^{-1} \sum_{i=1}^{N} \xi_{i\mu} S_i)^2 - \sqrt{\mathfrak{q} r} \sum_{i=1}^{N} h_i S_i \tag{11}$$

where the h_i are independent Gaussians with mean zero and variance one while $r = r(\mathfrak{q})$ is a given function [10] of $\mathfrak{q}$ and Λ_μ is the embedding strength [10] of pattern μ. So the extensively many patterns outside the cycle produce a Gaussian random field of variance $\mathfrak{q} r$. We then find, for instance, instead of (10),

$$\dot{m}_\mu = -\Gamma\{m_\mu - \langle\langle x_\mu \tanh[\beta(\sum_\nu x_\nu(m_\nu + \epsilon\overline{m}_{\nu-1}) + \sqrt{\mathfrak{q} r} z)]\rangle\rangle\}, \tag{12a}$$

while

$$\dot{\mathfrak{q}} = -\Gamma\{\mathfrak{q} - \langle\langle \tanh^2[\beta(\sum_\nu x_\nu(m_\nu + \epsilon\overline{m}_{\nu-1}) + \sqrt{\mathfrak{q} r} z)]\rangle\rangle\}. \tag{12b}$$

The double angular brackets denote an average not only over the $x_\mu = \pm 1$ but also over the Gaussian z. As compared to (10), the role of the extensively many patterns is to smoothen the solution through the Gaussian z. In fact, their role is quite similar to the one of *temperature*.

The above procedure has no claim of rigor, but as yet no exact solution to the problem of treating extensively many patterns has been found. Fig. 6 shows, however, that our Ansatz contains the essential physics. The agreement between the solution to (12) and the numerical simulation on a finite sample ($N = 1000$) is excellent. The pulse forms agree exactly and the periods differ by only two percent.

In summary, we have derived exact equations for the dynamical evolution of temporal sequences, at arbitrary temperature and with either parallel or sequential updating. The method applies not only to pure cycles but also to cycles with repetitions (and multi-spin interactions). This is the subject of the next section.

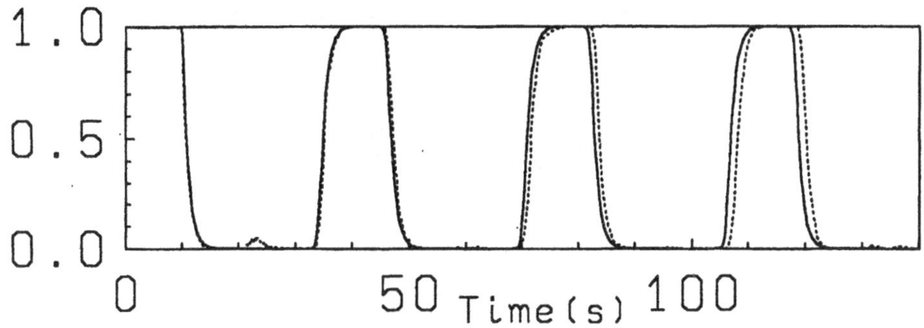

Fig. 6. Comparison between the analytic solution to Eq. (12) (solid curve) and numerical simulation on a finite sample of size $N = 1000$ with Glauber dynamics (dashed curve). Here we have $\beta = 10$, $\epsilon = 1$ and δ-function delay with $\tau = 10$ and $\Gamma = 1$. A cycle of length three is running in the presence of 100 other patterns ($\alpha = 0.10$). Only the overlap with the first of the cycle is shown.

6. COMPLEX TEMPORAL ASSOCIATION

In a temporal association such as producing a simple melody the activity patterns of a neural network follow one after the other in an unambiguous way. (This kind of association is also called linear.) Complexity occurs when, depending on its history, the system has to *choose* one out of several equivalent possibilities. For example, when the melody consists of several verses which all have the same refrain (or chorus). After a verse and the refrain have been finished, the system should not continue with the very same verse but make the transition to a new one. So at the final note of the refrain an ambiguity occurs: There are several verses which can be started but only a single one should be taken.

How to handle this ambiguity? The physics is simple. At the end of the refrain the system should be able to recall that it was in verse n, say, whereas the traces of $n-1, n-2, \ldots$ (et cycl.) should already have faded away. For exponential delay, which can be implemented easily in hardware, this is realized as follows. Details can be found in Ref. 2 - including a discussion of δ-function delay and *correlated* patterns, which are left out here.

Let us imagine that the *elementary* sequences P_ρ , $0 \leq \rho \leq r$, are to be stored and reproduced. For fixed ρ, an elementary sequence consists of a succession of p_ρ activity patterns (ρ, μ), with $1 \leq \mu \leq p_\rho$. As long as μ does not exceed p_ρ, the sequence is linear and transitions are unambiguous. To be specific, we require the sequences to be recalled in the order $P_1\ P_0\ P_2\ P_0 \ldots P_r\ P_0\ P_{r+1}$ and assume $r+1 \equiv 1(\mathrm{mod}\ r)$. We then get a complex cycle with repetitions. The P_ρ , $\rho \neq 0$ are the "verses" and P_0 is the "refrain". This setup may serve as a paradigm to illustrate our general theory.

The activity pattern of the neurons in the state (ρ, μ) is denoted by $\{\xi_i^{\rho,\mu}\ ;\ 1 \leq i \leq N\}$. For the sake of convenience we assume the $\xi_i^{\rho,\mu}$ to be independent random variables which take the values ± 1 with equal probability.

To encode a complex sequence we need *three* kinds of synapse. The synapses of the first kind,

$$J_{ij}^{(1)} = N^{-1} \sum_{(\rho,\mu)} \xi_i^{\rho,\mu} \xi_j^{\rho,\mu}, \tag{13}$$

are symmetric [6]. They stabilize the individual patterns. The synapses of the second kind [1,11,12]

$$J_{ij}^{(2)} = \epsilon N^{-1} {\sum_{(\rho,\mu)}}' \xi_i^{\rho,\mu\oplus 1} \xi_j^{\rho,\mu}, \tag{14}$$

are asymmetric. They generate transitions between successive states, *where "succession" is defined unambiguously.* The primed sum in (14) therefore excludes the state $(0, p_0)$, "the last note of the refrain". In addition, we define

$$(\rho, \mu \oplus 1) := \begin{cases} (\rho, \mu + 1) & , \text{if } \mu < p_\rho, \\ (0, 1) & , \text{if } \mu = p_\rho \quad \text{and} \quad \rho \neq 0, \end{cases} \tag{15}$$

so that P_0 is entered after each P_ρ, $(\rho \neq 0)$. To encode the proper succession at the end of P_0, a third kind of asymmetric synapse which provides a three-neuron interaction is proposed, *viz.*

$$J_{ijk}^{(3)} = \tilde{\epsilon}\, N^{-2} \sum_{\rho=1}^{r} \xi_i^{\rho+1,1} \xi_j^{0,p_0} \xi_k^{\rho,p_\rho}. \tag{16}$$

Finally, as in the models for linear temporal association [1,11,12], the synapses $J_{ij}^{(2)}$ and $J_{ijk}^{(3)}$ must be endowed with their own characteristic response times in order to recall the encoded complex sequence properly. In particular, *two different response times* will be needed for the two input channels j and k of $J_{ijk}^{(3)}$: A short one (τ_a) associated with j, to initiate a transition from $(0, p_0)$ to one of the P_ρ, $\rho \neq 0$, and a longer one (τ_b) associated with k, to "remind" the system of the previous P_ρ and thus provide necessary information for the decision as to which verse ($P_{\rho+1}$) comes next. We thus take the postsynaptic potential (local field) experienced by neuron i to be given by

$$\begin{aligned} h_i(t) &= h_i^{(1)}(t) + h_i^{(2)}(t) + h_i^{(3)}(t) \\ &= \sum_{j(\neq i)} J_{ij}^{(1)} S_j(t) + \sum_j J_{ij}^{(2)}\, \overline{S}_j^a(t) + \sum_{j,k} J_{ijk}^{(3)}\, \overline{S}_j^a(t)\, \overline{S}_k^b(t). \end{aligned} \tag{17}$$

Here $\overline{S}_j^\Delta(t)$, $\Delta = a, b$, denotes a convolution of $S_j(t)$ with a nonnegative memory kernel $w_\Delta(t)$ characterized by an internal time constant τ_Δ [1,11,12]; cf. Eq. (2).

The dynamics of the network is explained most easily in the limit $N \to \infty$, the total number of stored patterns being fixed. In this limit, the local field (17) may be expressed in terms of the overlaps $m_{\rho,\mu}(t) = N^{-1} \sum_i \xi_i^{\rho,\mu} S_i(t)$ as

$$\begin{aligned} h_i(t) = \sum_{(\rho,\mu)} \xi_i^{\rho,\mu}\, m_{\rho,\mu}(t) \;&+\; \epsilon {\sum_{(\rho,\mu)}}' \xi_i^{\rho,\mu\oplus 1}\, \overline{m}_{\rho,\mu}^a(t) \\ &+\; \tilde{\epsilon} \sum_{\rho=1}^{r} \xi_i^{\rho+1,1}\, \overline{m}_{0,p_0}^a(t)\, \overline{m}_{\rho,p_\rho}^b(t) \end{aligned} \tag{18}$$

where $\overline{m}_{\rho,\mu}^\Delta(t)$ denotes a convolution of $m_{\rho,\mu}(t)$ with the memory kernel w_Δ. Each of the $\overline{m}_{\rho,\mu}^\Delta(t)$ builds up while the system is in the corresponding state (ρ, μ), becomes of order one, if it has stayed there for a time of order τ_Δ (or longer), and *decays* on a time scale of the same order of magnitude once the system has left (ρ, μ). Through $h_i^{(1)}(t) + h_i^{(2)}(t)$, this mechanism stabilizes the linear part of each $P_\rho P_0$ (verse + refrain), inducing transitions at regular time intervals of order τ_a. We now turn to the role of τ_b and $h_i^{(3)}(t)$.

Suppose that the system has left the state (ρ, p_ρ), traversed the refrain P_0, and reached $(0, p_0)$, the final state of P_0. Then $h_i^{(3)}(t)$ becomes noticeable only if the system has spent a time of order τ_a in $(0, p_0)$ and has not forgetten (ρ, p_ρ) yet. This requires $\tau_b \approx p_0 \tau_a$. If, moreover, $\overline{m}_{\rho,p_\rho}^b$ dominates the other $\overline{m}_{\gamma,P_\gamma}$ with $\gamma \neq \rho$ and $\tilde{\epsilon}$ is large enough (a matter of easy tuning), then $h_i^{(3)}(t)$ will induce a transition to $(\rho + 1, 1)$, *i.e.*, the system starts a new elementary sequence (verse). Immediately after the transition, $h_i^{(3)}$ still favors $(\rho + 1, 1)$, but after a time of order τ_a this contribution has nearly disappeared and the system makes the transition to $(\rho + 1, 2)$. And so on.

We have verified [2] the above scenario through both numerical simulation on finite samples and solving the Eqs. (7)-(9). The agreement between theory and experiment is excellent and, as shown by Fig. 7, our system is able to neatly "sing a song with refrain".

In passing we note that, in a similar vein, one may also perform loop control - an important step in the direction of universal computing [2].

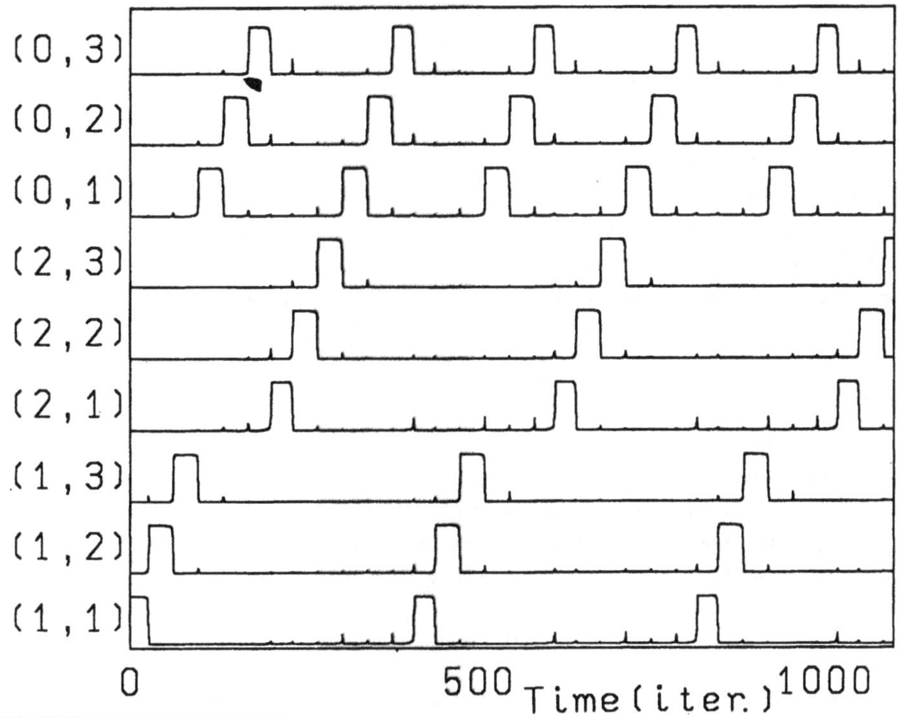

Fig. 7. Analytic solution to Eqs. (7) and (9) for the overlaps of the complex cycle P_1 P_0 P_2 P_0 P_1 $P_0\ldots$ with parallel dynamics at inverse temperature $\beta = 10$. Each horizontal track refers to a specific overlap (ρ, μ) with $1 \leq \mu \leq p_\rho$ and $0 \leq \rho \leq 2$. All P_ρ consist of three patterns, $p_\rho = 3$. The memory kernels w_a and w_b decay exponentially with $\tau_a = 15$ and $\tau_b = 3\tau_a = 45$ iterations. After having finished the refrain P_0, the network still remembers which verse it came from and continues with the *next* verse, thus resolving the ambiguity (going to either P_1 or P_2) at the end of P_0. The asymmetry parameters are $\epsilon = 1$ and $\tilde{\epsilon} = 17.75$.

7. THE HEBB RULE

One may wonder, though, how couplings as in (4), let alone (18), can arise. In this section I will indicate how Hebb's principle [4], if interpreted in a careful way, can be implemented mathematically [3] so as to handle both static objects (single patterns) and temporal associations such as tunes and rhythms. That is, after the network has been taught both single, stationary, patterns and temporal sequences - of course, by the *same* principle! - it will reproduce them when triggered suitably. As a special case, we then recover (4).

Synapses transmit information between neurons. According to Hebb's neurophysiological postulate for learning, they also store the information content of data presented to a neural net during a learning session. More precisely, the Hebb rule has two aspects. First, it is local. Given a synapse transmitting data from neuron j to neuron i, only the *local* information presented to neurons i and j determines the efficacy J_{ij}. Second, J_{ij} is allowed to increase if the activities of i and j *as noted by* i, are positively correlated.

Our key idea [3] is that signal *delays*, omnipresent in the brain and well known for their stabilization of temporal sequences [1, 11, 12], have to be taken into account *during the learning phase* as well. If this kind of Hebbian learning is combined with a *broad* distribution of delays, its performance is extremely robust. Neither does the performance of the network depend significantly on the characteristics of the distribution nor is it deteriorated by imprecise initial conditions such as noisy patterns or the theme BHCH instead of BACH. Our analysis also shows that pure Hebbian learning functions through *synaptic selection*, as advocated by Changeux *et al.* [17, 18].

For the moment we focus our attention on two specific neurons, say i and j, with J_{ij} as the synaptic efficacy for the information transport from j to i. If neuron j has fired, a soliton-like pulse propagates via the axon to the synapse at neuron i and it is here, at the synapse, where the information is stored, provided neuron i's activity is concurrent with or slightly after the arrival of the pulse coming from j. The signal transport through the axon takes a certain amount of time, the delay τ. So at time t the signal $S_j(t-\tau)$ has to be paired with $S_i(t)$, the state neuron i is in . This is δ-function delay. In general, delay can be modeled as a linear filter with a memory kernel *à la* Eq. (2). The delays vary from axon to axon and their distribution is very broad [3].

During a *learning session*, the system is offered a finite sequence of patterns $\{\xi_i^{\nu(t)}; 1 \leq i \leq N\}$ where $\nu(t)$ is a given function of t. According to Hebb's principle [4], at each instant of time the synaptic efficacy J_{ij} increases or decreases by an infinitesimal amount proportional to $S_i(t)\, S_j(t-\tau)$. Let us suppose that the learning session is of duration T and, for the sake of simplicity, that we start with a *tabula rasa* ($J_{ij} = 0$). Then we obtain, adding the partial increments,

$$J_{ij}(\tau) = N^{-1}\, \epsilon(\tau) \cdot \frac{1}{T} \int_0^T dt\; S_i(t)\; S_j(t-\tau) \tag{19}$$

In the integrand, $S_i(t) = \xi_i^{\nu(t)}$. The N^{-1} is a trivial scaling factor and $\epsilon(\tau)$ is a weight of the delay τ. In passing we note that the increments in (19) are linear (new data are just added) and that by imposing upper and lower bounds [19] or by allowing leakage one can induce forgetfulness. We will not pursue this issue here, however. It is also worthwhile to realize that the prescription (19) contains (4) as a special case. To see this, assume that during the learning session each pattern lasts for a time Δ and that *only* the delays $\tau = 0$ and $\tau = \Delta$ are present. The assertion then follows.

If the pattern shown to the network is stationary, i.e., $S_i(t) = \xi_i^{\mu}$ for some fixed μ and $0 \leq t \leq T$ while T exceeds all the τ's of the system (a natural consequence of the pattern being stationary), then the J_{ij} become symmetric and, despite the delays, the performance of the network turns out to be essentially that of the Hopfield model [6]. Plainly, in general the J_{ij} are asymmetric.

The Hebb rule (19) gives rise to a *retrieval* mechanism which is extremely robust. Neither does its performance depend on the specific model of synaptic transmission nor on the precise distribution of the delays τ. To illustrate this statement we have studied three models, to be denoted by A, B, and C.

(A) For each pair (i,j) there is a *large* number of axons (possibly, interneurons) whose delays τ have a distribution independent of i and j. Summing over the incoming signals we obtain the local field

$$h_i(t) = \sum_{j(\neq i)} \sum_{\tau} J_{ij}(\tau)\; S_j(t-\tau). \tag{20}$$

The weights $\epsilon(\tau)$ are chosen according to a given distribution of delays τ. Of course, one can also imagine that only a *single* axon links each pair of neurons. This idea has led us to consider two further models.

(B) In addition to the axonal delay, which is assumed to depend on j only, we have a synaptic (exponential) delay at i. Then

$$h_i(t) = \sum_{j(\neq i)} J_{ij}(\tau_{ij})\overline{S}_j(t), \tag{21}$$

where τ_{ij} stands for the pair (τ_i, τ_j), and where $\overline{S}_j(t)$ incorporates the different types of delay. If τ_i vanishes, then $\overline{S}_j(t) = S_j(t - \tau_j)$. We take $\epsilon(\tau) = 1$.

(C) For each pair (i, j) there exists a single axon with delay τ_{ij} which is sampled from a given distribution *independent* of i and j, so that $h_i(t)$ is of the form (21), with $\overline{S}_j(t) = S_j(t - \tau_{ij})$. Again, $\epsilon(\tau) = 1$.

The models A and B are random-site problems which are analytically soluble in terms of the sublattice magnetizations [9,20] of Sec. 3. Model C, however, is a random-bond problem and no exact solution is known yet. For detailed information concerning the Hebb rule, the reader may consult Ref. 3.

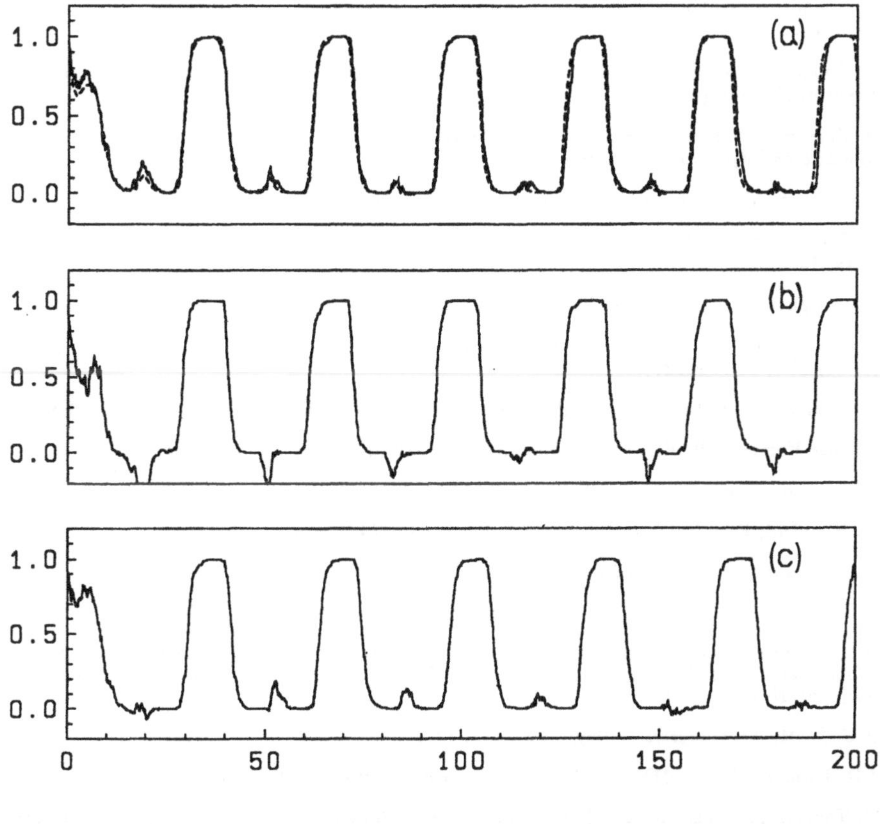

Fig. 8. Model dependence of the Hebb rule (19). The overlap (solid line) with the first pattern of a cycle consisting of three patterns is shown as a function of time (t): a. Model A, b. Model B, c. Model C. Though the transients are different, the long-term behaviour of the overlaps is strikingly similar. In all three simulations, the number of neurons is $N = 256$. Dynamics is sequential, $\Gamma = 1$, and $\beta = 10$. The initial conditions are $m_1(t) = 1$ for $-1 \leq t \leq 0$ and $m_\mu(t) = 0$ otherwise. We took a discrete distribution of axonal δ-function delays at $\tau = 0, 1, \ldots, 30$. The weights $\epsilon(\tau)$ are uniform and normalized to 1. During the learning session each pattern lasted $\Delta = 10$. The dashed line in a is the analytic solution to Eqs. (8) and (9), and refers to the case $N = \infty$.

Fig. 8 shows that the performance of the network hardly depends upon the specific model. Furthermore, it turns out that, once the cycle runs ($\Delta < \tau_{max}$), the retrieval quality hardly depends on the specific distribution of the delays either. This robustness is to be compared with the behavior of the usual cycle generating mechanisms [1,11,12], which the Hebb rule apparently outperforms.

Let me finish this review with an, in my opinion, surprising observation. Theorists may devise elegant theories, which provide nice toy models (cf. Secs. 2-6), but feedback to experiment and phenomenology then enriches theory in a manner which was not quite expected. The Hebb rule (Sec. 7) exemplifies how this may happen.

ACKNOWLEDGMENTS

I am deeply indebted to my collaborators, R. Kühn, A. Herz, U. Riedel, and B. Sulzer, without whom this work would not have been possible. I also gratefully acknowledge stimulating discussions with Prof.Dr.J. Honerkamp (Freiburg i.Br.) and Dr.H. Herzel (Humboldt-Universität, Berlin).

References

[1] U. Riedel, R. Kühn, and J.L.van Hemmen, Phys.Rev.A **A 38**, 1105-1108 (1988) and to be published.

[2] R. Kühn, J.L.van Hemmen, and U. Riedel, *Complex temporal association in neural nets*, SFB-Preprint No. **456** (1988).

[3] A. Herz, B. Sulzer, R. Kühn, and J.L.van Hemmen, *Hebbian learning reconsidered: Representation of static and dynamic objects in associative nets*, SFB-Preprint No. **463** (1988).

[4] D.O. Hebb, *The organization of behavior*. Wiley, New York, 1949.

[5] K. Binder (editor), *Monte Carlo Methods in Statistical Physics*. Springer, Berlin-Heidelberg-New York, 1979.

[6] J.J. Hopfield, Proc.Natl.Acad.Sci. U.S.A. **79**, 2554-2558 (1982), and **81**, 3088-3092 (1984).

[7] D.J. Amit, H. Gutfreund, and H. Sompolinsky, Phys.Rev.Lett. **55**, 1530-1533 (1985); Ann.Phys. (N.Y.) **173**, 30-67 (1987).

[8] G. Toulouse, S. Dehaene, and J.-P. Changeux, Proc.Natl.Acad.Sci. U.S.A. **83**, 1695-1698 (1986).

[9] J.L.van Hemmen, R. Kühn, Phys.Rev.Lett. **57**, 913-916 (1986).

[10] J.L. van Hemmen, Phys.Rev. **A 36**, 1959-1962 (1987).

[11] D. Kleinfeld, Proc.Natl.Acad.Sci. U.S.A. **83**, 9469-9473 (1986).

[12] H. Sompolinsky, I. Kanter, Phys.Rev.Lett. **57**, 2861-2864 (1986).

[13] R.B. Griffiths, C.Y. Weng, and J.S. Langer, Phys.Rev. **149**, 301-305 (1966).

[14] In a technical sense, these transitions are Hopf bifurcations. The first is supercritical, the second subcritical. For further information, see: J.K. Hale, *Theory of functional differential equations*. Springer, New York, 1977.

[15] A.C. Scott, *Neurophysics*. Wiley, New York, 1977.

[16] J.D. Farmer, Physica **4D**, 366 (1982); H.L. Swinney, Physica **7D**, 3 (1983).

[17] G. Toulouse, S. Dehaene, and J.-P. Changeux, Proc.Natl.Acad.Sci. U.S.A. **83**, 1695-1698 (1986).

[18] S. Dehaene, J.-P. Changeux, and J.-P. Nadal, Proc.Natl.Acad.Sci. U.S.A. **84**, 2727-2731 (1987).

[19] J.L.van Hemmen, G. Keller, and R. Kühn, Europhys.Lett. **5**, 663-668 (1988) and references therein.

[20] J.L.van Hemmen, D. Grensing, A. Huber, and R. Kühn, J.Stat.Phys. **50**, 231-257 and 259-293 (1988).

IMPROVED RETRIEVAL IN NEURAL NETWORKS WITH THRESHOLDS AND TERNARY NEURONS

A. Engel [1), H. Englisch [2), A. Schütte [3).

Dedicated to Elizabeth Gardner

Abstract: Hopfield's spin glass model of statistical physics simulates the error correction of noisy patterns in auto-associative memories. In order to increase the retrieval quality of this model, especially in the case of an overloaded memory, the information contained in the input is combined more efficiently with that of the memory by inserting two additional parameters into the model. The retrieval quality is calculated for one time step and in the limit of infinitely many time steps. Simulations with the projection rule for ternary neurons recommend also this variant of the standard network models.

Key Words: Neural net, pattern recognition, Hopfield model.

1. Introduction

Hopfield's spin glass model [1] has a multiple interpretation: The binary vector $\vec{\xi}=(\xi_1,\dots,\xi_N)$, $\xi_i\in\{-1,1\}$, can represent either a configuration of Ising spins or a binary pattern (+1 corresponds, for example, to a black, -1 to a white pixel) or a state of a system of formal neurons (+1 firing, -1 quiescent [2]) or an object (+1/-1 corresponds to yes/no as answer to the question: Has the object a certain feature?), where N is the number of spins, pixels, neurons or features, resp. For simplicity, we will mainly speak about patterns, for which the following problem is posed:

A memory shall store p patterns $\vec{\xi}^\mu$, $1<=\mu<=p$, and has the task to retrieve the original pattern if at some time t=0 a noisy version $\vec{S}(0)=(S_1(0),\dots,S_N(0))$ is presented. In the easiest form the corresponding original pattern is defined as that with maximal overlap $\max_\mu m^\mu(0)=m^{max}$ ("best matching" [3: 12.7], "minimum-distance classifier" [4: 2.3]) with

$$m^\mu(0)=\sum_{i=1}^{N}\xi_i^\mu S_i(0)/N. \qquad (1)$$

(The normalization 1/N guarantees $m\in[-1,1]$.) If the negative $-\vec{\xi}^\mu$ of a

1) Sekt. Physik Humboldt-Universität DDR-1040 Berlin Invalidenstr. 42
2) NTZ Karl-Marx-Universität DDR-7010 Leipzig Karl-Marx-Platz 10
3) Sekt. Elektronik Humboldt-Universität DDR-1040 Berlin Invalidenstr. 110

pattern is also a feasible solution then $\max_\mu m^\mu(0)$ has to be replaced by $\max_\mu |m^\mu(0)|$.

(If the probabilities p^μ for the occurence of the patterns (in perturbed form) are known as well as the probabilities q for the perturbations of the pixels then the classification can be optimized to get minimal likelihood of misclassification. Then one has to maximize

$$(\log p^\mu)/N+[(1+m^\mu(0))\log(1-q)+(1-m^\mu(0))\log q]/2 \tag{2}$$

[4: 3.5]. Since we are interested in the case $N\to\infty$, where one can expect that p^μ scales as O(1/p), we see that only $m^\mu(0)(\log(1-q)-\log q)$ has to become maximal, i.e. $m^\mu(0)$ itself. That is why we do not treat further the likelihood method which is important for patterns of finite length [5].)

In the next section the basic properties of the Hopfield model are mentioned; an important one is that it can act many time steps. For one time step the model is a special case of a perceptron [3, 4]. By optimally adjusting the self-interaction of the "Hopfield perceptron" its performance is improved, cf. Section 3. In Section 4 the usual Hopfield model where the time t tends to infinity is considered. Two input-dependent possibilities for thresholds are proposed which also increase the retrieval quality. While the case t=0 can be treated exactly by standard means of probability theory, the case $t\to\infty$ needs an approximation from statistical physics, the replica trick (cf. [6, 7, 8]). Instead of only considering the limiting cases t=0 and $t\to\infty$ (in simulations with small samples the stationary state is typically reached for t<4) one could think of looking for that t with maximal $m(t)=\sum_i S_i(t)\xi_i^\nu/N$, where ξ^ν is the pattern searched for. But already the calculations for t=1 are so complicated [9] that this way seems to be impracticable.

The last section is devoted to first simulations with ternary neurons.

2. The Standard Hopfield Model

The grandmother network [7] as the most suggestive solution for the determination of the pattern with maximal $|m^\mu(0)|$ has the Hopfield model as its descent. In the parallely working version the Hopfield model obeys

$$S_i(t+1)=\mathrm{sgn}(\sum_j J_{ij}S_j(t)+h_i), \tag{3}$$

where we included additionally pixel-dependent thresholds h_i.

$$\mathrm{sgn}(x)=\begin{cases}1 & \text{for } x>0\\ -1 & \text{for } x<0\\ -1 \text{ or } 1 & \text{for } x=0\end{cases} \tag{4}$$

is a sign function modified for the purpose of a bipolar output. The coefficient J_{ij} is interpreted as the strength of the synapse between neuron i and j. In the Hopfield model it is for $i \neq j$ given by

$$J_{ij}=\sum_{\mu} \xi_i^{\mu} \xi_j^{\mu}/N, \tag{5}$$

i.e. $J_{ij}=J_{ji}$, and for i=j usually by $J_{ii}=p/N$ (according to (4)) or $J_{ii}=0$. If the dynamics (3) has a fixed point $\vec{S}(\infty)$ this stationary vector is considered to be the output pattern for the input $\vec{S}(0)$.

The serial version to the parallel algorithm (3) reads

$$S_i(t+1/N)=\mathrm{sgn}(\sum_j J_{ij}S_j(t)+h_i), \quad S_j(t+1/N)=S_j(t) \text{ for } j \neq i, \tag{6}$$

where i is a randomly or systematically chosen index. As time step we use 1/N in order to be able to compare with the parallel algorithm, where after one time step also N new S-values are calculated. The serial algorithm has the advantage that one can prove the existence of $\vec{S}(\infty)$ for arbitrary $J_{ij}=J_{ji}$ (for $i \neq j$) and $J_{ii} \in [0,\infty)$ [7], where for $J_{ii}=0$ and $\sum_j J_{ij}S_j(t)+h_i=0$ we have to define $S_i(t+1/N)=S_i(t)$. Counterexamples show that the parallely working network does not always has - like the serial one - a stationary state. The easiest example is a network with N=2, $J_{12}=-1$, $J_{11}=J_{22}=h_1=h_2=0$ and $S_1(0)=S_2(0)=1$. Then the system oscillates between two states; for every $n \in \mathbb{N}$ $S_1(2n)=S_2(2n)=1$, $S_1(2n+1)=S_2(2n+1)=-1$. Our counterexample is typical in the sense that cycles with a period larger than 2 cannot occur [7]. Under the stronger conditions $J_{ii}>=p/N$ and equation (5) for i=j the existence of a limit state for the parallel network can be proved [7]. In the networks with $J_{ij}=J_{ji}$ [10] and in the serially working networks with $J_{ii}<0$ arbitrarily large cycles can occur.

The physicists would consider rule (6) as a zero-temperature dynamics. The notation indicates that there must be also a rule for positive temperature T: $\mathrm{prob}(S_i(t+1/N)=1)=(1+\exp(-y_i(t)/T))^{-1}$, where $y_i(t)=\sum_j J_{ij}S_j(t)+h_i$ and prob(X) denotes the probability that the event X is true. Obviously for $T \to 0$ the probabilistic rule tends to the deterministic one. A related procedure called simulated annealing became a common tool of stochastic optimization (for a mathematical treatment cf. [11].)

The replica trick yields that for random independent patterns and $\alpha > \alpha_0 \approx 0.14$ ($\alpha=p/N$ is the ratio between the number of patterns and pixels, α_0 is the critical ratio) $m(\infty)$ tends to zero for $N \to \infty$ independently of m(0), whereas for $\alpha < \alpha_0$ $m(\infty)$ is large (>0.97) and independent of m(0).

The following sections show how to use the information especially of overloaded memories, i.e. for $\alpha>\alpha_c$, without introducing multipixel interactions [12], time-consuming calculations of error-corrections [13] or of the projection operator (cf. Section 5).

3. The Hopfield Perceptron with Optimal Self-Interaction

The Hopfield model is for t=0 a special case of a fully connected two-layer perceptron [3, 4], where the number of input pixels coincides with that of the output pixels and the strengths of the synapses are given in advance by (5). As we have already remarked in the preceding section, the values of J_{ii} can be chosen arbitrarily from $[0,\infty)$ in order to get a stationary state for the serial dynamics. Our aim is to fix $J_{ii}=h$ in an optimal manner, this corresponds to the replication rate control in [14]. The limit cases $J_{ii}\to\pm\infty$ are not interesting, since they only mean that the output coincides with the input or its negative, resp. But our intuition tells us that a moderate positive J_{ii} would be desirable: If $\sum_{j\neq i} J_{ij}S_j(0)\approx 0$, then the decision $S_i(1)=\mathrm{sgn}(\sum_{j\neq i} J_{ij}S_j(0))$ is not reliable and it seems to be more favourable to put $S_i(1)=S_i(0)$. This competition between information from the other pixel values and the stability of the pixel value considered can be taken into account by (3) with $J_{ii}>0$. This is for t=0 equivalent to a threshold $h_i=J_{ii}S_i(0)$, i.e. an external field parallel to the input spin configuration.

The following monotonicity behaviour has to be expected:

- For fixed h m(1) increases with respect to m(0) and decreases with respect to α.
- The optimal h increases with respect to α and m(0), i.e. with increasing number of disturbing patterns or with improving input the input gets a higher weight.
- m(1) is for the optimal h a decreasing function of α with m(1)>m(0). (The equality holds for $h=\infty$, which is not optimal.)

The restriction to random independent patterns with expectation value $\langle\xi_i^\mu\rangle=0$ is essential for the (only in the limit $N\to\infty$) rigorous derivation of

$$m(1)=[(1+m(0))\mathrm{erf}((m(0)+h)/\sqrt{2\alpha})+(1-m(0))\mathrm{erf}((m(0)-h/\sqrt{2\alpha})]/2 \qquad (7)$$

with the error function $\mathrm{erf}(y)=2\int_0^y e^{-x^2}dx/\sqrt{\pi}$.

For h=0 the fixed point equation

$$m(1)=m(0) \qquad (8)$$

was often studied whereby the solution was interpreted as an approximation for $m(\infty)$ [15]. The fixed points of (8) are decreasing with respect to with $m(1)=1$ for $\alpha=0$, $1>m(1)>0$ for $0<\alpha<2/\pi\approx0.637$ and $m(0)=0$ for $\alpha>=2/\pi$. Differentiation of (7) with respect to h yields the optimal value for the strength of the self-interaction term

$$h_{opt}=(\alpha/2m(0))\ln[(1+m(0))/(1-m(0))]. \qquad (9)$$

All expectations offered at the beginning of this section prove true as it it can be read off from formula (7) and (9). For the two limit cases $m(0)\to0$ and $m(0)\to1$ we get that $h_{opt}=\alpha$ and that h_{opt} diverges as $-(\alpha/2)\ln(1-m(0))$, resp. In the first limit h_{opt} coincides with the naive value $J_{ii}=p/N$ derived from equation (4).

4. The Hopfield Model with Input-Dependent Thresholds

4.1 The Input as Threshold

In the previous Section the self-interaction $J_{ii}S_i(t)=hS_i(t)$ coincides with an external field $h_i=hS_i(0)$. This is no longer the case for $t>0$. The self-interaction J_{ii} seems to be a trivial constant which does not change the fixed points, but the basins of attraction of these points are altered such that the real dynamics changes. Surely, it is very difficult to describe this change analytically, in [16] computer simulations are presented. For the alternative interpretation of the additional h-term in Section 3 as an input-dependent threshold $hS_i(0)$ an approximative analytical treatment for the case $t\to\infty$ is possible.

Whereas for h=0 the analytical treatment yields that $m(\infty)$ is independent of m(0) this does not hold anymore for h=0. On the other hand, it seems to make sense to transfer all expectations for m(1) expressed in Section 3 to $m(\infty)$. Due to the complicated structure of the equations (10)+(11) we cannot give an explicit formula like (9) for the optimal h, but simulations and numerical solutions of these equations [7] confirm the expectations for $m(\infty)$. The methods of ref. [6] (cf. [7]) yield

$$m(\infty)=[(1+m(0))\mathrm{erf}((m(\infty)+h)/\sqrt{2\alpha r})+(1-m(0))\mathrm{erf}((m(\infty)-h)/\sqrt{2\alpha r})]/2. \qquad (10)$$

It looks - despite the additional quantity r - very similar to (7). The quantity r is a measure for the influence of the disturbing patterns and has to be determined simultaneously with (10) from

$$1-1/\sqrt{r}=\sqrt{2/\pi\alpha r}[(1+m(0))\exp(-(m(\infty)+h)^2/2\alpha r)+(1-m(0))\exp(-(m(\infty)-h)^2/2\alpha r)]/2. \qquad (11)$$

4.2 The Field Generated by the Input as Threshold

A comparison of the solutions of equations (7) and (10)+(11), resp., indicates that for $m(0)=0.4$ the simple choice $h=0$ yields a better retrieval quality $m(1)=\mathrm{erf}(1/\sqrt{2})\approx 0.683$ than the optimal $h\approx 0.68$ for $m(\infty)$ (≈ 0.62). Thus we can predict that $m(\infty)$ will be immediately improved if instead of $hS_i(0)$

$$h_i=h' \sum_{j\neq i} J_{ij}S_j(0) \qquad (12)$$

is used with sufficiently large h', since for $h'\to\infty$ $m(\infty)$ tends to the $m(1)$-value belonging to $h=0$. Both, computer simulations and the numerical solution of equations (13)-(15) show that $m(\infty)$ as a function of h' has a relatively flat maximum which does not exceed much $m(\infty)$ for $h'=\infty$. (To choose (12) as external field in the calculation of $m(1)$ is useless since it only multiplies the argument in (3) with the factor $(1+h')$ which has no effect on the result.)

It is a curiosity that (12) was already used in [15] due to a programming error. Without identifying (12) as an input-dependent threshold Kinzel remarked in his erratum that in simulations a non-zero value for h' can improve the retrieval quality.

The replica symmetric approximation for (12) is the solution of the following system of 3 coupled equations:

$$m(\infty) =[(1+m(0))\mathrm{erf}(y_1)+(1-m(0))\mathrm{erf}(y_2)]/2 \qquad (13)$$

$$m'(\infty)=[(1+m(0))\mathrm{erf}(y_1)-(1-m(0))\mathrm{erf}(y_2)]/2 \qquad (14)$$

$$C=\sqrt{1/2\pi\alpha r}[(1+m(0))\exp(-y_1^2)+(1-m(0))\exp(-y_2^2)], \qquad (15)$$

where r, y_1, y_2 are abbreviations for

$$r=(1+2hm'(\infty)+h^2)/(1-C)^2, \qquad (16)$$

$$y_1=(m(\infty)+hm(0)+hC/(1-C))/\sqrt{2\alpha r}, \qquad (17)$$

$$y_2=(m(\infty)+hm(0)-hC/(1-C))/\sqrt{2\alpha r}. \qquad (18)$$

The new term $m'(\infty)$ is the scalar product of the final state with the input state: $m'(\infty)=\sum_i S_i(\infty)S_i(0)/N$.

5. The Projection Rule and Ternary Neurons

A drawback of the Hopfield model (5) consists in the deterioration of the correct patterns $\vec{S}(0)=\xi^\nu$ by the algorithm (3) for $p>N/(2 \ln N)$ [17] while the choice of the J_{ij} as the matrix elements of the orthogonal projection J onto the (at most p-dimensional) subspace in R^N, spanned by the ξ^μ, guarantees due to $\vec{S}(1)=\mathrm{sgn}(J\xi^\nu)=\mathrm{sgn}(\xi^\nu)=\xi^\nu$ $\vec{S}(1)=\vec{S}(0)$ for any initial vector $\vec{S}(0)=\xi^\nu$. If $\alpha>=1$ then the subspace, spanned by p random vectors, coincides with R^N with probability 1 [17]. Thus the critical ratio is not larger than 1 since for $\alpha>=1$ the operator J becomes the identity. The refined analysis in [18] shows $\alpha_c=1/2$. Neglecting the difference between binary and real operations Venkatesh and Psaltis [17] quote the effort of $(\alpha+\alpha^2+\alpha^3/2)n^3$ multiplications for the calculation of J in comparison to $\alpha n^3/2$ multiplications for rule (5). The table 1 shows the results of simulations for the projection rule applied to highly correlated (maximum 0.59) patterns representing the figures "0" till "9", confer below.

```
-------------------------------------------------------------------------
I  xxxx  I     xx I   xxx  I   xx   I   x    I xxxxxx I    xxx IxxxxxxxxI
I xx  xx I    xxx I  xx xx I  xxxxx I   x    I x      I   xx   Ix      xI
Ixx    xxI   xxxx I xx   xxI xx   xxI  xx    I x      I  xx    I      x I
Ixx    xxI  xx xx I     xx I     xx I xx     I x      I x      I     x  I
Ixx    xxI xx  xx I    xx  I    xx  Ixx  x   I x xxx  Ixx xx   I    x   I
Ixx    xxIxx   xx I   xx   I     xx Ix  xx   I xxx xx Ixxx  xx I   x    I
Ixx    xxI     xx I  xx    Ix      xxIxxxxxxxxI      xxIx     xxI xxxxx  I
Ixx    xxI     xx I xx     Ixx    xxI   xx   I      xxIxx    xxI   x    I
I xx  xx I     xx Ixx     xI xx  xx I   xx   Ixx   xx I xx  xx I   x    I
I  xxxx  I     xx I xxxxxx I  xxxx  I   xx   I xxxxx  I  xxxx  I   x    I
I        I      **I    **  I    ****I  **    I **   **I  ****  I  ******I
-------------------------------------------------------------------------
I   xx   I   xx   I
I  x  x  I xx  xx I
I x    x Ixx    xxI
I  x  x  Ixx    xxI
I   xx   I xx  xxxI
I xx  xx I   xx xxI
Ixx    xxI      xxI
Ixx    xxIxx    x I
I xx  xx I xxx xx I
I  xxxx  I   xxx  I
I**      I**    **I
-------------------
```

The figures "0" to "9" in a 8x11-array, i.e. $\alpha=10/88\approx 0.11$. The 11-th row contains the binary code of the corresponding figure whereby 2 pixels represent 1 bit.

The parallel version (3) is compared with the random serial one (6) and the maximal misfit version. The latter one also obeys equation (6), where that index i is chosen with maximal misfit $-S_i(t)y_i(t)=\max_j -S_j(t)y_j(t)$.

m(0)		1.0	0.9	0.8	0.7	0.6	0.5	0.4	0.3	0.2
parallel	c	100	100	100	100	99.1	94.9	80.0	40.8	10.4
	e	0.0	0.0	0.0	0.0	0.1	0.1	0.7	5.0	8.5
serial	c	100	100	100	99.8	98.5	93.8	78.8	46.2	14.9
random	e	0.0	0.0	0.0	0.0	0.0	0.5	1.9	5.9	13.2
serial	c	100	100	100	100	100	98.4	89.9	56.9	16.3
misfit	e	0.0	0.0	0.0	0.0	0.0	0.2	2.1	7.8	18.9

Table 1: Percentage of correctly (c) and erroneously (e) classified perturbed patterns for the projection rule; every data was calculated after 100 trials with every of the 10 figures

The e-rows show the percentage of perturbed patterns whose final state is erroneously one of the 9 other patterns. The difference between 100 % and the sum of the c- and e-row is the percentage of final states agreeing with a "spurious" state, i.e. a stationary state which differs from all ten memorized patterns. A spurious state as answer can be interpreted as "I do not know" which is not as bad as a wrong answer. For an initial retrieval quality not too small the misfit version - as could be expected - provides the best results.

In table 2 the results for simulations with the projection operator J are reported where the coefficients J_{ii} are put zero. The positive definiteness of J ensures the existence of $\vec{S}(\infty)$ also in the parallel version [19] whereas in the altered parallel version with $J_{ii}=0$ cycles with period 2 can occur. The choice $J_{ii}=0$ enlarges the attractor basins of the memorized patterns which leads to an increased number of correct and unfortunately also of wrong classifications.

m(0)		1.0	0.9	0.8	0.7	0.6	0.5	0.4	0.3	0.2
parallel	c	100	100	100	100	99.8	98.7	93.2	62.0	26.5
	e	0.0	0.0	0.0	0.0	0.0	0.6	2.4	12.4	23.4
serial	c	100	100	100	100	99.4	94.8	81.6	48.1	18.2
random	e	0.0	0.0	0.0	0.0	0.5	1.9	6.1	15.4	25.4
serial	c	100	100	100	100	100	98.6	92.2	64.8	25.2
misfit	e	0.0	0.0	0.0	0.0	0.0	0.8	3.4	13.3	23.0

Table 2: Percentages for the projection rule, but $J_{ii}=0$

If the input consists of incomplete (instead of only noisy) patterns then ternary elements can take this into account where $S_i(0)=0$ corresponds to an unknown input. As a further step, the introduction of ternary processing elements $S_i(t)$ with

$$S_i(t+1)=\begin{cases}\operatorname{sgn}(y_i(t)) & \text{for } |y_i(t)|>c(t)\\ 0 & \text{otherwise}\end{cases} \tag{19}$$

with a time-dependent threshold $c(t)$ aims at the elimination of the influence of undecided pixels, i.e. those with too small $|y_i(t)|$. For $t\to\infty$ our thresholds $c(t)$ tend to zero in order to get a binary output $S_i(\infty)$. Simulations with such ternary elements and $c(t)=0.2\cdot 2^{-t}$, performed with the parallel version for the projection operator, but $J_{ii}=0$, are outlined in table 3. Perhaps, the poor results indicate that $c(0)$ is too large. Too much information is lost when many $S_i(1)$ belong to the undecided pixels.

That is why the next simulation starts with $c(0)=0$ and continues with $c(t)=0.4\cdot 2^{-t}$. The effect is convincing; it seems that in the first time step the pattern moves into the neighbourhood of one of the given figures and then $c(t)$ prevents the network from staying in a spurious state near this figure.

m(0)		1.0	0.9	0.8	0.7	0.6	0.5	0.4	0.3	0.2
$c(0)=0.2$	c	100	100	100	99.3	90.6	67.1	34.4	19.6	8.4
$c(t)=0.2\cdot 2^{-t}$	e	0.0	0.0	0.0	0.3	4.2	10.6	20.9	24.1	24.2
$c(0)=0$	c	100	100	100	100	100	99.6	96.0	68.3	27.4
$c(t)=0.4\cdot 2^{-t}$	e	0.0	0.0	0.0	0.0	0.0	0.2	2.1	11.9	26.5

Table 3: Projection rule with $J_{ii}=0$ for ternary elements

The above-mentioned remarks concerning the existence of $\vec{S}(\infty)$ apply also to $\lim_{t\to\infty} c(t)=0$. Additional considerations are necessary for $\lim_{t\to\infty} c(t)>0$, for simplicity let us assume $c(t)=c$. The output $S_i(\infty)=0$ indicate that a feature is only partially present. Neural networks with continuous values have been investigated for a long time [10]; to our knowledge papers about neurons with a finite number of states are rare, cf. [20] for simulations with 11-ary neurons, resp., and [21] for Potts neurons.

The proofs for the existence of a binary limit vector $\vec{S}(\infty)$ or limit cycle with period 2 use Ljapunov functions $E(t)$ [7] which have to be modified for ternary neurons to

$$E(t)=-\sum_{i,j} J_{ij}S_i(t)S_j(t)/2-\sum_i (h_iS_i(t)-cS_i(t)^2) \tag{20}$$

or

$$E(t)=-\sum_{i,j} J_{ij}S_i(t)S_j(t+1)-\sum_i [h_i(S_i(t)+S_i(t+1))-c(Si(t)^2+S_i(t+1)^2)]. \tag{21}$$

They coincide for $c=0$ with the original functions from [7]. The proofs for $c>0$ follow the lines of those in [7].

At the end of the paper it should be mentioned that not only ternary neurons have been investigated, but also ternary synapses [22]. In this case equation (5) in the Hopfield model has to be replaced by

$$J_{ij}=\begin{cases} \mathrm{sgn}(\sum_\mu \xi_i^\mu \xi_j^\mu) & \text{for } |\sum \xi_i^\mu \xi_j^\mu|>a\sqrt{p} \\ 0 & \text{otherwise,} \end{cases} \tag{22}$$

where the parameter a can be optimally adjusted. These synapses simplify hardware realizations of networks with continuous connections to such with binary or deleted (for $J_{ii}=0$) connections. A simple approximation gives us a hint for the optimization of the parameter a: If the J_{ij} will be independent of each other then for 1/3 dilution of all connections the maximal information would be stored in the synapses, i.e. a≈0.43. Thus it is not surprising that the network with a=0 is improved by moderate dilution; the correct optimal value lies at a≈0.612 [22].

A further improvement is obtained for the inclusion of an external field $hS_i(0)$ into the models with ternary synapses, for the optimal h cf. [23].

References

[1] Hopfield, J.J.: Proc. Natl. Acad. Sci. USA **78** (1982) 2554-2558.
[2] Mc Culloch, W.S. and W.A. Pitts: Bull. Math. Biophys. 5 (1943) 115-133.
[3] Minsky, M. and S. Papert: Perceptrons: An introduction to computational geometry. MIT Press, Cambridge MA - London 1969.
[4] Nilsson, N.J.: Learning machines. Mc Graw-Hill, New York e.a. 1965.
[5] Bechstein, J.: these proceedings.
[6] Amit, D.J., H. Gutfreund and H. Sompolinsky: Ann. Phys. 173 (1987) 30-67.
[7] Engel, A., H. Englisch and A. Schütte: submitted to Europhys. Lett. Englisch, H., A. Engel and A. Schütte: to appear in J. New Generation Computer Systems.
[8] Engel, A.: in preparation.
[9] Amari, S. and K. Maginu: Neural Networks 1 (1988) 63-73. Their theorem 3 coincides for t=2 (for t>2 it is only an approximation) with equation (3.15) in Gardner, E., B. Derrida and P. Mottishaw: J. Physique **48** (1987) 741-755.
[10] Grossberg, S.: Neural Networks 1 (1988) 17-61.
[11] Holley, R. and D. Stroock: Commun. Math. Phys. **115** (1988) 553-569.
[12] Abbott, L.F. and Y. Arian: Phys. Rev. A **36** (1987) 5091-5094. Feigelman, M.V. and L.B. Ioffe: Int. J. Mod. Phys. B 1 (1987) 51-68. Gardner, E.: J. Phys. A **20** (1987) 3453-3464. Giles, C.L. and T. Maxwell: Appl. Optics **26** (1987) 4972-4978. Krey, U. and G. Pöppel: A dynamical learning process for the recognition of correlated patterns in symmetric spin glass models. To appear in Proc. Conf. Measures of complexity, Rom 29.9-2.10.'87. Lee, Y.C. e.a.: Physica D 22 (1986) 276-306. Personnaz, L., I. Guyon and G. Dreyfus: Europhys. Lett. **4** (1987) 863-867.
[13] Diederich, S. and M. Opper: Phys. Rev. Lett. **58** (1987) 949-952. Gardner, E.: Maximum storage capacity in neural networks. Preprint Edinburgh Univ. 87/395.
[14] Voigt, M.: In: Lotka-Volterra approach to cooperation and competition in dynamic systems; eds.: W. Ebeling and M. Peschel; Akademie-Verlag, Berlin 1985.
[15] Kinzel, W.: Z. Phys. B **60** (1985) 205-213; **62** (1986) 267.
[16] Fontanari, J.F. and R. Köberle: J. Phys. A 21 (1988) L667-671
[17] Venkatesh, S.S. and D. Psaltis: Linear and logarithmic capacities in associative neural networks. To appear in IEEE Transactions on Information Theory.
[18] Kanter, I. and H. Sompolinsky: Phys. Rev. A **35** (1987) 380-392.
[19] Goles Chacc, E.: In: Disordered systems and biological organization; eds.: E. Bienenstock, F. Fogelman Soulié and G. Weisbuch; Springer-Verlag Berlin/W. e.a. 1986.
[20] Banzhaff, W.: In Proc. IEEE 1. Int. Conf. Neural Networks; eds.: M. Candill and C. Butler; SOS-Printing, San Diego 1988.
[21] Kanter, I.: Phys. Rev. A **37** (1988) 2739-2742.
[22] Sompolinsky, H.: Phys. Rev. A **34** (1986) 2571-2574. van Hemmen, L.: Phys. Rev. A **36** (1987) 1959-1962.
[23] Engel, A., H. Englisch, A. Schütte and M. Stcherbina: in preparation.

Organization of Neural Networks by Learning

W. Weller [1)]

Summary

From the performance point of view a selforganizing artifical neural network is introduced for modelling the sensomotorical behaviour of a human operator acting in an a priori unknown environment. The interconnections between the two layers of the model are expressed using a stochastic concept. For modelling the input/output behaviour a decision algorithm based on the principle of maximum likelihood is discussed. The aspect of selforganization is induced by learning. For updating the stochastic parameters several predominantly new versions of an adaption algorithm are presented and investigated by means of simulation experiments.

1) Humboldt-Universität zu Berlin, Sektion Elektronik
Invalidenstr. 110, 1040 Berlin, DDR

I. Introduction

In the course of technological development there are many examples which show that by studying phenomena of the animating nature insights have been gained whose application induced a fundamental technological progress. This likely explains the strong interest of the systems theoreticians and computer scientists in results of the research work into the field of neurophysiology and psychology about neural compounds and the human brain. Their endeavours are directed to the modelling and implementation of abilities like recognition, understanding, learning, planning, problem solving etc. to fit out man-made systems with a certain degree of intelligence. Corresponding to that they consider the computer as a human-like being. On the other hand the natural scientists are interested in a better understanding of the mechanisms of information processing of such neural working structures. The point of view, as they take it, is the interpretation of the human brain as complex automaton.

As one of the results motivated by neurobiological and psychological research of the human brain, the concept of the artificial neural systems (ANS) was introduced trying to make use of some of its abilities to associate, to adapt, and to learn for artificial systems. Such ANS's can be understood as nets with the topology of directed graphs built up by artificial neurons as elements with the peculiarity that internal memories are contained in the connections.

The problem which shall be treated in this paper is to apply the ANS approach to the modelling of the human sensomotorical behaviour. We are here interested mainly in network organization where certain statistical properties in the behaviour of human operator are regarded.

II. The human sensomotorical and its representation of an ANS - model

A man who is interacting with an unknown environment produces actions given to the outside. In his dialogue with the environment he will gradually accumulate experience which is useful to reorganize his behaviour plastically. Therefore an evolutionary process takes place during which the operator more and more learns to assign purposeful reactions to current observations.

Trying a modelling of the human behaviour which reflects the reality in a sufficient manner the following features are to be taken into considerations

- immediate assignment of observations and actions
- fuzzy decision reduced with the increase of experience
- memorization of the actual knowledge (short and long term memory)

- generalization of the knowledge
- continuous processing of new information increments
- aim oriented improvement of the behaviour

The admissibility to apply ANS's for modelling the sensomotorical behaviour results from two reasons. On the one hand it is to be pointed the fact that the behaviour within the original system - the acting human operator - is realized by such neural structures. On the other hand ANS's have frequently proved their prominent qualification to describe processes containing aspects of pattern recognition, association, and learning.
Resulting from neurophysiological research it is known that sensomotorical behaviour is realized by an extraordinarily complex neural system consisting of different substructures organized in an hierarchy /1/. Whereas at the lower levels, such as the movement apparatus, spinal cord, and cerebral trunk, relatively simple neural compounds with fixed organization dominate, preferably for the realization of mono- and polysynaptical reflexes, the higher substructures - specially the related areas of the cortex as the location of thinking and consciousness - disposes of neural structures of enormous complexity with a highly flexible organization.
According to that we have no real prospect to elaborate a homomorphical model imitating the sensomotorical behaviour. Instead we suppose a fairly simple ANS-model as shown in fig. 1.

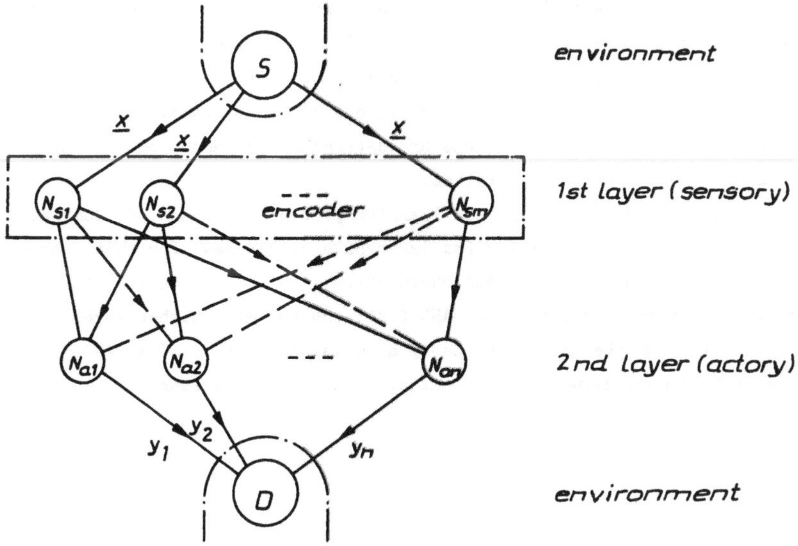

Fig. 1

It is to emphasize that this structure reflects mainly the input/output behaviour whereas the aspects of adaption and learning as the more intelligent functions are hidden in this representation. As to be seen in the figure the environment is only taken into consideration as it is both source and drain of information referring to the ANS. This source S emits a bundle of m signals $x_1, x_2, \ldots, x_m$ or a vector input $\underline{x} = [x_1, x_2, \ldots, x_m]^T$. At the opposite side the drain D receives an output signal y. Because of the nature of the actions the signal is adopted to be discrete valued $y \in Y^n = (y_1, y_2, \ldots, y_n)$,

For the ANS model a two-layered structure is underlain. The 1st layer (sensory layer) the actual input signal $\underline{x}(j) \in X$ is processed referring its membership to one of in total l situations $s(j) \in S^l$. That means exactly one neuron N_s "fires" in response to the signal $\underline{x}(j) \in X_s \subset X$ but is not excited by any other signal $\underline{x}(j) \in X_t \neq X_s \subset X$. In other words, the actual firing neuron N_s can be considered as a detector or representative cell of the situation $s \in S^l$.

It should be noticed that a layer with a function as described is frequently called an encoder. In general such an encoder works as a classifyer and performs the property of generalization as requested.

The 2nd or actory layer is designated to contain n neurons N_k, $k = 1,2,\ldots,n$ corresponding to the set of actions. For the organization of the ANS two types of variables are of relevance like in natural neuron nets: signals and interconnections /2/. Signals can be interpreted in terms of the neurophysiology as action potentials propagated along the axons. Connections are axonal links and their branchings by collaterals. Their efficacy can be characterized by weights. Different weights are indicated in fig. 1 by full and dotted lines.

The ability of synaptic plasticity contained in neural nets enables us to model selforganizing processes. For this purpose in our ANS model parameters valueing the strength of neural interconnections are determined and adjusted gradually by means of suitable adaption algorithms.

It is worth mentioning that during the learning process more than one dominating interconnections to a neuron of the 2nd layer have originated. For that reason it can be said that the 2nd layer has OR-functional character. On the other hand the 1st layer realizes in some sense AND functions but at a higher level. As it is well known from the automaton theory a serial connection of an AND - and OR - network is a good structure for realizing any (logical) function.

III. Algorithmic description

III. 1. Basic concept

In contrary to the customary modelling of neural nets using a deterministic description based on differential equations we prefer a stochastic concept which considers incertainties in the human behaviour in a better way.
For that purpose a learning discrete probability distribution is introduced to explain the structural modifications in our ANS.
Let

$$\underline{p}_s = \left[p_1\ p_2\ \cdots\ p_n\right]_s^T \quad , s \in S^1$$

be a probability vector representing a discrete distribution which describes statistically when each neuron N_k of the 2nd layer fires if a neuron N_s of the 1st layer fires (fig. 2).

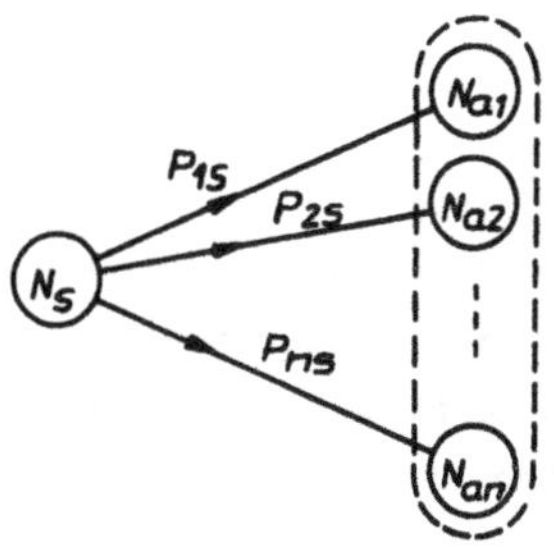

Fig. 2

Equivalently $\underline{p}_s$ expresses the conditioned probability distribution underlying a human operator if he selects special actions y_k in response to an observation $\underline{x}$ belonging to the situation $s \in S^1$.
Because of the effect of learning the distributions $\underline{p}_s$ forming an array underlie dynamical variations, i.e. $\underline{p}_s$ depends on the discrete time j. To explain the efficacy of the learning on the adaption of the probability vector $\underline{p}_s$ the distinguished states as shown in fig.3 can be emphasized.

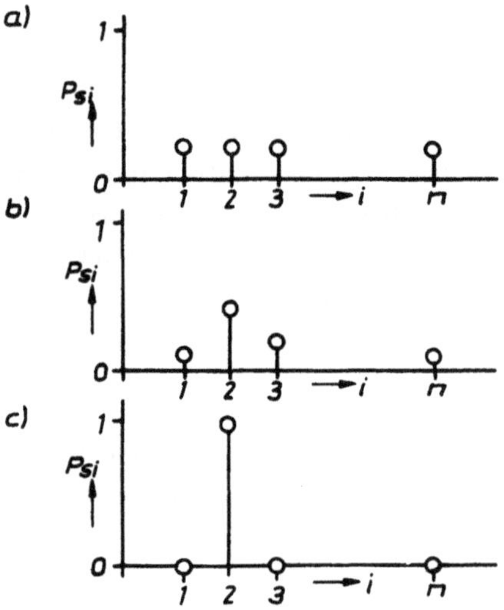

Fig. 3

a) initial state: The vector $\underline{p}_s(0), \forall s \in S^1$ describes the initial distribution. If there is no a priori information available $\underline{p}_s(0)$ represents the equal distribution. The system behaves as a stochastic automaton.

b) temporary state: In the course of the adaption some of the discrete probabilities may have increased while others have decreased.

c) final state: After having reached the goal, one or a few discrete probabilities have adopted their maximum while all others are zero. That means the distribution has become one-point or few-point. The system reacts deterministically.

In order to describe the behaviour of our selforganizing ANS algorithmically it is useful to give a separate presentation of the input/output behaviour and the dynamics of the selforganization by learning.

III. 2. Description of the input/output behaviour

The apparatus of the classical systems theory is not very favourable to express learned stimulus - response - relationships. Instead mathematical mappings are used as a suitable concept. Correspondingly an overall description of such systems can be given by

$$S: \ \underline{x} \xrightarrow{(j)} y \ ; \forall \underline{x} \in X \ , \forall y \in Y^n, \tag{1}$$

where the mapping S is time dependent.

Because of the two-layered structure of our ANS a twofold mapping will be used:

$$\text{ANS:}\quad \begin{array}{l} \underline{x} \longrightarrow s \; ; \; \forall \underline{x} \in X \; ; \; \forall s \in S^1 \\ s \longrightarrow y \; ; \; \forall s \in S^1 \; ; \forall y \in Y^n \end{array} \tag{2a,b}$$

The mapping in the 1st layer referring to (2) is strongly determined by the kind of the surrounding process. If it is a discrete or discretizised process $\underline{x}$ is represented by patterns. Then, in the simplest case, each neuron of the 1st layer represents such an input pattern. Algorithms which describe such modyfiable neurons can be found in the literature /3/. If otherwise the input vector is analogically valued the preclassification by an hypercube-type classifyer is favourable /4/. The difficulties arise if the environmental process contains stores or delays and no state variables are accessible. In such a case instead of singe input signals $\underline{x}(j)$ sequences of input signals and, if necessary, supplemented by sequences of the output signal have to be analyzed /5/. The evaluation of signal sequences requires the existence of short term memories of a certain length to aquire the "history" of the systems movement. With respect to the variety of the possible cases and the existing solutions we abstain from a more detailled presentation here.

Concentrating our endeavours towards the mapping in the 2nd layer (equ.2) the ANS model has to make a concrete decision referring to an action $y(j) \in Y^n$ having recognized a certain situation $s(j) \in S^1$ which underlies the actual valid distribution $\underline{p}_s(j)$. For that purpose a stochastic mechanism is proposed based on the principle of maximum likelihood. This can be described by the way of example as followes. Let z_i be n counting variables initialized before starting the decision procedure by the inverse of the corresponding single probabilities

$$z_i(0) = \frac{1}{p_{is}} \quad , \forall i = 1,2,\ldots,n \; . \tag{3}$$

Using a sequence of randomly generated integers

$$r = \text{RND} \;\Big|\; r \in N = 1,2, \ldots,n$$

the counting variables are decremented according to

$$z_i = \begin{cases} z_i - 1 & \text{if} \quad i = r \\ z_i & \text{if} \quad i \neq r \; . \end{cases} \tag{4}$$

Then the stochastic decision is made by

$$k = \arg_{i=1}^{n} z_i \;\Big|\; \exists \quad z_i = 0 \tag{5}$$

III. 3. Description of the dynamics of selforganization by learning

For the selforganization of the ANS the prinziple of learning by success is applied. For this a reward or punishment is granted depending on whether or not the last correction of the valid probability vector $\underline{p}_s$ has led to am improvement of the behaviour.

Let $w_x(j) \in Y^{(n)}$ designate a goal variable analyzed with the input vector $\underline{x}(j) \in X$, we introduce a valueing variable corresponding

$$c(j) = \begin{cases} c_o & \text{if } y(j) = w_x \\ -c_o & \text{if } y(j) = w_x \end{cases} \quad ; \quad c_o > 0 . \tag{6}$$

Then, if a selection $y(j) = y_k \in Y^n$ has been made, the mathematical structure of a suitable adaption algorithm for correcting the elements of the valid probability vector $\underline{p}_s$ can be given by

$$p_{ks}(j+1) = p_{ks}(j) + a \begin{cases} \Delta p_{ks}(j) & \text{if } c(j) > 0 \\ -\Delta p_{ks}(j) & \text{if } c(j) < 0 \end{cases}$$

$$p_{is}(j+1) = p_{is}(j) + a \begin{cases} -\Delta p_{is}(j) & \text{if } c(j) > 0 \\ \Delta p_{is}(j) & \text{if } c(j) < 0 \end{cases} \tag{7}$$

$$\forall i = k \in N,$$

where a denotes an attenuation coefficient adjustable within $a \in (0,1]$. The structure of such an adaption is visualized in fig. 4 .

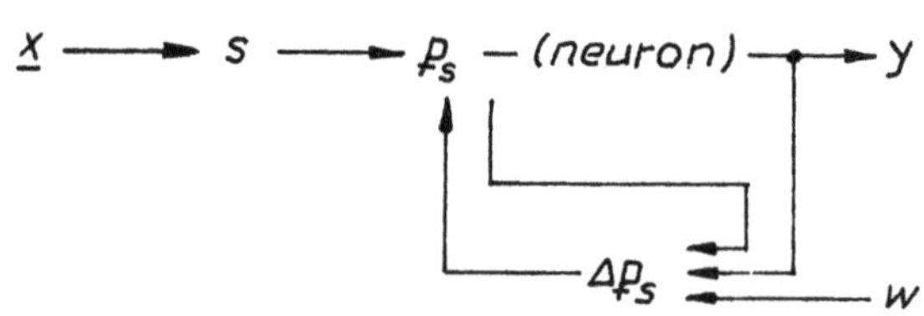

Fig. 4

With respect to equ. (6) the algorithm of adaption can equivalently be described by

$$p_{ks}(j+1) = p_{ks}(j) + a\, c_o\, \Delta p_{ks}(j)$$

$$p_{is}(j+1) = p_{is}(j) - a\, c_o\, \Delta p_{is}(j) \ , \quad \forall i \in N. \tag{8}$$

Before starting the adaption process it is necessary to initialize all probability vectors by given a priori distributions

$$p_{is}(0)\ ,\forall i \in N\ ;\forall s \in S^1 \tag{9}$$

If there is no a priori information about them an equal distribution

$$p_{is}(0) = \frac{1}{n}\ ,\forall i \in N\ ,\forall s \in S^1. \tag{10}$$

should be adopted.

IV. Spezifications of the adaption algorithm

Now it is necessary to specify the adaption algorithm as suitable functions for the correction term

$$p_{ks}(j) = f\ (p_{ks}(j))$$
$$p_{is}(j) = g(p_{is}(j)),\ \forall i \neq k \in N \tag{11a,b}$$

are to be proposed. In order to do this certain constraints have to be taken into consideration.

IV. 1. Constraints

By definition the single probabilities and the total probability underlie the conditions

$$p_{is} \in \left[0,1\right]\ ,\forall i \in N\ ,\forall s \in S^1 \tag{12}$$

and

$$P_s = \sum_{i=1}^{n} p_{is} = 1\ . \tag{13}$$

From addition the equ.s (8) and with respect to equ. (13) receives the important relation

$$\Delta p_{ks} = \sum_{i \neq k}^{n} \Delta p_{is}\ . \tag{14}$$

Furthermore the application of equ.s (12, 13) to the equations of adaption (8) delivers the set of constraints

$$p_{ks} + p_{ks} \leq 1$$
$$p_{is} - p_{is} \geq 0\ ,\quad i \neq k \in N$$
$$p_{ks} - p_{ks} \geq 0 \tag{15a-d}$$
$$p_{is} + p_{is} \leq 1\ ,\quad i \neq k \in N\ .$$

Additionally, following from equ. (12) introduced in (15b, 15c) the corrections have to satisfy the condition

$$\Delta p_{is} \geqq 0 \ , \forall i \in N \ , \forall s \in S^1 . \tag{16}$$

This system of constraints restricts the area of possible solutions as shown in fig. 5 .

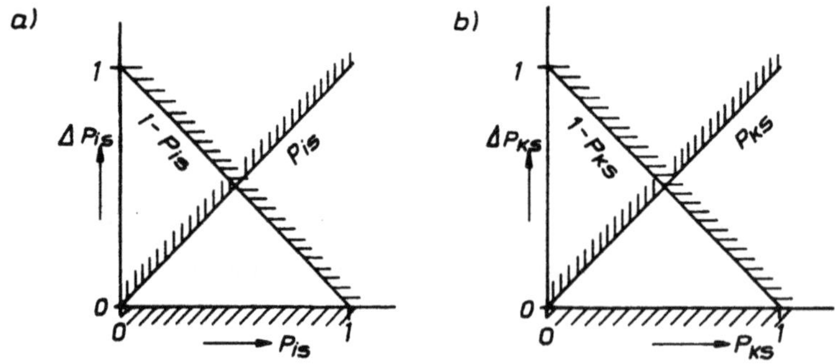

Fig. 5

IV. 2. <u>Correction algorithms of the type I</u>

First of all it can be stated that it is sufficient to derive suitable terms of Δp_{is} only because it is simpler to evaluate Δp_{ks} from equ. (14), i.e. using

$$\Delta p_{ks} (j) = \sum_{i \neq k}^{n} \Delta p_{is}(j) \ . \tag{17}$$

In the sequel we propose some functions of correction with parameters satisfying the constraints stated in IV. 1 .

As an analysis results the satisfaction of equ. (15a) is the more critical problem. Corresponding to this we reduce the corrections Δp_{is} referring the upper boundaries by division of n - 1. Consequently instead of equ.s (11) we use the functions

$$\Delta p_{is}(j) = g \left(\frac{p_{is}(j)}{n - 1} \right) \tag{18a,b}$$

and

$$f(\Delta p_{ks}(j)) = (n - 1) \sum_{i \neq k}^{n} f \left(\frac{p_{is}(j)}{n - 1} \right) .$$

Based on this formulation the following algorithms of correction can be proposed:

a) algorithm of piecewise linear correction (PLC)

The solution area can be exploited mostly if the equation of the boundary itself is based on the design of the correction equation. Because this boundary is piecewise linear a corresponding correction algorithm PLC with the discontinuity at $p_{is} = 0.5$ can be proposed as

$$\Delta p_{is}(j) = \begin{cases} \dfrac{p_{is}(j)}{n-1} & \text{if } p_{is}(j) \leq 0.5 \\[2ex] \dfrac{1 - p_{is}(j)}{n-1} & \text{if } p_{is}(j) > 0.5 \end{cases} \qquad (19)$$

$$\forall i \neq k \in N.$$

The diagram of the PLC-algorithm equ.(19), (17) is shown as curves 1a, 1b in fig. 6 .

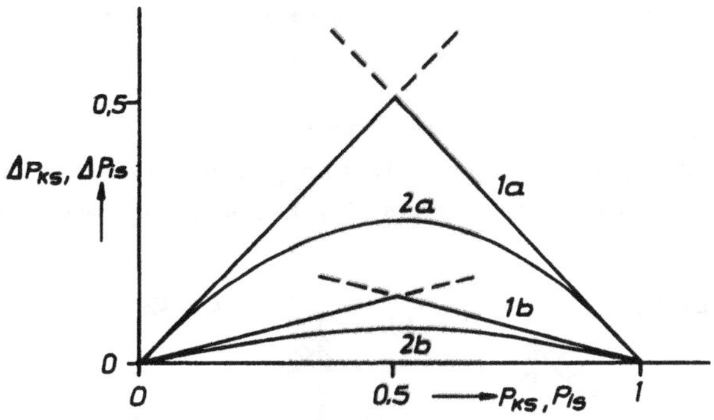

Fig. 6

b) algorithm of quadratic correction (QUC)

To avoid the discontinuity any other function, possibly symmetrical to $p_{is} = 0.5$, can be used as far as the constraints are satisfied. Using an appropriate quadratic function the following algorithm of correction QUC is given as an example:

$$\Delta p_{is}(j) = \frac{p_{is}(j)\,(1 - p_{is}(j))}{n-1}, \quad \forall i \neq k \in N. \qquad (20)$$

In fig. 6 the curves 2a and 2b illustrate the equ.s (20), (17).

IV. 3. Correction algorithms of type II

Considering the adaption functions corresponding approach I (see fig. 6) it is obvious that corrections become the smaller the more the probabilities are approaching the values 1 or 0 respectively. Consequently the adaption process will not quickly converge.

To overcome this disadvantage a more detailled analysis was made resulting in the fact that the constraints equ.s (15a), (15b) are only of importance in case of succes whereas equ.s (15c), (15d) are relevant having no success. Based on that knowledge a new types of more effective correction algorithms have been elaborated containing heuristic elements.

The first idea is to apply two different algorithms for correction

$$\Delta p_{is}(j) = f_1\ (p_{is}(j))$$

$$\Delta p_{is}(j) = f_2\ (p_{is}(j)) \qquad (21a,b)$$

between them a selection is made depending on success ($c(j) = c_o$) or failure ($c(j) = -\ c_o$). The second feature of this method is its operation in two steps.

The 1st step is designed in such a way that a possibly rapid progress in correction is made. Therefore preliminary corrections $\Delta p'_{is}(j)$ are determined first where the harder constraints for Δp_{is} (equ.s 15b, 15d) only have been taken into account (fig. 7).

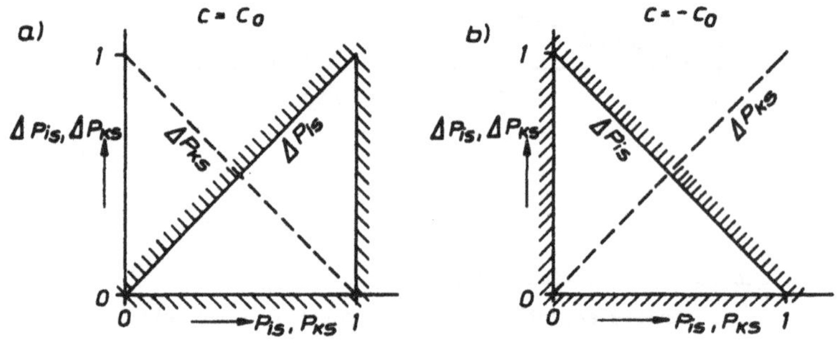

Fig. 7

Two examples of such preliminary correction algorithms are proposed as follows.

a) algorithm of linear correction depending on success (LCS)

With reference to fig. 8 a so-called linear correction algorithm LCS can be presented by

$$\Delta p_{is}'(j) = \begin{cases} p_{is}(j) & \text{if } c(j) = c_0 \\ (1 - p_{is}(j)) & \text{if } c(j) = -c_0 \end{cases} \qquad (22)$$
$$\forall i \neq k \in N.$$

Because this algorithm is based on the equations of the actual valid boundaries as shown in fig. 8, curves 1a and 1b, the corrections caused by that algorithm will be fairly rapid.

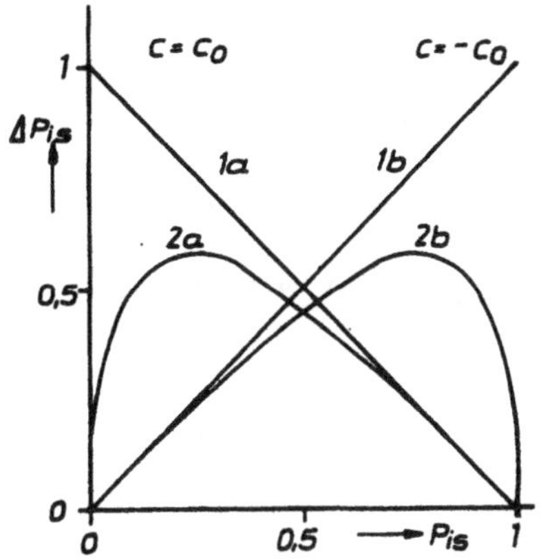

Fig. 8

b) algorithm of cubic correction depending on success (CCS)
More gentle corrections can be expected using suitable nonlinear functions. As an example the CCS-correction algorithm using symmetrical cubic functions can be given by

$$\Delta p_{is}'(j) = \begin{cases} p_{is}(j)\,(0.5 + 2\,p_{is}(j) - 2.5\,p_{is}(j)^2) & \text{if } c(j) = c_0 \\ p_{is}(j)\,(3 - 5.5\,p_{is}(j) + 2.5\,p_{is}(j)^2) & \text{if } c(j) = -c_0, \end{cases}$$
$$\forall i = k \in N. \qquad (23)$$

The curves 2a and 2b in fig. 9 represent that algorithm.

As mentioned before the algorithms of type II may produce correction values which do not satisfy the constraints referring $\Delta p_{ks}'$. Therefore an additional treatment of the preliminary values $\Delta p_{is}'$ and $\Delta p_{ks}'$ must follow corresponding step 2 to make that procedure of correction applicable.
To solve that problem algorithms based on the prinziples of both a general reduction and a conditioned reduction have been developed and tested /6/.

Among them the modification algorithm by condioned reduction (MCR) has proved to be the best one and therefore shall be reproduced here.
The basic idea of the MCR algorithm is to make only a modification if the Δp_{ks} does not satisfy the boundary condition valid for c and, if that is necessary, to make the reduction so that the overshoot becomes just zero. Therefore the MCR algorithm encloses an analysis and a determination.
Let d denote the overshoot evaluated by

$$d(j) = \begin{cases} \Delta p'_{ks}(j) + p_{ks}(j) - 1 & \text{if } c(j) = c_o \\ \Delta p'_{ks}(j) - p_{ks}(j) & \text{if } c(j) = -c_o \end{cases} \tag{24}$$

then the decision and modification is to perform using

$$\Delta p_{is}(j) = \begin{cases} \left(1 - \frac{d(j)}{\Delta p'_{ks}(j)}\right) \Delta p'_{is}(j) & \text{if } d(j) > 0 \\ \Delta p'_{is}(j) & \text{if } d(j) \leqq 0, \\ & \forall i \neq k \in N \end{cases} \tag{25a}$$

and

$$\Delta p_{ks}(j) = \begin{cases} \sum_{i \neq k}^{n} \Delta p'_{is}(j) & \text{if } d(j) > 0 \\ \Delta p'_{ks}(j) & \text{if } d(j) \leqq 0. \end{cases} \tag{25b}$$

V. Properties of the algorithms modelling the ANS

After having produced algorithms for modelling both the input/output behaviour and the dynamics of adaption of an ANS, tests should be added to prove the ability of operation and to get insights into their functional properties. For that purpose the PC runable program LERNAUT was developed. The program is menue oriented and offers options referring to different algorithmical versions, dimensions, functional parameters, and kinds of displaying the results.
After it has been shown with some experiments that the proposed algorithms do work, special attention was given to clear up their convergence and effectiveness. For that reason first of all in some pretests the algorithms with the worst features have been detected in order to exclude them in the following test. After that the algorithms assorted in tab. 1 are taken to be examined in deeper investigations.

algorithms of adaption	correction	modification
A A 1	PLC	-
A A 2	QUC	–
A A 4	LCS	MCR
A A 5	CCS	MCR

tab. 1

In a 1st series the algorithm of adaption have been tested due to their convergence. All of them have be found to show a monotonic convergence. Corresponding to the expectation the algorithms of approach II show the highest speed of adaption. This is illustrated by the diagram in fig. 9 visualizing the behaviour of adaption of the goal element $p_{k^*s}(j)$ of the probability vector $\underline{p}_s$.

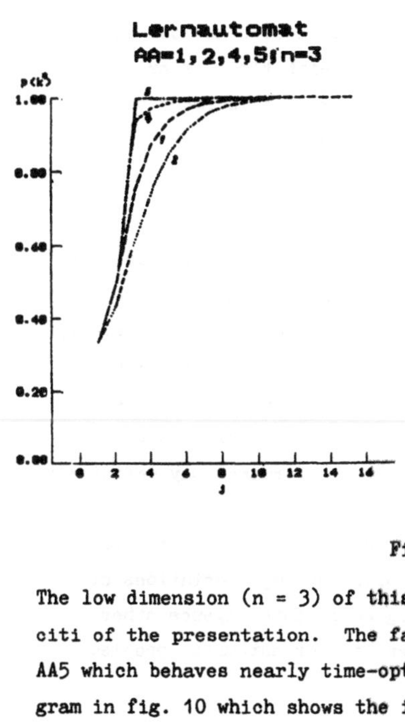

Fig. 9

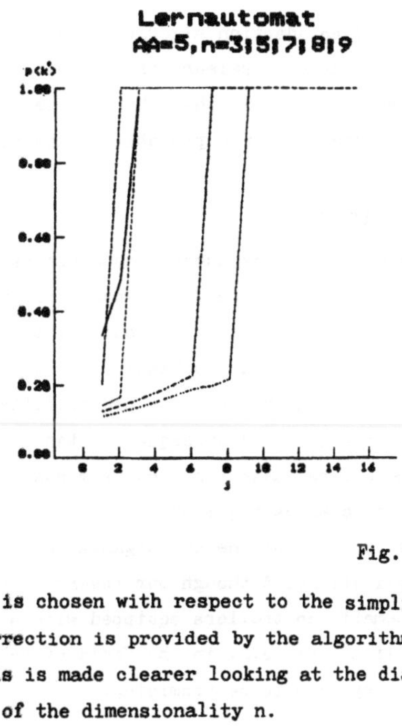

Fig.10

The low dimension (n = 3) of this example is chosen with respect to the simpliciti of the presentation. The fastest correction is provided by the algorithm AA5 which behaves nearly time-optimal. This is made clearer looking at the diagram in fig. 10 which shows the influence of the dimensionality n.
An impression of the influence of the attenuation factor a to smoothen the corrections taking the algorithm AA5 as an example is to be seen from fig. 11 .

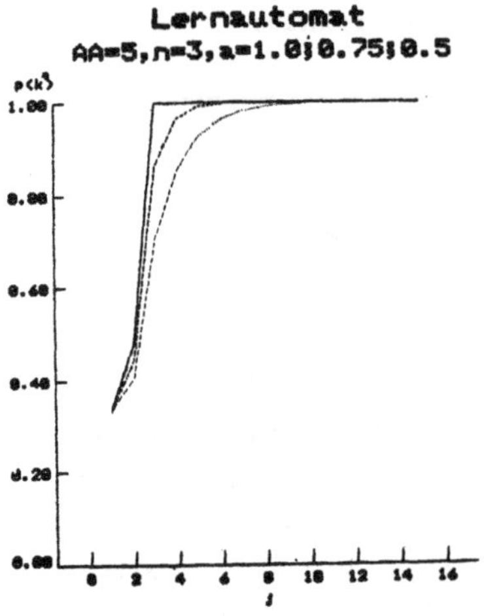

Fig. 11

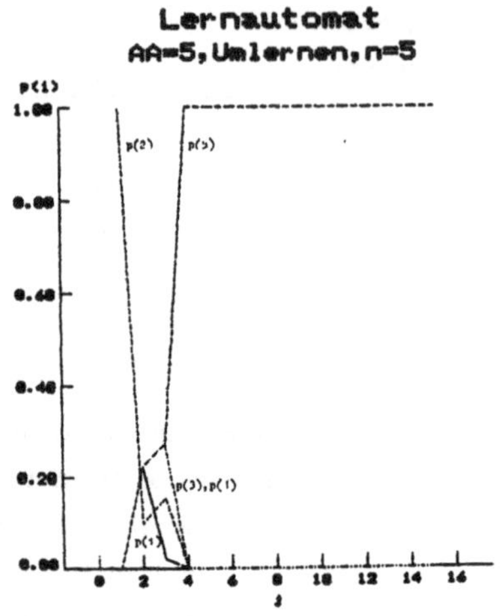

Fig. 12

Finally an adaption algorithm modelling human sensomotorical behaviour should also be able to relearn if the environment may change with time. We are happy to show in fig. 12 that the proposed algorithm as an example is ready to reconfigure a learned probability distribution by a new one.

VI. Conclusion

For modelling the human sensomotorical behaviour a selforganizing ANS is used to explain both the fast dynamics of input/output assignment and the slow dynamics of learning. In contrary to a full deterministic description normally used, we prefer a stochastic concept based on a learnable random decision.
For updating the decision probabilities some versions of the adaption algorithm are presented and subsequently tested. Resulting from this a new in a way time-optimal adaption algorithm has been found whose performance may definitely be adjusted as required.
The versions of the selforganizing ANS described may be useful for different applications. Although our research is focussed upon the implementations of automatic controllers equipped with a certain degree of intelligence other applications, e.g. in the field of pattern recognition or automatic problem solving seem to be promising.

REFERENCES

/1/ Schmidt, R.F.: Motorische Systeme. in: Physiologie des Menschen. Eds. Schmidt, R.F., Thews, G. Springer-Verlag, Berlin, Heidelberg, New York, 1983, pp 87 - 118

/2/ von der Malsburg, C ; W. Singer: Principles of Cortical Network Organization. in: Organization of Neural Networks. Eds. von Seelen, W.,Shaw, G., Leinhos, U.M. VCH Verlagsgesellschaft mbH, D-6940 Weinheim (BRD) 1988, pp. 109 -126

/3/ Amari, Shun-ichi: Mathematical Theory of Self-Organization in Neural Nets. in: Organization of Neural Networks. Eds. von Seelen, W., Shaw, G., Leinhos,U.M. VCH Verlagsgesellschaft mbH, D-6940 Weinheim (BRD), 1988, pp. 399 - 413

/4/ Weller, W.: Ein selbstorganisierender Klassenregler. messen, steuern, regeln. Berlin 31 (1988) 9, pp. 391 - 394

/5/ Weller, W.: Lernende Steuerungen. VEB Verlag Technik, Berlin 1985, and R. Oldenbourg, München, Wien 1985

/6/ Weller, W.: Entwicklung und Untersuchung von Adaptionsalgorithmen für lernfähige Automaten. report AT 87 - 12, Humboldt-Universität zu Berlin, Sektion Elektronik 1987 (not published)

CONCEPT FOR THE REALISATION OF A LEARNING NETWORK

Marius van der Meer [1)]

1. Abstract

After a short review about recent tendencies in producing and marketing artificial neural networks some proposals for a low cost neural network of discrete universal processing units are given. Underlying the well known error back propagation algorithm the details for forward and error back propagation through such a universal processing element and the learning phase controlled by a master unit are described.

2. Recent Tendencies in Development and Application of Artificial N.N.

It is an old idea to simulate a biological neural structure which has found recently a rising market for so called artificial neural networks (ANN's).
There are great differences between the representation and processing of knowledge in biological and technical systems. Hence the scientific background for the artificial neural networks finds its place in the broad area between cognitive psychology and neurosciences.
Kohonen defined the artificial neural networks as massively parallel interconnected networks of simple (usually adaptive) elements and their hierarchical organisations which are intended to interact with the objects of the real world in the same way as biological neuron systems do /4,5/.
At the First Annual International Conference on Neural Networks (ICNN) in San Diego in 1987 the exhibition of the participating industries reflects the actual international level in producing and marketing first attempts of neural networks development systems and some applications of these tools. The most of these products of about ten firms are diverse hardware and software tools for simulating the bahaviour of a neural network, no real network was shown. The most of the companies are offering different types of special boards as stand alone systems or as extensions in PC's or work stations up to VAX level completed by smart software packages for simulating the most of the known neural network paradigms. The aim of these products is to support research and development, education and commercial and military applications developments.

---

1) Humboldt-Universität zu Berlin, Sektion Elektronik,
DDR-1086 Berlin, PSF 1297

At most the applications represent the analysis of very complex data bases for real time controls, e.g. radar or sonar analysis, image processing, strategy planning and knowledge processing.
Examples for such offers are

* the ANZA System of the Hecht-Nielson Neurocomputing Corp. as a board for IBM PC's with standard software for network modelling following Grossbergs and Kohonens ideas,
* the Sigma-1 workstation with a dual-slot board high speed neural network processor Delta-1 of SAIC (Science Application International Corporation), which allows to proceed in forward propagation 10 millions of inferences per second,
* the NDS (development system) of Nestor Incorp. for modelling 15,000 neurons with 15 millions of interconnections on PC AT, SUN or APOLLO workstation,
* the MARK neuro computer series, which consists e.g. in the MARK III system of 8 up to 15 monoboard processors for diverse environments.

An intersting example for the application of such simulation or modelling systems is the so called NETtalk system, developed by Terrence Sejnowski on a VAX 11/780 at the Johns Hopkins University in Baltimore. The aim of this simulation program for an error back propagation machine is to demonstrate the possibility of applications of a neural network for automatic speech synthesis from optical reading a printed text. Each read letter activates its corresponding line of 29 lines for all letters of the alphabet in the input layer of the network. The network can select after learning as its output the right characteristics for the generation of the phonem corresponding to this letter. Because of the context dependence of the pronounciation of a letter this machine read not only one letter but also the three neighboured letters before and behind the actual reading position simultaneously. This program simulates 203 input lines, 80 hidden units, and 26 output lines. In the phase of learning this machine was trained by reading 1024 words (e.g. from a school beginners reading book or from Merriam-Websters Pocket Dictionary). Then 50 cycles of learning these words are enough for speaking the known text with 5% errors. But the more exciting fact is that 77% of all the words of the dictionary (about 20,000 words) can be spoken with the right pronounciation after learning of only 1000 words. The memory used for this feature in the network is equivalent to 10 KBytes instead of 2 MBits for the explicit storage of the phonem characteristics for the 20,000 words.
The first steps into the direction to produce devices with a real network architecture were made in the AT&T Bell Laboratories /7/.
There are several chips for such tasks under development:

* the Interconnection Matrix Chip contains 54 amplifiers as "neurons" which can be connected with each other with one of three coupling strengths. This chip has digital inputs and outputs, but uses intern

analog multiplication and current summing. The chip contains on 7*7 mm 75,000 transistors, fabricated using 2.5 micron CMOS technology.

* a learning chip is soon to be submitted for fabrication in 1.25 micron CMOS technology allowing 1,200 connections between 50 inputs and 24 outputs with network updates which will be done at frequencies of about 10 MHz. There are implemented special adaptive learning rules optimized for limited resolution of the connection strengths.

3. Concept of a Low-Cost Experimental Processing Unit for a Learning Machine

3.1. Paradigm of the Error-Back Propagation

Some fundamental ideas for the learning algorithm as internal representation of the context between given inputs and the corresponding outputs of a network were proposed by D.E. Rumelhart, G.E. Hinton and R.J. Williams as a generalization of the so called delta rule. They used a multilayered network where the information coming to the input units is recoded into a suitable internal representation. The outputs of each element of the input layer and of the several hidden layers of the network serve as one input of in general all elements of the next layer. In the output layer finally it is possible to transform the internal representation of information flow between the layers into the desired form of output. During this forward propagation of information input in order to get a corresponding output in each node of the network a summing up of all its weighted inputs takes place. This result represents the activation level of this node. Here the weight factors for all input lines are adjustable in the learning phase of the network, the output of one node is represented by the sigmoid function value of the activation. So the weight factors of all input lines in the network are the result of the learning phase and represents the stored knowledge. The activation levels of all nodes are an expression of the actual input for the network and determine by forward propagation its corresponding output /8,9/.

That means that the behaviour of such a network as a classification or recognition machine results from the suitable choise of all the weight factors of the nodes. The aim of the error back propagation phase is to determine these right weight factors by means of the generalized delta rule as a correction of initial weight factors in dependence of the difference between the desired and the actual output for a given input of the network.

An essential question which cannot considered here is the nessesary number of elements (especially hidden elements and hidden layers) for such a network. This is of course dependent of the special aim for the network and nevertheless also a problem of theoretical considerations of these networks. But the number of input and output elements can be optimized easier in dependence of the given information income and the desired output coding for the problem to solve.

3.2. Algorithms

The learning process by iteration described above can be written in some formulae in analogy to the notation of Rumelhart, Hinton and Williams. The activation a_i of each node i of the layer m is

(1) $$a_i^{(m)} = \sum_j s_j^{(m)} W_{ij}^{(m)}.$$

The output of this network element results in use of the sigmoid function

(2) $$s_i^{(m+1)} = f(a_i^{(m)}) = 1/(1+\exp(-a_i^{(m)})).$$

The starting point for the error back propagation is a suitable measure for the error between the desired (s_{ip}^*) and the observable output $s_{ip}^{(n)}$ of the output layer (n) of the network for a given input pattern p. As such a measure serves E_p with

(3) $$E_p = 1/2 \sum_i (s_{ip}^{(n)} - s_{ip}^*)^2.$$

The correction of the weight factors starts from the bottom of the network following

(4) $$W_{ij}^{(m)} := W_{ij}^{(m)} - \eta D_i^{(m+1)} * a_j^{(m)}$$

with

(5) $$D_i^{(n)} = (s_i^{(n)} - s_i^*) * \frac{\partial}{\partial a_i^{(n-1)}} f(a_i^{(n-1)}) = (s_i^{(n)} - s_i^*) * \frac{\partial}{\partial a_i^{(n-1)}} s_i^{(n)}$$

and has to be continued backward with

(6) $$D_j^{(m)} = \left(\sum_i D_i^{(m+1)} * W_{ij}^{(m)} \right) * \frac{\partial}{\partial a_j^{(m-1)}} s_j^{(m)}.$$

3.3. The Flow Chart and the Corresponding Architecture

In Figure 1 is shown the flow chart for the evaluations in one node corresponding the algorithm described. On the left hand side is shown the simpler part for the forward propagation of the information from the input to the output following (1) and (2). On the right hand side is shown the more interesting part of the error back propagation handling in one processing unit. Here the first difficulty in the design of a universal processing unit follows from the inversion of the data flow direction compared with forward propagation. Furthermore from all the input lines of the next layer in the network, which in forward direction receives the same output of a certain element, this element in the error back propagation phase has to receive another error measure date to evaluate the correction values for the weight factors. These error dates have to be summed up following (5) and have to be multiplied by the derivative of the element output. Then the values D_i serve on one side for the correction of the input weight factors of a given node with a learning rate coefficient η which has to be determined during the initialization of the network or during the learning phase in any dynamic appropriate manner. On the other hand these values D_i have to be multiplied by the specific input weight for further sending back, i.e. upwards to the corresponding node of the next upper layer.

3.4. The Processing Unit

On the top of Figure 2 as a scheme of one node are shown the input lines (up to 48 for using three multiplexers 4067). These inputs reach the standard serial input line of a single chip processor (e.g. Z8) via a switching unit. This processor is completed in a common way by a static (CMOS-) RAM for the data of inputs, the weight factors and the error measures, the ROM is used to store the algorithm of the behaviour of each node during the several phases of working. To the bottom of the scheme leads from the serial output of the processor via the switching unit the one output line of this processing element. The switching unit itself serves for the inversion of the data flow direction for the error back propagation phase.

3.5. A Possible Structure of a Layered Network with Units Described Above

It should be explained briefly the scheme of Figure 3 for the working of a network composed of universal processing units described above. In the learning phase an error back propagation network needs a master which offers the tasks as pairs of given inputs and desired outputs. The master of the network described here is an external control unit which serves as such a task generator.

This means that it produces successively different pairs of input and output from a given finite set of such patterns which have to be learned by the network. Moreover this control unit synchronizes the data flow through the network in the error back propagation phase, because each element of a certain layer has to send a line number specific error date without any conflict to other simultaneously sending nodes of this layer to the right node of the next upper layer. For this aim the control unit sends a line counter date to the actual learning layer. This line counter is decremented until all input lines of the actual learning layer have send out its error date. This is detected by the control unit and its response is a signal that the error back propagation phase for this layer has ended.

According this procedure it is obvious that the learning phase of such a network is time expensive compared with the forward propagation phase. The time is proportional to the number of layers and the number of elements per layer. But after learning the layered structure and parallel working of all elements in each layer allows to get the output of the network after a time proportional to the number of input lines of each node and to the number of layers. The shorter algorithm for forward propagation and the possibility of pipelining may serve for rather prompt response of the trained network.

4. Acknowledgement

I wish to thank Professor W. Ebeling for the possibility to work in his group and also his colleages Th. Pöschel and Dr. Boseniuk for a lot of interesting discussions and remarks on the topic of this paper.

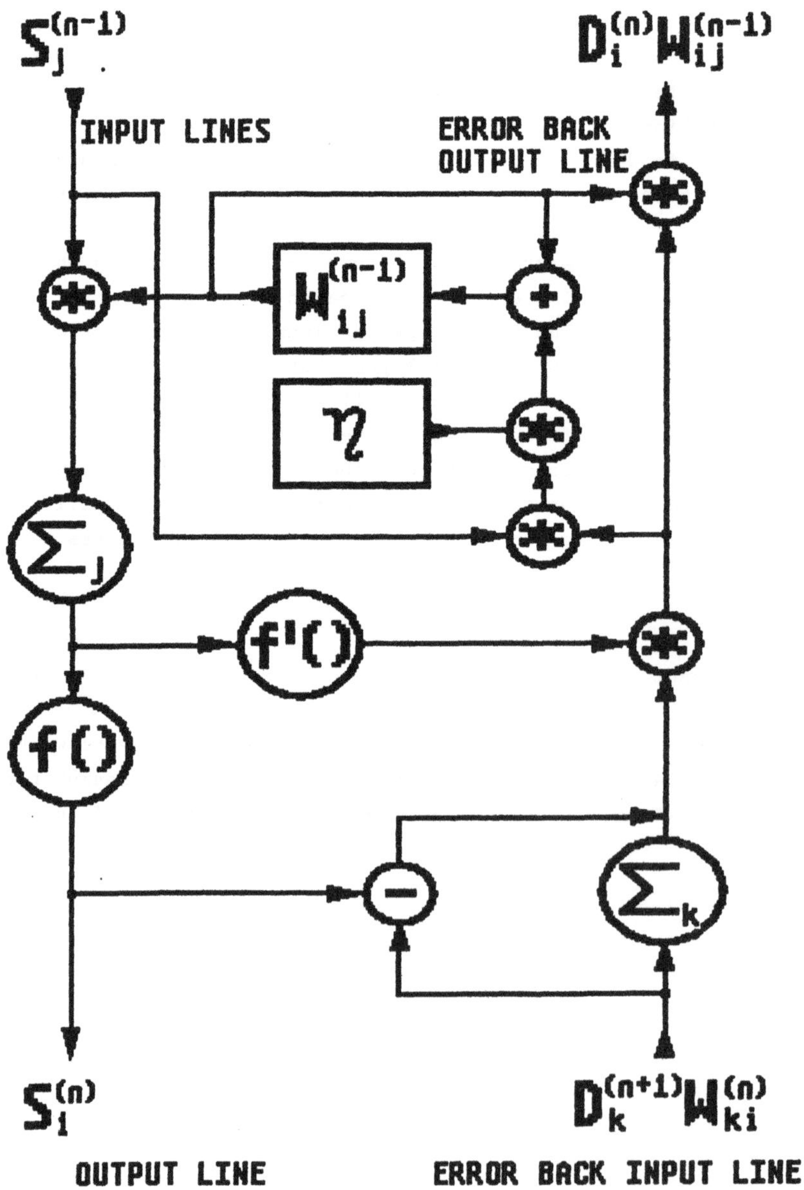

Fig. 1: Flowchart for the algorithms of forward processing of network inputs to the outputs and of error back propagation to correct the weight factors of the links in the network

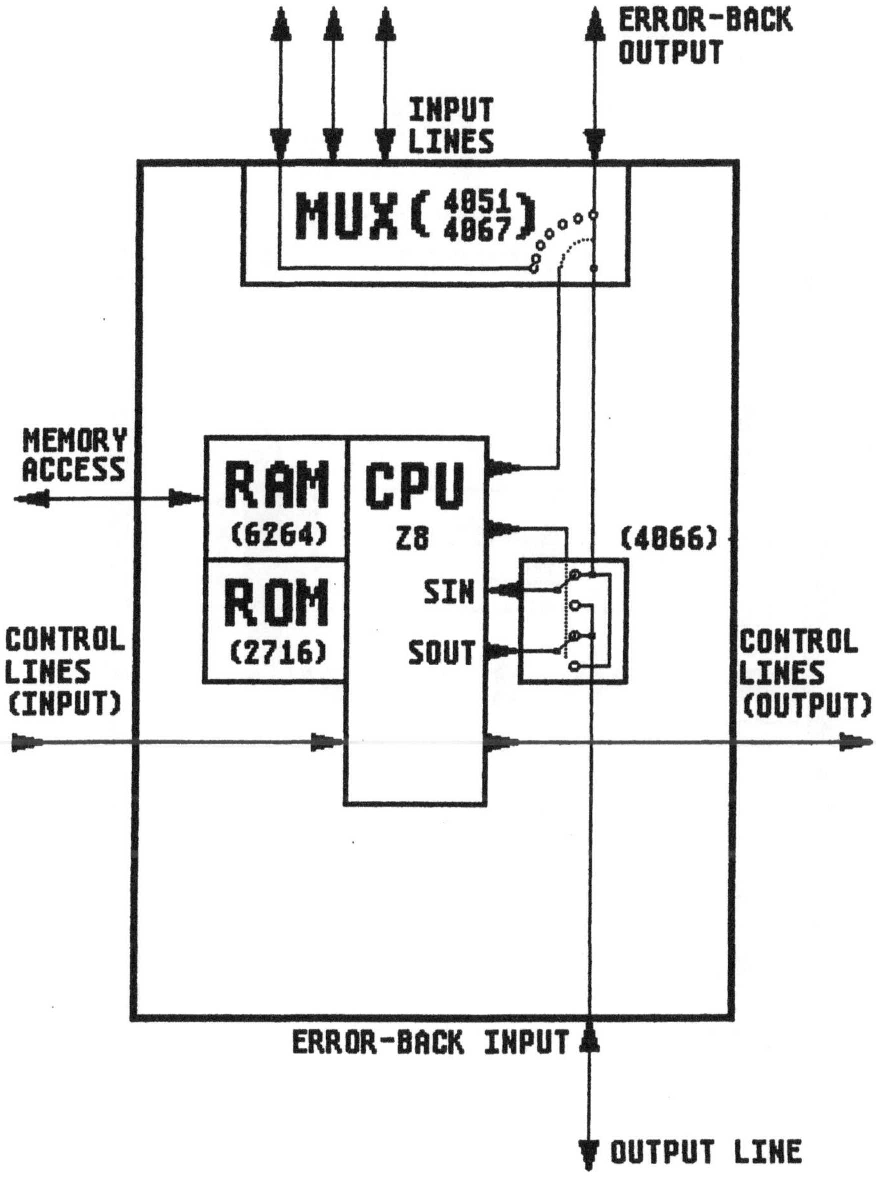

Fig. 2: Scheme of one node with up to 48 input lines and one output line based on Z8 microprocessor

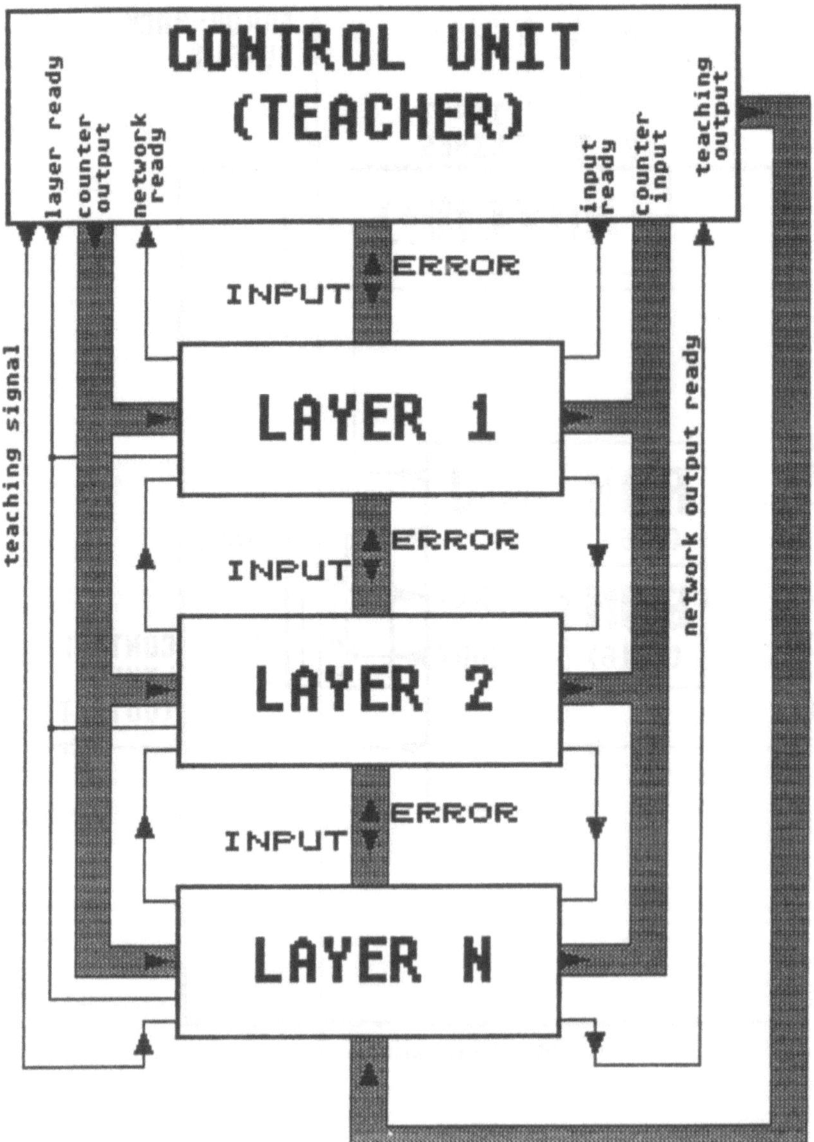

Fig. 3: Layered structure of network composed by the proposed structure of processing units as nodes

6. Literature

/1/ Corrado, J.: Artificial Neural Networks, Spang Robinson Review, 1987

/2/ Grossberg, St.: Nonlinear Neural Networks: Principles, Mechanisms, and Architectures. Neural Networks, Vol.1, pp. 17-61, 1988

/3/ Kemke, Ch.: Tagungsbericht ICNN '87 San Diego. KI Vol.4, pp. 22-25, 1987

/4/ Kohonen, T.: An Introduction to Neural Computing. Neural Networks, Vol.1, pp. 3-16, 1988

/5/ Kohonen, T.: State of the Art in Neural Computing. Proceedings ICNN 1987, June 21-24, 1987, San Diego, pp. I-77 to I-90

/6/ Kohonen, T.: The "Neural" Phonetic Typewriter. Computer, Vol. 3, pp. 11-22, 1988

/7/ Mackie, S., Graf, H.P., and Schwartz, D.B.: Implementation of N.N. Models in Silicon. in: Neural Computers, NATO ASI Series Vol. F 41, ed. by R. Eckmiller and Ch. v.d.Malsburg, Springer-Verlag, Berlin Heidelberg, 1988

/8/ Palm, G.: 20 Modellvorstellungen auf der Basis neuronaler Netze. in: Wissenspsychologie, ed. by H. Mandl and H. Spada, Psychologie Verlags Union, Muenchen, 1988, pp. 291-300

/9/ Sejnowski, T.: Neural Network Learning Algorithms. in: Neural Computers, NATO ASI Series Vol. F 41, ed. by R. Eckmiller and Ch. v.d.Malsburg, Springer-Verlag, Berlin Heidelberg, 1988

Simulation of Network Machines

Thorsten Pöschel - Humboldt Universität zu Berlin, GDR

1. Introduction

The simulation of neuronal systems has got two aims:

First to get information about the mechanism of human information processing systems. That means to find out the relations between the microstructure, which is well investigated by biology and physiologie, and the macrostructure investigated by cognitive psychology. Both sciences are highly developed; the working mechanism of a single or some neurons as well as many properties about the behaviour of whole nervous systems are well understood. The cognitive psychologie tries to develop models, which conclude from the reactions of test persons to information processing mechanisms at a lower level. By means of psychological experiments it seems possible to verify or falsify macroscopical neuronal models /7/.

From the microstructure one tries to approach more complex systems by investigating Neural Networks. The investigation of two special types of the so called Network Machines is the subject of the presented contribution.

The System Theory also tries to conclude from the behavior of simple elements to the properties of more complex systems and also in invers direction. However in difference to neuronal systems with about 10^{10} simple elements the objects of System Theorie are much smaller.

The second aim of the investigation of neuronal nets concerns the development of artificial intelligent systems, e.g., learning by example presentation machines, which change an inherent state according to the presented task, the required result and the error the machine has made, by means of a special feed back mechanism.

2. Network Machines

A network machine as we will understand it in this paper consists of a large number N of simple uniform processing elements. Each of them is characterized by its activation E_i and its output s_i, which is a analytic or probabilistic funtcion of the activation /14/:

$$s_i = f(E_i) \qquad (1)$$

The processing elements are connected by weighted links in a special manner, which is characterized by the type of network machine. These links w_{ij} transfer the output s_i of an element to the input of another. Some of the elements serve as interface to the environment. The information, which should by processed (the problem) expressed in binary numbers or real numbers out of a limited interval, is clamped onto the input elements of the net. Then the other elements get an activation transferred by the links and change their output according to the output function (1). In this way also the states of the output elements vary. From these numbers the output of the network can be obtained. Now the deviation of the output from the required by a teacher result has to be determined and the weights must be varied is such a manner, that the deviation will reduce /11/.

In the following sections we will discuss two special types of Network Machines and present some of the results of computer simulations we have done.

3. The Boltzmann Machine

The Boltzmann Machine consists of bistable elements, which can acquire the values 0 or 1. Each of them is designated by its bias Θ_i. The weights of the links are real numbers $w_{ij} \in \mathbb{R}$; w_{ij} connects the output of the j-th element with an input of the i-th one. The weights are symmetrically, e.g. $w_{ij} = w_{ji}$. All working elements are connected with each other. The output of an element s_i here is a stochastical function of its activation. With probability

$$p(E_i) = \frac{1}{1 + e^{\left(\frac{-E_i}{T}\right)}} \tag{2}$$

the state of the element i is set to 1 otherwise it becomes 0. This formula is well known from the Metropolis Algorithm, used to calculate partition functions. In this algorithm T has the meaning of the thermodynamic temperature. Assuming that E is the internal energy of the Boltzmann Machine

$$E = \sum_{i=1}^{N} \Theta_i - \sum_{i=1}^{N} \sum_{j=1}^{i-1} w_{ij}\, s_i\, s_j$$

$$E_i = \sum_{\substack{j=1 \\ j \neq i}}^{N} w_{ij}\, s_j - \Theta_i = E(s_i{=}0) - E(s_i{=}1) \tag{3}$$

it is shown, that obeying these formulae processing elements converge to a probability distribution

$$P(\{s\}) = C\, e^{\left(\frac{-E(\{s\})}{T}\right)} \tag{4}$$

where $\{s\}$ is the statistical ensemble of the ouputs of the workimg elements.

To describe the learning rule of the Boltzmann Machine we define a measure for the deviation of the networks result from the desired one, called information gain:

$$G = \sum_{\{s\}_o} P(\{s\}_o) \ln \frac{P(\{s\}_o)}{P'(\{s\}_o)} \tag{5}$$

P' is the probability, that the configuration $\{s\}_o$ of the output elements occures when the network is running freely and P is the desired by a teacher probability for this configuration. That means P is obtained by running the Boltzmann Machine according to the Metropolis algorithm where the input elements and the ouput elements are clamped to the inputs given by a teacher and all others are freely running. Corresponding P' is the probability which the Boltzmann Machine finds themselfes if the network is connected to the teaching input and all other elements are running the Metropolis algorithm. G has got the property:

$$G \begin{cases} = 0 \text{ , for } P' = P \\ > 0 \text{ , otherwise} \end{cases} \qquad (6)$$

G = 0 is the aim of the learning procedure, e.g. in this case the network comes to the same equilibrium state, independent of the clamped or unclamped output elements. For this reason we may use G as measure of the deviation of the networks output to the teaching one. That means, we will change the weights according to:

$$\Delta w_{ij} = -\varepsilon \left\langle \frac{\partial G}{\partial w_{ij}} \right\rangle \qquad (7),$$

and $w_{ij} := w_{ij} + \Delta w_{ij}$

where $\langle \partial G / \partial w_{ij} \rangle$ is an averaged over some different input patterns value. As result of a long calculation one finds /1/ :

$$\frac{\partial G}{\partial w_{ij}} = -\frac{1}{T} (p_{ij} - p'_{ij}) \qquad (8),$$

where p'_{ij} is the probability that s_i and s_j are 1 for freely running outputs; p_{ij} is the correspondent probability for the case, that the outputs are clamped, ε is a constant /1/.

4. Performance of the Boltzmann Machine

In the sections 4.1. and 4.2. we present computer simulations of the Boltzmann Machine we performed with a personal computer ATARI 260 ST (4.1.) and with a SM 52 computer (4.2.). It turns out that even such simple problems as our examples require a large amount of computer power. More complex examples, as in the case of the Error Propagation Machine have not been done for this reason.

4.1. The 4-2-4 Encoder

The 4-2-4 Encoder is a standard example to test the performance of learning networks proposed by /1/. The 4-2-4 Encoder consists of 4 input elements, 2 inner elements and 4 output elements (fig.1). There are 4 allowed different input configurations and also for a fixed task 4 teaching outputs, two examples of tasks are shown in fig. 2.

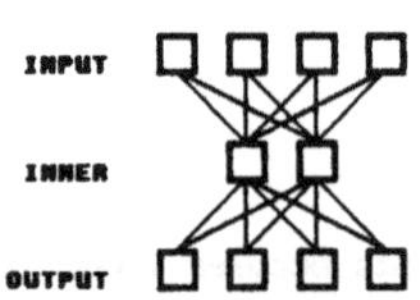

fig.1

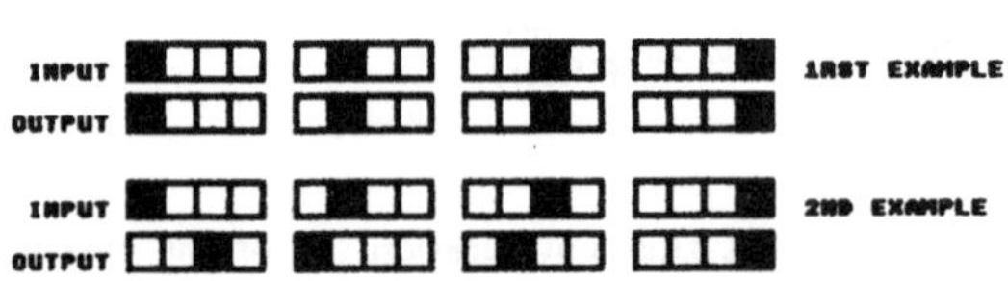

fig.2

The difficulty is to press the 4 bit information of the input elements through the bottleneck of 2 inner ones. For this reason of course the input elements are not directly connected with the output ones, otherwise the task turns out to be trivial. After about 80 representations of every input pattern the network found the correct output with a reliability of 100 %.

In fig. 3 the normalized values of the inner energy as defined in (3) of the completely taught with example 2 in fig.2 network is drawn for the 4 possible input configurations and the corresponding 5 configurations of the inner and output elements which correspond to the lowest inner energy values. As expected it is obvious that the configuration with the lowest inner energy corresponds to the taught output.

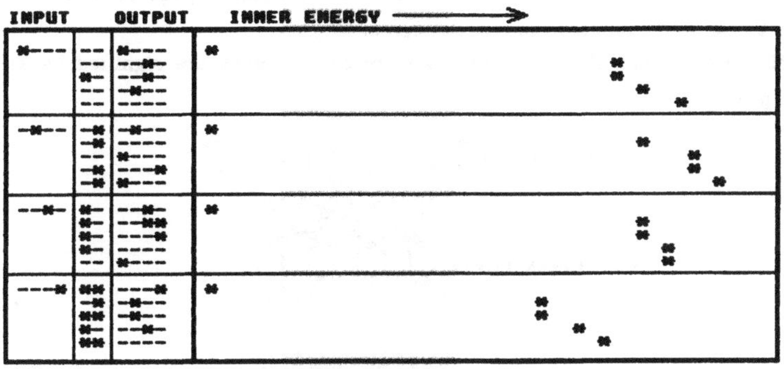

fig. 3

4.2. Simple Pattern Recognition

In our second example we want to discuss a simple problem of pattern recognition. The machine, consisting out of 25 input, 20 inner and 20 output elements was taught to recognize 20 different 3 x 3 patterns independent of their location within a 5 x 5 raster as shown in fig. 4 /2/:

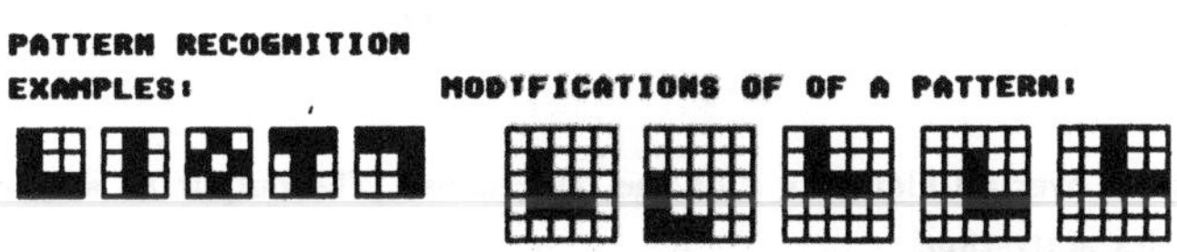

fig.4

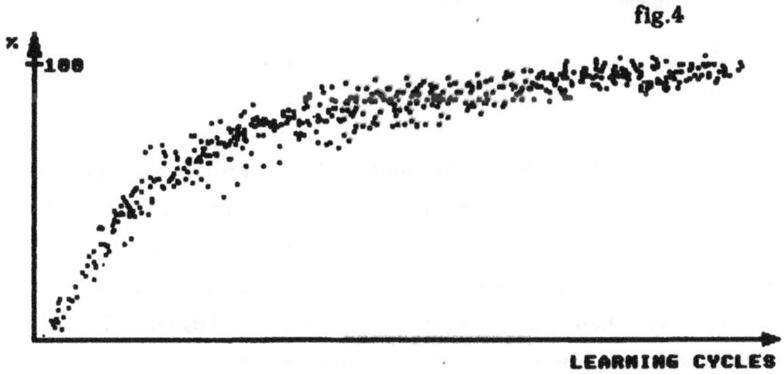

fig.5

Also this very computing time consuming task was solved and after learning the machine recognized the different patterns with a rather high reliability (fig. 5).

5. Error Propagation

The second example for Network Machines we want to discuss is the Error Propagation Machine. In difference to the Boltzmann Machine it consists of elements whose output is a real number out of the interval (0,1). The processing elements are arranged in layers, the first layerr consists of input elements, the last one of output elements and all others of inner elements. In our calculations we used only 1 layer of inner elements; the incorporation of more layers appears to be not reasonable in our examples.

The weights of the links that are directed from top to down are signified by a real number, $w_{ij} \in \mathbb{R}$. (fig. 6)

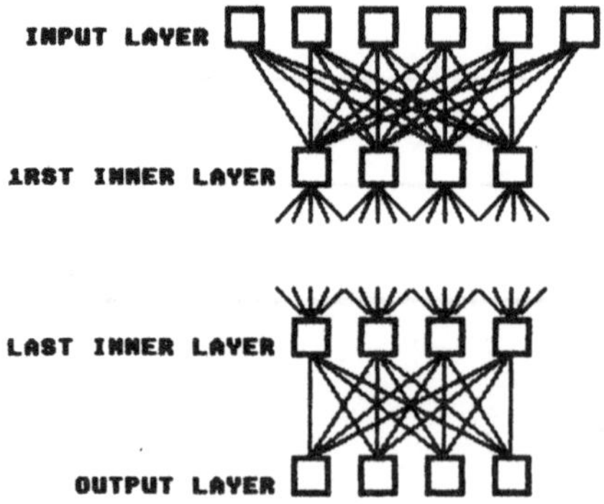

fig. 7

The activation E_i of an element is given by:

$$E_i = -\sum w_{ij}\, s_j + \Theta_i \qquad (9),$$

where the summation runs over all elements s_j of the layer above. The output of an element is an analytic function of its activation:

$$s_i = f(E_i) = \frac{1}{1 + e^{-E_i}} \qquad (10)$$

The working mechanism acts as follows: First the input of a learning example given by a teacher is clamped to the input elements of the network. Then the output values of the inner elements from the 2 nd layer are calculated according (9) and (10). The output values of the next layer, either an inner one or the output layer is calculadet in the same manner and so on, until the output layer is reached. Then we determine the deviation ERROR of the networks output $\{s_i\}$ from the teachers correct answer $\{s_i^T\}$ as Euklid distance (11).

$$\text{ERROR} = \sum_i (\, s_i - s_i^T \,)^2 \qquad (11)$$

The summation runs over all output elements. Then, very similar to the Boltzmann Machine, the weights of the links are varied in a manner, that the ERROR will reduce. Again $\langle \partial \text{ERROR} / \partial w_{ij} \rangle$ is the averaged derivative over some different output patterns. In our Simulations we averaged by means of an exponentially decaying filter /10,12,13/.

$$\Delta w_{ij} = -\varepsilon \left\langle \frac{\partial\ \text{ERROR}}{\partial w_{ij}} \right\rangle$$

$$w_{ij} := w_{ij} + \Delta w_{ij} \qquad (12)$$

6. Performance of the Error Propagation Machine

In the next two sections we present some Examples of the performance of the Error Propagation Machine. This Simulations have been performed with an IBM XT (6.1., 6.2.) and an ATARI PC (6.3.).

6.1. The Enhanced (4+N)-2-4 Encoder

The Enhanced Encoder consists of 4+N input, 2 inner and 4 output elements. The problem the network has to solve is similar to the encoder problem in 4.1. with the additional difficulty that only 4 of the 4+N input elements carry an information. These 4 elements are hidden within the input layer. The teaching inputs of the others are randomly chosen, e.g. the additional task consists in finding out which input elements are significiant for the output by means of examples. As in 4.1. the net solves this task very quickly.

Analyzing the number of connection values w_{ij} out of an given interval (fig. 8) it turns out that only very few weights have got a meaningful value. The peak at the value around zero originite from the weights of the links from the not significant input elements to the inner ones. These inputs should have no influence to the output of the network and for that reason the weights connected with this elements are about zero.

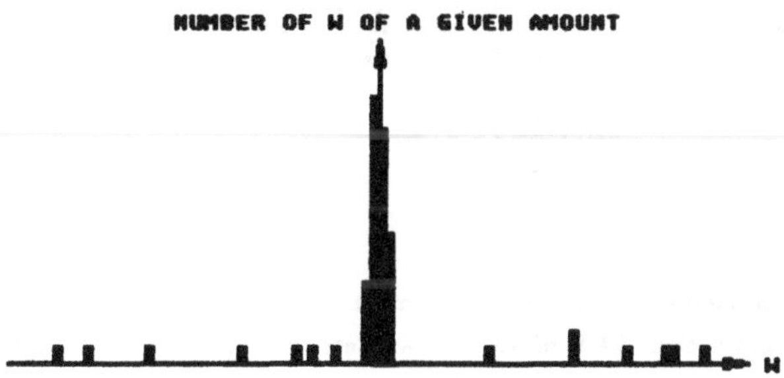

fig. 8

6.2 Comparison of Binary Numbers

The task consists in finding out whether the binary number of the first 8 input elements greater then the binary number of the last 8 ones. The used network has got 16 input, a single inner and 1 output element. (fig.9)

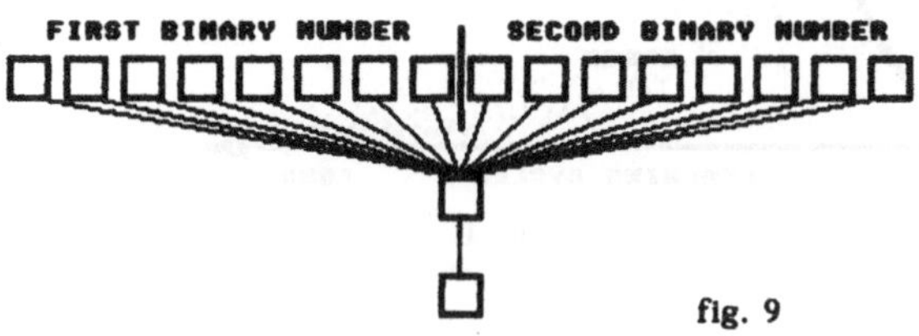

fig. 9

If the output element s had a value > 0.5 the output was interpreted to be 1, otherwise 0. If the network didn't capture any information obout the problem yet, in the beginning of the learning procedure it will decide correct with a reliability of about 50%, if it captured the meaning of the most significiant bits of both binary numbers it decides with 75% reliability. When the net knows the meaning of both next significiant bits it decides with 82,5% correct and so on. After 300-400 teaching procedures the reliability was about 100%, e.g. the net learned to classify the input elements with reference to their importance.

6.3. Pattern Recognition

One of the most discussed problem in modern informatics is pattern recognition. However it is evident that other (older and highly developed) technics attain a higher reliability yet /2/ in this section we want to demonstrate, that networks are also capable to recognize simple patterns as capital hand drawn letters.

For this example we used a network of 150 input, 20 inner and 26 output elements. The input elements were arranged in a 10 x 15 matrix. The machine was taught with 12 alphabets by different authors. Four of this alphabets are shown in fig. 10.

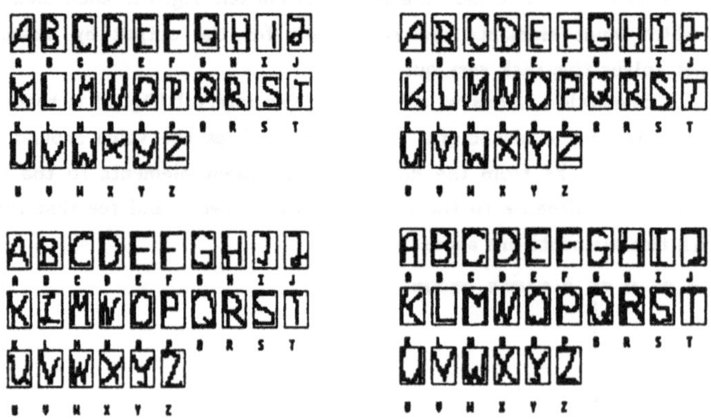

fig. 10

In fig. 11 the ERROR and the reliability of correct assignment of the net is drawn. After learning the network recognized more than 99 % of the shown letters correctly. Not shown ones (unknown) were recognized with reliability of about 70 %.

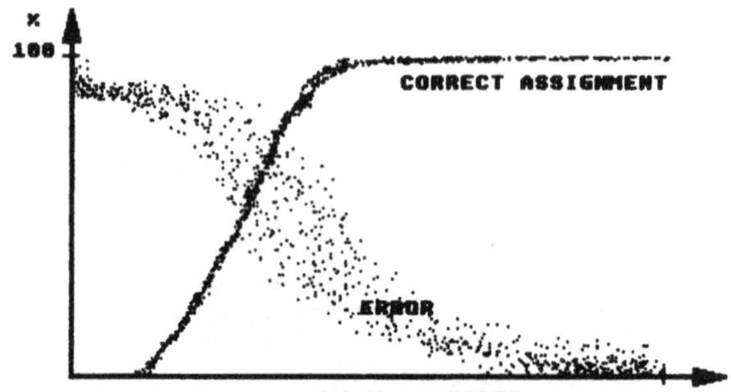

fig. 11

To demonstrate the ability of the taught network to classify the input patterns we have drawn the normalized spectrum of the Hamming distances of all input patterns (fig.12, left) and the averaged over all different letters Hamming distances of all input patterns which belong to the same letter, for instance of all different hand drawn letters "A" (right). The Hamming disdance was calculated according (13).

$$D_H^{NM} = \sum_{i=1}^{150} \text{abs} \left(\text{sgn} \left(s_i^N - 0.5 \right) - \text{sgn} \left(s_i^M - 0.5 \right) \right) \qquad (13)$$

It is obvious that the shape of the curves is different, but the peak is nearly at the same point at an Hamming distance of about 55.

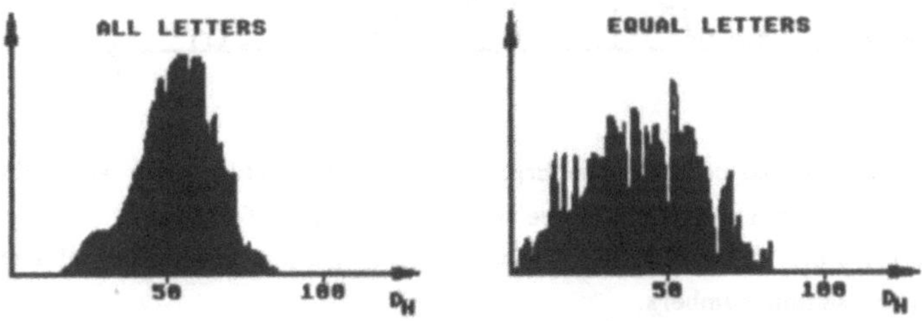

fig. 12

Fig. 13 shows the equivalent spectrum of the inner working elements. It is evident that the peak is shifted to the lower distances, e.g. the network classified the input patterns. The same spectrum at the output layer would be shifted extremely to the left, as our reliability value of 99 % indicates.

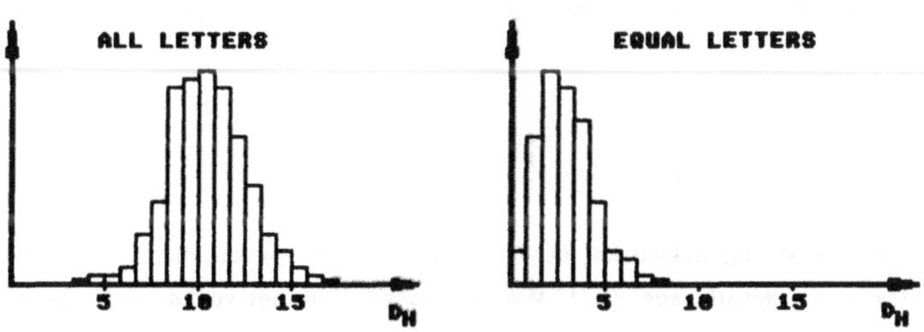

fig. 13

7. Evolution Algorithm

Analyzing the distribution of the w_{ij} values of the former pattern recognition task we found that the majority of the elements of the taught matrix are around zero (fig. 14). That means they have nearly no influence on the performance of the network. We set all the w_{ij} whose values lie in the hatched area to zero (fig. 15), e.g. we disconnected the corresponding working elements. It turns out that the reliability of the network remains the same.

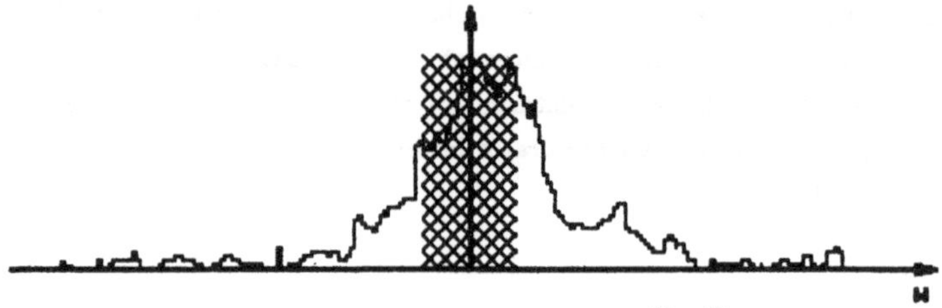

fig. 14

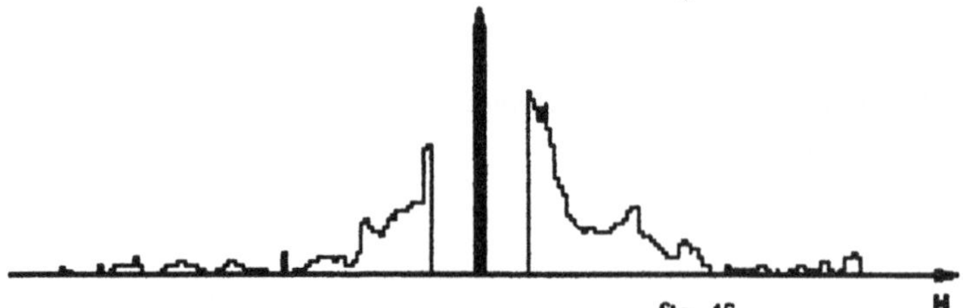

fig. 15

This fact induces the idea to combine the Error Propagation Machine with an evolution algorithm /3,6,9/. This algorithm runs for a three layered network as follows:

1. Connect every inner element with a certain number of input and output elements. Initiate them with random numbers.
2. Perform a number of learning cycles.
3. Disconnect from every inner element links with a small w-value
4. Connect the inner elements with other input and output elements using the free links originating from the former step.

Applying this algorithm to the pattern recognition task from 3.3. we did not get a significiant improvement yet; it took us nearly the same computational time to achieve the same reliability as in the fully connected net. Until now the advantage consists in the fact that we need only 706 weighted links instead of 3566, e.g. we use only about 20 % of the memory to store the matrix w.

8. Conclusions

Two different types of learning networks were investigated as special cases of self organization of networks (for more details see /8/). We have seen that networks with the same structure are able to solve very different tasks only by presenting learning examples, e.g. not using any kind of a program. The question what kinds of tasks network machines are suitable for is unsolved yet. We think, that the Cognitive Psychology is able to supply a lot of experiences and experimental data to give a reasonable answer to this question. Another question is: how complex must a network machine of a certain kind be to solve a given problem, e.g. how to define the complexity of a problem for a given network type, similar as for Touring Machines or for other types of computers. A great advantage of the Boltzmann Machine as of the Error Propagation Machine is the simple applieability of parallel working special hardware /4,5/.

9. Ackknowledgement

The author want to express his gratitude to the initiator of this investigations, Prof. W. Ebeling, for the steady support and stimulation of this work. Thanks also to Dr. T. Boseniuk for many fruitful discussions.

10. References

/1/ Ackley, D.H., G.E. Hinton, T.J. Sejnowski: A Learning Rule for Boltzmann Machines. Cognitive Sc. 9 (1985)

/2/ Arkadiew, A.G., E.M. Brawermann: Zeichenerkennung und maschinelles Lernen. R. Oldenbourg Verlag, München und Wien (1966)

/3/ Boseniuk, T.: Modellierung komplexer Systeme durch Computersimulation. Dissertation A, Humboldt Universität zu Berlin (1987)

/4/ Boseniuk, T., W. Ebeling, M. v.d. Meer, T. Pöschel: Schaltungsanordnung und Verfahren zur deterministischen oder probabilistischen Bildung eines diskreten Outputfeldes aus einem diskreten Inputfeld. Patent WP G06F/313564

/5/ Boseniuk, T., W. Ebeling, M. v.d. Meer, T. Pöschel: Schaltungsanordnung und Verfahren zum Abarbeiten von Lernprozessen auf parallel arbeitenden Digitalrechnern. Patent WP G06F/313563

/6/ Ebeling, W., R. Feistel: Physik der Selbstorganisation und Evolution. Akademie-Verlag Berlin (1986)

/7/ Ebeling, W.: Physik komplexer nichtlinearer Netzwerke und neue Wege der Informationsverarbeitung. Sitzungsberichte der Akademie der Wissenschaften der DDR 4N, Akademie-Verlag Berlin (1987)

/8/ Ebeling, W.: Selforganisation and Information Processing by Networks (contribution to this volume)

/9/ Feistel, R.: Physik und Evolution. Wissenschaftliche Zeitschrift der Humboldt Universität zu Berlin, MNR 35, 412-417 (1986)

/10/ McClelland, J.L., D.E. Rumelhart: An Interactive Model of Context Effects in Letter Perception, Part 1. An Account of Basic Findings. Psychological Review Vol. 88 Number 5, Sept. (1981)

/11/Rumelhart, D.E., J.L. McClelland, eds.: Parallel Distributed Processing: Explorations in the Microstructure of Cognition. Vol.1 and 2 Cambridge: MIT Press, (1986)

/12/ Sejnowski, T.J., C.D. Rosenberg: NETtalk, a program which converts text into spoken English. Technical Report JHU/EECS-86/01 Baltimore Maryland (1986)

/13/ Sejnowski, T.J., C.D. Rosenberg: Parallel Networks that Learn to Pronounce English Text. Complex Systems 1 (1987)

/14/ Williams, R.J.: Unit Activation Rules for Cognitive Network Models, Institute for Cognitive Science, San Diego, California ICS Report No. 8303 (1983)

THE FIRMWARE MODEL OF A NEOCORTICAL COLUMN AS A SELF-REGULATING CONTROL STRUCTURE FOR AUTONOMOUS RECOGNITION AND LEARNING

E. Koerner[1)], H.-M. Gross[1)], H. Shimizu[2)] and I. Tsuda[3)]

1. Structured versus unstructured neural networks

Most of current popular neural network schemes are composed of homogeneous arranged simple processing elements. The recent progress in learning algorithms for parallel distributed processing has led to the belief in some part of the community that there is no need for a-priori structure but the system (the network) may self-organize, self-structure, under working by means of general learning algorithms alone. The convincing results of these schemes like autoassociators, Boltzmann machines, spinglass systems and other popular model approaches with and without backpropagation, however, hold only in case of severe restrictions imposed on the input such as stationary environment, selected and limited number of input patterns which do not fully use the potential memory capacity of the networks. The problem is to get ultrastability without loosing the wanted flexibility, adaptability of neural networks in case of real world (nonstationary, highly parallel) inputs.

First, without a selfstabilizing mechanism for learning, stored representations may be washed out or modified unwantedly as long as no external teacher supervizes the learning and the learning process is shut off before the memory is overloaded. Hence, this type of systems performs well in well controlled environments only. Second, as pointed out by Carpenter & Grossberg (1988), in systems with external control of learning the mismatch of desired and actual output often determines learning. The learning with that criteria has to be slowly and in a

---

1) The Ilmenau Institute of Technology
Section Engng. and Biomedical Cybernetics
PF 327, Ilmenau, 6300, GDR
2) Faculty of Pharmaceutical Sciences, Department
of Biophysics, University of Tokyo, Hongo, Bunkyo-ku,
Tokyo 113, Japan
3) Bioholonics Research Project, Research Development
Corporation of Japan, Nissho-Bldg., 5F, 14-24 Koishikawa
4-chome, Bunkyo-ku, Tokyo 112, Japan

stationary environment to be not at risk of unstable oscillations. The tendency of getting trapped in local minima inherent in such models requires additional measures to escape local solutions and to approach global ones, which slow down the learning speed even more (c. f. the use of externally controlled internal noise in Boltzmann learning and simulated annealing). In contrast, structured networks like Grossberg's ART 1 which use the approximate-match criteria learn rapid and stable while protecting the already estabilished memory. Third and the keypoint, in any case other than restricted simple input patterns an attentional control of both relaxation and, logically also learning is a prerequisite to prevent a combinatorical explosion of the identification problem in completely parallel matching. Without such a selfregulating control structure that prevents the system from being trapped in spurious memory states or local minima there is no guarantee of a smooth interpretation process towards a globally consistent solution.

Complex systems for pattern recognition should therefore employ a processing state dependent on switching between two different modes of operation,

a) a completely in-parallel automatic matching in case of completely known input pattern approximately matching the stored template, and
b) a cognitive mode which is a complicated sequence of formulating and testing of hypotheses on the input (Hecht-Nielssen 1982).

The point for enabling this processing mode to do we want it to do is in the following: With unknown or uncompletely known inputs an in-time formulation of a hypothesis on the input is taking the risk of ending up in partial matches. The more complex the scene the more serious the consequences of combinatorical explosion of the decision problems. To guarantee a rapid and smooth recognition process, this associative search for a hypothesis has to be guided by a kind of intuitive control, that means by priming the system by its own recall which represents knowledge on some parts of the input. To do just that the system has to be able to concentrate first on this known part of the input which makes already some sense to it, hereby seletively reducing the dimension of the accepted parallel input and shifting its focus of attention in the course of making the hypothesis globally consistent. Attentional control in its full sense of meaning requires thus the parallel development of even conflicting hypotheses within the same system each of which has to be sharpened by a competitive (winner-takes-all) mechanism, and its reformation into a global consistent one.

There is no conventional neural network model which can do the job satisfactorily. However, these problems mentioned above are serious ones concerning the applicability of neural network paradigms to real world problems. Despite the fact that the models should be simplified and formalized as much as possible to stress the decisive aspects of neural processing only, here seems to be the need for conceptual extension of neural network modeling by looking for frameworks which embed the known schemes of competitive learning and pattern matching into a selfregulating control structure for autonomous recognition and learning.

Brains do have this ability. And seemingly, this is not a question of levels only but of functional architecture (a-priori structure) of neural network systems. Cortical systems with its especially high flexibility and plasticity of processing like e. g. Cerebellum, Neocortex or Hippocampus exhibit a different functional organization compared to formal neural networks, namely they resemble homogeneous nets but composed of complex processing nodes instead of simple one element nodes. Cortices are composed of columnar or lamellar elementary units each of which representing a reappearing firmware organization of different characteristic neuron types. Based on a computational theory on early vision which satisfies all known facts on morphology and electrophysiology of primary sensory cortex we proposed a model of an elementary cortical processor as a node with just that selfregulating control structure in its firmware enabling autonomous recognition and learning procedures mentioned above. It is worth noting that despite the different starting point and implementation of this approach compared to Grossberg's ART-systems /Grossberg 88/, the functional characteristics are in some respect similar.

2. Cortical control of sensory input to thalamic interface

The cortex does not get a pre-selected set of objects from the sensory input to be decided on but a parallel byte of millions of pixels. And it's the job of the cortex to solve this puzzle within several hundreds of milliseconds to get a meaningful interpretation. It is well known that the brain makes extensive use of eye movements to scan the scene at important parts to focus attention and reducing input complexity. However, at any such fixation point the problem of combinatorical explosion of alternative decision states is just the same, and further, what a mechanism is controlling this movement? There is psychophysical evidence that even within the about 300 ms between the fixation saccades a kind of internal scanning of the visual image at the thalamic input to the cortex takes place /Julesz 84, Treismann 87/. Following Crick's suggestion that the cortex may control its thalamic input /Crick 84/, we proposed a model approach to a flexible thalamic interface and its flexible processing-state-dependent control by cortical pattern formation. It was shown that the known experimental data on neocortical columnar organization support strongly the 6-layered structure of any such column to be approached as a hierarchy of self-regulating control of cortical processing (for details see Koerner et. al. 1987). Any thalamic channel feeds its activity to and is controlled by a model minicolumn (or elementary cortical processor) which code relational information with regard to this input channel and give a feedback to its thalamic input. The thalamic interface is a sheet of relay neurons being controlled by an inhibitory network. The strength of inhibition across all the thalamic channels is

$$LP_{ij} = c1 * RO_{ijm} + c2 * I_{ij} - c3 * RO_{ijm}$$

where RO_{ijm} is the cortical feedback from column ijm which is the recall of memory provoked by inputs I_{ij}. With sensory input at IF1, the analog activity distribution over all thalamic channels is normalized by $L_{ij} = L$. With entraining the cortical feedback however, L is increased to block all IF1-channels except those which get the strongest feedback RO_{ijm} to its position. Since in neural computing pattern recognition means the formation of an internal activity distribution matching the related active input channels, those channels are carved out of the inhibitory block by locally suppressing inhibition which could entrain a representation (which contribute to a highly probable decision on the input byte). Hence, the image on the input is created in the "cortical" system and it can set free all channels that are expected to contribute to that decision provided the entrainment is strong enough to create a inhibitory level L at the interface which can mask all other analog inputs. The selective attention is a result of hiding all other channels than the wanted, so the original input is readily accessible.

3. Cortical layers as a content-dependent self-regulating control architecture

The proposed model structure of an elementary cortical processor /Koerner et. al. 1988/ consists of a syntactic detector R0 (c. f. Fig. 1) with local connectivity, a semantic classificator R1 and a semantic linker R2 both of which have global connectivity patterns. The inputs I_{ij} cause a recall of R0 consisting of an autoassociative memory (AAM) with winner-take-all mechanism (WTA) continuously communicating with an adaptive filter (IF2). This priming feedback supports only those channels with the highest local and global syntactic complexity/ Koerner et. al. 87/.

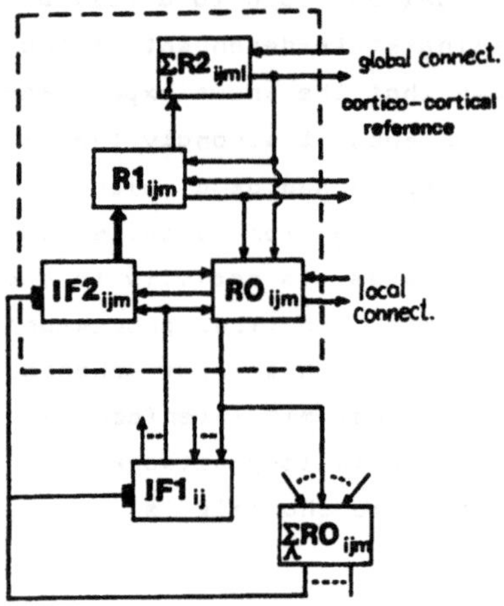

Fig. 1:
Model of the elementary cortical processor with a self-regulating control structure in its firmware which manipulates its thalamic interface (IF1). The RO, R1, R2-modules of the system represent different levels of order formation, which produce description rules of growing complexity (RO-syntactic detector with local connectivity; R1-semantic classificator and R2-semantic linker; R1 and R2 have global connectivity patterns). Which of the R-modules dominatly rules the system depends both of the state of processing and the inhibitory feedback of weighted global cortical acitivity ($\sum_{\lambda}$ RO)

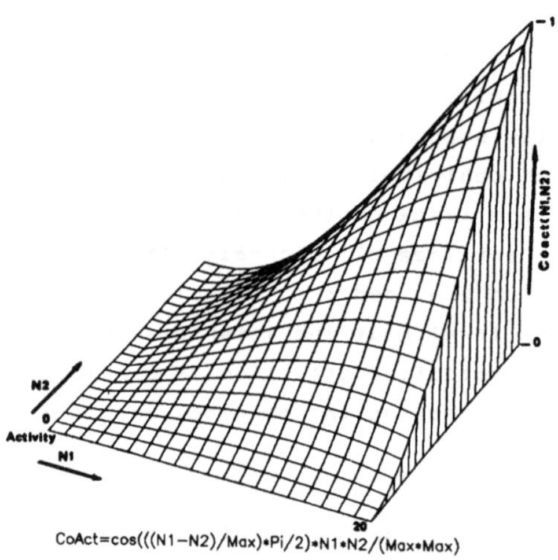

Fig. 2:
Part of the control function of a modified Malsburg-type rapid learning at R2 level which determines the Coactivity between antisynchronous (Activity-difference more then 50 % of Maximum) and synchronous (difference smaller then 50 %) neural events at Neurons N_i and N_j (N_1, N_2).

Because of the nonlinear characteristics of L-inhibition at IF1, the parallel input byte is drastically reduced to only a small dimension containing the probably most important aspects of the input the cortex has to decide on. This reduced input is fed to R1-systems which code as an AAM with WTA more global relations. R1 turns the local RO-decisions a globally consistent one, since with R1-entrainment the L-inhibition level is rapidly increased and only the channels with both

R0- and R1-support-priming can be kept open. If R1 is maximum entrained cortical module inhibition switches off all elementary processors at R0 which contributed to this decision (consistent with psychophysiological results) and the next-grade syntactic complex input configuration will start this process anew. However, this time there is already a feedforeward from the previous decision in R1 which supports pulling out those aspects of the input out of the inhibitory masking next that may have semantic relations to the former decision. This random access grouping at R0 is a kind of syntactic guessing reducing the burden of the "cortex" drastically to start a decision on the input. The R1 recall reorganizes this packaging of input channels. And with its priming bonus to those channels (processing nodes) which would make sense in relation to the former decision, the parallel input is decomposed to a time sequence of subsequent decisions (bytes of smaller dimension) the phase relation of which is due to its semantic relation. By this mechanism the first decision gets the lead in rebuilding the input back to a parallel representation in the course of its interpretation, an autonomous object/background decision is done. This is a primitive form of guiding the associative search for pattern matching by intuitive control, reducing the probability of partial matches increasingly in the course of interpretation.

The benefit of this decomposition of the parallel input into a time sequence of flashing decisions is that the system has not to test the matching of the input image with the stored items one after each other but that the optimization towards the best matching can be done in parallel at all processing levels, since the time sharing group formation prevents the WTA mechanisms to block their related nodes from being accessed and taken by other more globally matching decisions. Therefore, even a switching of object/background decision is feasible.

In /Koerner et. al. 1988/ we have shown that a modular array of 5*5*3*3 such elementary processors will properly decompose an input image into a sequence of smaller dimensional bytes and that in case of fitting to stored knowledge the sequence is rapidly synchronized and reassembled to a complete parallel representation matching all relevant channels at the input. In case of a new scene, the known parts are recalled in a reappearing sequence of the known relations of the scene ranked according to its relational complexity. However, how to learn new relations between such already existing relational clusters in this network without the need of external control? Simple hebbian learning will not do the job in this competitive environment. To overcome this difficulty we implemented a modified Malsburg-type rapid learning in connection with the concept of eligibility for learning introduced by Edelman (1982), Barto and Sutton (1981) for the learning in R2 (which is a degenerate extension of R1).

4. Learning by linking known aspects of the input

If a sequence of R0 and R1-decisions reappears several times then the input is sufficiently different to known pattern relations and on the other hand the new pattern may be stable enough to be worth memorizing. Only that part of the input can be perceived and subsequently learned which could be synchronized within time spans of several hundreds of milliseconds /Koerner et. al. 1987/. The rapid learning at R2 mediated by

$$W_{ij}(k+1) = (1-B(W_{ij}(k))) * W_{ij}(k)+dW_{ij}(W_{ij}(k)) * CoAct(N_i,N_j,k) * norm_{Hebb}(N_i,N_j,k) \qquad (1)$$

with

$$dW(W_{ij}) = dW_{max} * (1-(W_{ij}-W_o)/(W_{min}-W_o)^2) \qquad (2)$$

$$CoAct(N_i,N_j) = Cos((N_i-N_j/ActMax) * \; / \; 2) \qquad (3)$$

$$norm_{Hebb} = N_i * N_j/ActMax^2 \qquad (4)$$

$$(ActMax = 20, \; W_o = 0...1, \; dW_{max}=0,1)$$

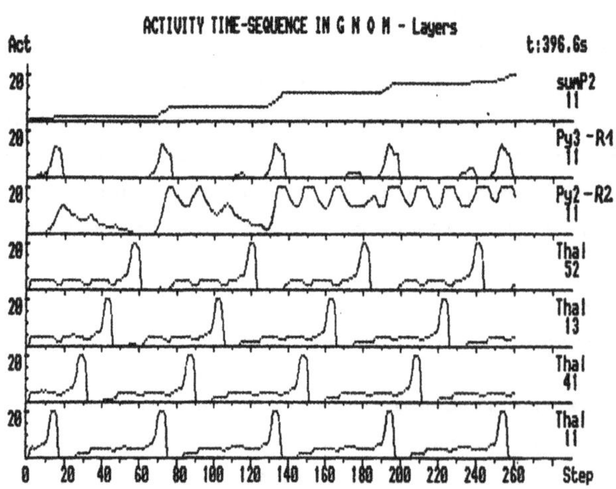

Fig. 3:
Shows the time sequence of decomposition of an parallel input image (visual byte) into a sequence of smaller dimensional bytes. Because of no fitting to stored knowledge and an inactive dynamic learning at R2-level the sequence is not synchronized and not reassembled to a complete parallel representation.

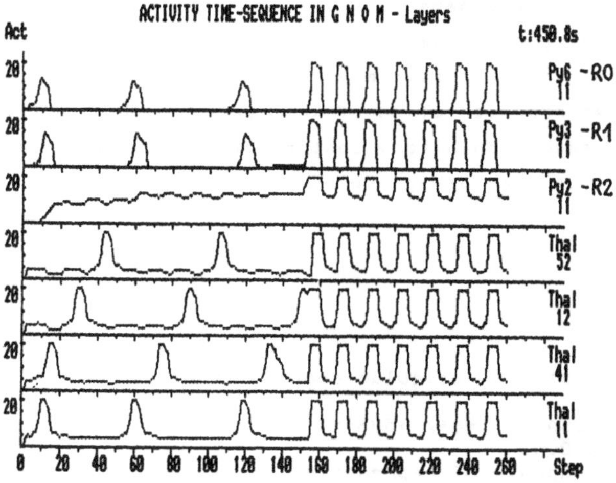

Fig. 4:
Sequence of R0 (Py 6) and R1 (Py 3) decisions which reappears several times because of differences between input and known internal pattern relations. With the semantic linker R2 (modified Malsburg-type rapid learning) the sequence is synchronized towards a dynamically stable parallel representation which is learned into the longtime network's connectivity in R1.

enables the rapid entrainment of synaptic weights from a base level w to its maximum value, but also its rapid decay. In fig. 4 the input is the same as in fig. 3, but with the linker R2 the sequence is after stable reappearing several times synchronized towards a dynamically stable parallel representation which then is learned into the network's connectivity as a new entity by changing the base level of the respective synaptic weights by dW if $w>w_0$ continuously for a number of time steps k*dt>T.

5. Discussion

The model described is a minimum configuration for enabling this processing-state dependent attentional control which is a flexible self-regulation scheme with potential ability to start-up, direct and sharpen the associative search in the distributed memory. Contrary to systems R0 and R1 which are sufficiently consistent to the neocortical columnar structures both in its architectures and coding characteristics, R2 is an artificial construct merging features of both neocortical layer 2 at different hierarchical coding levels and aspects of hippocampal control of cortical processing.

The working-in-principle of this scheme of self-regulation for autonomous recognition and learning could be demonstrated. To enable the system's working under more a realistic environment we are going to add a hierarchic multilayer representation of knowledge in the system and to include the necessary inhibitory control of learning which protects the stored knowledge from being overwritten.

References

/ 1/ **Crick, F.**
"The function of the thalamic reticular complex: the searchlight hypothesis"
Proc. Nat. Acad. Sci. USA 81(1984) 4586-90

/ 2/ **Edelmann, G.M.; Reeke, G.N.**
"Selective networks capable of representative transformations, limited generalizations, and associative memory.
Proc. Nat. Acad. Sci. USA 79 (1982) 2091 - 2095

/ 3/ **Grossberg, S.**
"The ART of adaptive pattern recognition by a self-organisation neural network"
Computer 21 (1988)3, 77 - 88

/ 4/ **Hecht-Nielsen, R.**
"Neural analog processing"
Proc. SPIE, 360, 1982, 180 - 189

/ 5/ **Julesz, B.**
"Towards an axiomatic theory of preattentive vision" in Dynamic Aspects of Neocortical Function; G.M.Edelmann, W.E.Gall, W.M.Cowan (eds.)
Wiley: NY, Chichester, Brisbane, Toronto, Singapore, 1984

/ 6/ **Koerner, E.; Tsuda, I.; Shimizu, H.**
"Parallel in Sequence-towards the Architecture of an Elementary Cortical Processor"
in: "Proc. of Int. Workshop on Parallel Algorithms and Architectures", Suhl (GDR), May 25 - 30, 1987, Akademie-Verlag, Berlin 1987, S. 37 - 47

/ 7/ **Koerner, E.; Gross, H.-M.; Richter, A.; Shimizu, H.**
"Control of Sensory Processing - a Hypothesis on and Simulation of the Architecture of an Elementary Cortical Processor"
(Subm. to publication at Parcella 88, Berlin Okt. 88)

/ 8/ **v.d.Malsburg, Ch.; Schneider, W.**
"A Neural Cocktail-Party Processor"
Biol. Cybern. 54 (1986), 29 - 40

/ 9/ **Sutton, R.S.; Barto, A.G.**
"Towards a Modern Theory of Adaptive Networks: Expectation and Prediction"
Psychological Review 88 (1981), 135 - 170

/10/ **Treisman, A. M.**
"Merkmale und Gegenstaende in der visuellen Verarbeitung"
Spektrum der Wissenschaft, 1 (1987), 72 - 82

The Performance Landscape of a Metabolic Network

Jens Georg Reich

Central Institute of Molecular Biology
Academy of Sciences of the GDR
Berlin-Buch 1115

Abstract

The stationary rate of an essential reaction is taken as index of performance of a metabolic network. Its value is studied as function of the rate constants of the system. Extending previous work along this line in this paper not only the optimal parameter set, but also the performance surface in the whole accessible parameter space is investigated.

The main result is that the performance of a tightly entangled nonlinear network is remarkably robust with respect to parameter changes over a large region of the parameter space. This was tested and demonstrated on paradigmatic models of metabolic networks. The importance of the optimal parameter vector must not be overstressed.

Introduction

The theoretical representation of a metabolic system comprises a set of reactions connecting a certain number of metabolites, and all sorts of rate coefficients. A model is satisfactory, if reaction rates, metabolite concentrations and their time course are close to what is observed *in vivo*. To develop such a descriptive model, one usually accepts the rate parameters as fixed quantities, prescribed "by nature", and tries to estimate them from observed data.

One might, however, pose the problem the other way round. What would be the optimal set of rate parameters? Could such an optimum be reached by stepwise trial and selection? How long would it last to attain a new optimum in new circumstances? Questions of this type concern the *design* of a metabolic system. This problem has been addressed by several theorists including ourselves (Atkinson, 1977; Savageau, 1977; Reich and Selkov, 1981; Heinrich and Sonntag, 1981; Reich, 1984a,1984b, 1985; Heinrich et al.,1987; Schuster, 1988). It brings at once the notion of *optimal performance* into play. One might argue in a qualitative manner and arrive at general principles. Or one might look for calculable (and measurable) criteria of performance and study them as function of those parameters which can be changed and adapted.

This paper is dedicated to the *performance landscape* of a metabolic network. I consider not only, as previous papers did, *the* optimum, but also its surroundings, the steepness of the path leading, as it were, to "the summit" of the landscape. Very simple paradigmatic model systems will be studied, with emphasis on entangled network connections (in contrast to chains that were dealt with in several predecessor papers).

Performance Criterion

Performance in a metabolic system is a complex and multidimensional phenomenon and therefore difficult to define and to measure. But there are special cases whose treatment is easier. Consider the situation of a microorganism in a competitive environment such as the Pacific Ocean, the guts of an animal or a flow-through culture. Apart from the stability of the cellular integrity, the main factor that determines the competitive fitness of an organism is the rate of proliferation. It will ultimately decide which of the competing species will win the race. For this reason we take an idealized version of this rate of proliferation as a model of a performance criterion. It is easy to define and has direct biological significance, at least in life situations of the specified type. We will call this rate by r throughout, and try to optimize it as function of cellular rate parameters.

Distribution of Resources: Types of Networks

In order to proliferate, our cell has to assimilate the available resources: substrates, energy, and metabolic building moieties of all sorts. The rate of proliferation depends on a smooth interplay of dozens, even hundreds, of partial reactions. Two types of networks may be distinguished in accordance with the degree of complexity of the network.

One type is characterized by weak interaction. Each partial pathway functions on its own account and contributes to the overall process. For instance, every one of the 20 amino acids has to be provided simultaneously for the rate of protein synthesis to proceed. With some idealization one may assume that these linear stoichiometries work independently of each other, and that the overall proliferation rate is the mathematical product of the individual rates. The actual situation is more intricate, but the product is the simplest way to express two basic properties: each partial process stimulates proliferation as a whole, and each of them is essential, so its rate must be > 0 for biosynthesis to be possible at all.

There is the alternative type of strong interaction. During biosynthesis from a medium with one dominant substrate, for instance, nearly everything has to be made from the same building stone: be it energy equivalents, reducing equivalents, carbon backbone equivalents, important cofactor backbones, etc. Not only the final assembly of macromolecules, but already the production of precursors is then a highly interactive process. For instance, ATP, GTP, NADH, NADH, di- and tricarboxylates contribute in a cooperative manner to any biosynthesis, and also their regeneration is tightly coupled. A strongly interacting network is therefore a tangle of interwoven cofactor cycles rather than a set of parallel routes converging into the same final pathway.

Allocation of Total Catalytic Capacity as Limit to Growth

The main task of the proliferating cell is biosynthesis of macromolecular substances, mainly protein (see the detailed calculations of Forrest and Walker, 1971, and Stouthamer, 1973). Since the overall capacity for biosynthesis is limited (by number of genes, by limited rate of transcription, translation, limited cell volume, etc.), its balanced allocation is the main determinant of performance. The regulatory apparatus of operon control is dedicated to this task. This limitation may included into any performance model in the form of a restricted sum of macromolecules (protein, enzymes, etc.):

$$\sum_i E_i = E_o \qquad (1).$$

Here E_i is the amount of protein made for the i-th partial process. E_o is the total biosynthetic product of the cell. A scale factor converts this sum to unity, and comparability of different pathways (indexed by i) is ensured by counting allocated equivalents of unit cost (amino acid equivalents, energy equivalents, etc.). A restriction of type (1) will accompany any performance model that will follow.

The Basic Two-Parameter Model

In previous papers, I studied an idealized two-component model of proliferation with competing allocation of resources (see Reich, 1984a; 1984b):

$$\xrightarrow[\text{precursor supply}]{E_1} \quad X \quad \xrightarrow[\text{biosynthesis}]{E_2} \qquad (2),$$

where

$v_1 = k_1 E_1 (X_o - X)$ rate of supply

$v_2 = k_2 E_2 X$ rate of biosynthesis

X : amount of "charged" precursor (e.g. NADPH, ATP)

$X_o - X$: amount of discharged precursors ($NADP^+$, ADP)

E_1, E_2 : allocated amount of catalysts

k_1, k_2 : specific rate parameter of process.

By suitable coice of scales one obtains the following steady-state rate of proliferation (our performance criterion):

$$r = h_1 f_1 (1-x) = h_2 f_2 x \qquad (3)$$

with allocation restriction

$$f_1 + f_2 = 1 \qquad (4),$$

where

x : dimensionless "charge" of precursor

h_1, h_2 : dimensionless rate parameters

f_1, f_2 : allocated fractions (special form of eq.(1)),

which simplifies to

$$r = \frac{h_1 h_2 f_1 f_2}{h_1 f_1 + h_2 f_2} \qquad (5).$$

The parameters h_i may be considered for our study as natural constants, while f_i may be varied by trial and error, selection of higher rates being the decisive criterion.

The performance function (5) has a maximum. Fig.1 shows the simplest, symmetric ($h_1=h_2$, called h) case, and displays a remarkable property which is of interest for the adaptive quality of the system, its <u>robustness</u>. Denote a value of the parameter h as <u>acceptable</u>, if the performance is better than 50% of the maximal value, and as <u>excellent</u>, if better than 95%. Then it follows from the parabolic character of the performance function that the fraction of acceptable and excellent values among all possible parameter values is SQRT(1-c) with c=0.5 and 0.95, respectively.

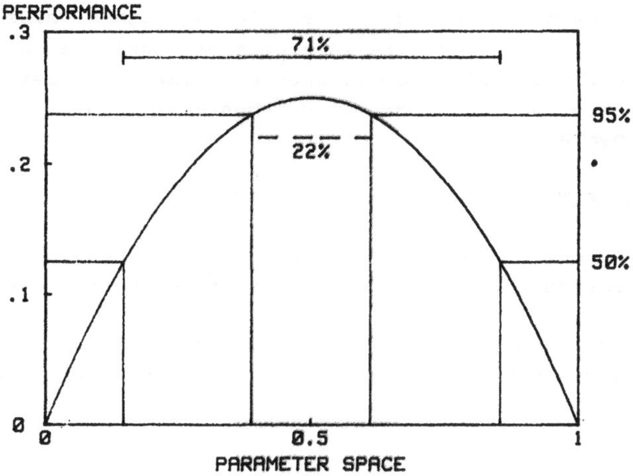

Fig. 1. Performance Landscape of the Symmetric Two-Pathway Network

The model is described in scheme (2), the stationary rate is eq.(5) with one independent parameter ($h_1 = h_2$), i.e. $r = h_1*(1-h_1)$.

The parameter points showing exactly 95% and 50% performance are indicated. In this way the broadness of the region of near-optimal and acceptable performance is visualized. 22% of all possible parameter values perform better than 95%-optimal, and 71% of all values are better than 50%-optimal.

In other words, 71% of all randomly selected h-values will be acceptable, 22% excellent. With a few die castings one may find acceptabe, even excellent parameter values! To formulate it more pointedly: there is not much left to optimize - only an odd fringe of parameters is not acceptable. I propose to study this phenomenon on more subtle models.

Asymmetric Case and Effect of Cooperativity of Rate Laws

When h_1 and h_2 are not equal then it can be shown by application of calculus that excellent parameter sets become rarer, but even in extreme cases is their density > 5%. The fraction of acceptable parameters drops less sharply and remains always over 50%.

By kinetic cooperativity we denote the biologically relevant situation that the metabolites appear non-linearly in the rate equations, giving the stationary values as implicit equation:

$$v_1 = f_1 (1-x)^a = (1-f_1) x^b = v_2 \qquad (6).$$

With $a = b = 1$ we have the previous model. Taking higher values for both coefficients, $a = b = 3$, one obtains an acceptable performance in 80% and an excellent one in 27% of all randomly chosen parameter values - cooperativity slightly increases parameter robustness! Table 1 shows this finding on other examples.

Dimensionality of the Network (Case of Weak Interaction)

The basic model has just 2 reactions with only one independent parameter. Do its properties extend to networks of many interacting pathways?

With n interacting pathways, each with allocation fraction f_i, we get the following performance expression for the case of weak interaction:

$$r = \prod_{i}^{n} f_i \tag{7a}$$

$$\sum_{i}^{n} = 1 \tag{7b}$$

We call a network with such a performance criterion as "product-of-flow measuring". Each pathway has stationary rate proportional to the allocated catalyst, whose sum is, again, restricted by limits to growth. The optimal allocation predicts identical f's equal to $1/n$, and the optimal rate is proportional to $1/2^n$. The density of acceptable and excellent parameter sets in the parameter space can be calculated by cumbersome multiple integration, but I preferred estimation by a Monte-Carlo procedure. Random sets of positive parameter values with a prescribed sum were drawn (this is not quite easy to do, but technicalities would take too much space here), and the fractions of acceptable and excellent sets were recorded.

Table 2 shows a typical result. As expected, with increasing number of dimensions the fraction of acceptable and excellent sets decreases, so that it becomes more difficult to find them by a random procedure. However, the share of parameter sets with more than 50% of the optimal performance is very robust, much more than the fraction of excellent sets (>95%). One would conclude that it is comparatively easy to localize a "viable" parameter constellation, but difficult to find the optimum.

It is to be noted that one partial reaction may have a rather small rate constant and the performance nevertheless remain well. To give an example for ilustration: If n=10 and 9 of the f's have a value of 0.11 and the one remaining is 0.01, then the rate is still 24% optimal instead of the 10% we anticipate if one rate parameter is smaller by more than ten times. This is compensation of le Chatelier type, and its effect will, as will be shown, increase with strength of pathway interaction.

Influence of Cooperativity in a Network

Model (7) can be extended to include cooperativity exponents, which in logarithmic notation reads:

$$\log r = \beta_i \sum_i^n \log f_i \tag{8}$$

$$\sum_i f_i = 1 \tag{8a}$$

The optimal set of allocation factors for such a model, obtained by maximizing $\log r$, is

$$(f_i)^{opt} = \beta_i / S \tag{9}$$

where

$$S = \sum_i \beta_i \tag{10}$$

is the "number of interactions" required for proliferation (precursors and cofactors may be used up several times in the whole process - hence the cooperativity!). The optimal rate belonging to this parameter set is given by

$$\log r^{opt} = \sum \beta_i \log \beta_i / S \tag{11}$$

an expression reminiscent of information entropy. Table 3 shows the fluctuation of this optimal rate for the cases n=3 and n=5 and several series of ß-values (for simplicity identical for all i). The robustness of the parameter values with respect to increasing cooperativity is remarkable. One should take into account that one fraction f entering with an exponent $\beta > 1$ is stoichiometrically equivalent with β different components (3 ATP in one pathway replacing, say, ATP,GTP and CTP, each by one). Consider, for instance, the fact that for n=5 pathways, each one with a cooperativity factor of $\beta=4$, i.e. for 20 kinetically vital interactions, the fraction of excellent parameter sets is still 1.4% and can be found after approximately 50 random trials (ln2/0.014)!

Metabolic Networks with Strong Interaction

So far we had virtually independent pathways whose rate product was counted as performance, with the allocation sum being the only link between them. A necessary extension is the case of <u>strong interaction</u>. We take as model case three weakly interacting regeneration pathways and bundle the consumption of their resulting cofactors(precursors) in one biosynthetic process,

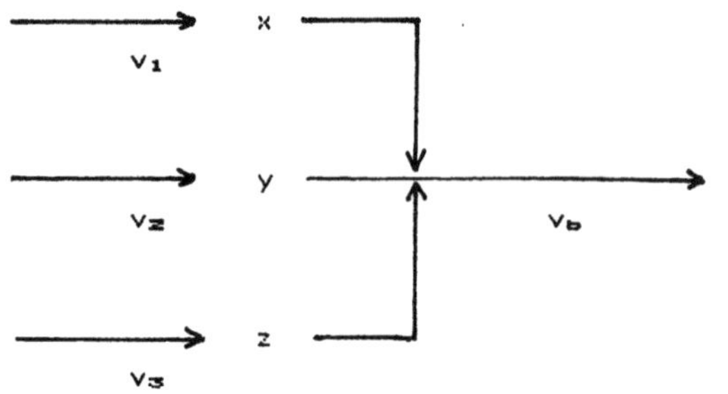

(12)

with fluxes in terms of normalized factor concentrations x,y,z :

$$v_1 = h_1 (1-x)^{\alpha_1} \qquad (13a)$$

$$v_2 = h_2 (1-y)^{\alpha_2} \qquad (13b)$$

$$v_3 = h_3 (1-z)^{\alpha_2} \qquad (13c)$$

$$v_b = h_b x^{\beta_1} y^{\beta_2} z^{\beta_3} \qquad (13d)$$

$$v_1 = v_2 = v_3 = v_b \quad \text{(stationarity condition)} \qquad (13e)$$

$$h_1 + h_2 + h_3 + h_b = 1 \quad \text{(allocation restriction)} \qquad (13f)$$

The optimal set of parameters h_i may be calculated by a r-maximizing hill-climbing procedure, while the fluctuation studies can again be done as Monte-Carlo sampling. Table 4 shows several experiments (1000 trials each) with different sets of cooperativity coefficients. The result is surprising: in a tightly coupled network the robustness increases with cooperativity! A low value of one of the parameters (say, h_1) is compensated by an increased value of the pertinent cofactor ((1-x)) , and the accompanying drop in its complement (x) is neutralized by the higher value of its rate parameter (h_b) which goes along with the reduced value of the former (h_1). Le Chatelier coupling is so strong that the majority of parameter sets has more than 50% of the optimal proliferation rate.

Discussion

To understand selection and improvement of competing metabolic networks it is not sufficient to study the optimum performance, on the tacit assumption that evolution has had enough time to find it by trial and error. This is not so obvious, because the environment may change permanently and drive the optimum away. A system may be on the road, but never quite close, to its optimum. Furthermore, the production of parameter sets by gene mutation is a stochastic process, which may even be envisaged as a statistical ensemble as in theoretical mechanics (Berg and Hippel, 1987, have developed this concept for the case that gene expression is regulated by promoter strength). For all these reasons, it is useful to study the whole of the performance landscape and not only its highest point.

The synopsis of our results is that metabolic networks appear to have a smooth and well-behaved performance landscape. A considerable part of the parameter space shows acceptable performance, and the maximum seems to be broad and not difficult to find (see fig.1). With increasing number of interacting partial reactions the relative volume of acceptable parameter sets decreases slowly, as expected, but to a moderate extent.

It was further found that the robustness increases with the complexity of interactions in the network. For example, 3 components with interaction coefficient 2 (we took the cooperativity coefficient as model of complexity of interaction!) have a more robust surface than 6 components interacting only once (see tables 2 and 3: 29% vs. 12% acceptable parameter sets in the space).

We have then distinguished <u>weakly</u> from <u>strongly</u> interacting networks. In the former case the linkage is by a restricted sum of catalytic power and the performance is the product of partial rates. In strongly interacting networks the partial pathways are tightly interwoven, and only one output rate is measured. The restriction on the total catalytic power is the same. The case of strong interaction corresponds more to the usual situation in intermediary metabolism with its numerous cofactor cycles. Such strongly entangled networks behave approximately like the weakly entangled counterparts, if there is no cooperativity (compare the case of $\alpha = \beta = 1$ in table 4 with n=3 or n=4 in table 2). However, they become surprisingly more robust which increasing cooperativity of partial pathways and of the final bundle.

What is the interpretation of these findings?

1. Under restricted total catalytic capacity (= cellular protein content) the network, once "knowing" its stoichiometric structure, has no particular problem in finding a parameter set of acceptable performance - a random set has a good chance to do well.

2. The true optimum may bemore difficult to find, in particular in higher parameter dimensions. Only a very strict selection pressure will drive an evolving system into this optimum. One should keep in mind that the mutation game cannot measure the steepest gradient towards the optimum in the way a mathematician can gather it: component by component. Evolutionary hill-climbing will therefore become increasingly expensive with increasing dimension of the optimization problem.

3. Strong kinetic interaction within and between the pathways leads to a strong tendency of le Chatelier type compensation of effects. The network may thus tolerate and adapt itself to a partial defect (small catalytic capacity: time hierarchy (Heinrich et al., 1987)), and still remain in an acceptable region. I suspect this becomes more pronounced when alternative routes and multiple interconnections become involved.

4. One should be careful not to overinterprete the importance of the kinetic structure at the optimum. Quite different parameter constellations may show similar performance.

The general, though tentative, conclusion is: Metabolic networks are sufficiently specified by their stoichiometry. Their kinetic self-organization is no grave evolutionary problem. I am at present playing with more realistic models (feedback control, multiple entanglement), in order to corroborate the hypothesis. Such models are difficult to be cast into a systematic conceptual framework, however.

Table 1

Robustness of the Model Parameters agaist Changes in Kinetic Cooperativity

In model (6) the density of acceptable and excellent parameter combinations in the accessible parameter space was evaluated by an iteration scheme. Note how close the values are to each other although the inner dynamics of the system varies greatly.

cooperativity		performance	
a	b	acceptable (>50%)	excellent (>95%)
1	1	.22	.71
2	2	.26	.80
3	3	.27	.80
1	3	.25	.75
1	10	.26	.76

Table 2

Density of Acceptable (>50% optimal) and Excellent (>95% optimal) Parameter Sets in a Metabolic Network Measuring the Product of Component Flows (Weak Interaction)

Eqs.(7a) and (7b) define the mathematical model. 10 000 randomly selected parameter sets were evaluated and the number of acceptable and/or excellent performances was recorded. The numbers are the mean of 3 trials, they are given as fractions of unity. It was established that the standard deviation of the recorded case numbers was approximately equal to the square root of these numbers, as in a Poisson process.
The mean factor at the bottom of the table is the average ratio of fraction(x_i) / fraction(x_{i+1}) downward the column. The results show that excellent performance becomes very rare with increasing n , whereas an acceptable behavior is more accessible even in higher dimensions.

dimension n	performance >50%	>95%
2	.7075	.2250
3	.5097	.0485
4	.3405	.0158
5	.2124	.0014
6	.1215	.0004
7	.0697	.0001
8	.0356	0
9	.0179	0
10	.0082	0
12	.0038	0
mean decay factor (per n)	0.6	0.2

Table 3

The Performance Landscape is Robust with Respect to Cooperativity of Pathways in a Product-of-Flow Measuring Metabolic Network

The model is the same as in table 1, only an exponent $ß_i$ accompanies each rate parameter. Only models with identical exponent for each i were studied. Random allocation of 10 000 parameter sets was done as in the previous table (mean of two trials). It is seen that the region of acceptable and of excellent performance sets depends only weakly on the cooperativity index. Note that the case of e.g. n=3, ß=2 is to be compared with n=3*3 = 9 diffeerent partial processes in table 1. The parameter robustness would appear to make networks with multiple usage of few cofactor systems preferable to those with many diversified ones.

dimension	cooperativity	performance	
n	ß	>50%	>95%
3	1	.5105	.0468
3	2	.2856	.0236
3	3	.1982	.0158
3	4	.1522	.0108
5	1	.2137	.0012
5	2	.0621	.0002
5	3	.0274	.0001
5	4	.0142	.0001

Table 4

Density of Acceptable (>50% optimal) and Excellent (>95%) Performance in the Parameter Space of the Model described by eqs. (13), with strong coupling of 3 cofactors in a biosynthetic reaction bundle. 1000 randomly selected sets of parameter vectors (with sum restricted to be unity) were examined. The set of cooperativity coefficients α and β was the same for each component.

cooperativity coefficient		fraction of acceptable parameter values	fraction of excellent parameter values
α	β		
1	1	.534	.017
2	2	.655	.023
3	3	.718	.027
5	5	.751	.035
3	1	.595	.022
5	1	.622	.031
1	3	.638	.020
1	5	.653	.023

References

Atkinson, D.E. (1977): Cellular Energy Metabolism and its Regulation. Academic Press: New York

Berg, O.G. and Hippel,P.H.(1987): Selection of DNA Binding Sites by Protein. J. molec. Biol. 193, 7230-7250

Ebeling, W. and Feistel, R. (1982): Physik der Selbstorganisation und Evolution. Akademie Verlag: Berlin

Forrest,W.W. and Walker, D.J.(1971): The generation and utilization of energy during growth. Advan. Microb. Physiol. 5,213-274

Heinrich, R. and Sonntag, I. (1981): Analysis of Selection Equations for a Multivariable Population Model. J. theor. Biol. 93, 325-361

Heinrich, R., Holzhütter, H.G. and Schuster, St. (1987): A theoretical approach to the evolution and structural design of enzymatic networks; linear enzymatic chains, branched pathways and glycolysis of erythrocytes. Bull. Math. Biol. 49,535-595

Kacser, H. and Beeby, R. (1984): Evolution of Catalytic Proteins. J.molec. Evol. 20, 38-51

Reich, J.G. (1984a): Zur Ökonomie im Proteinhaushalt der lebenden Zelle. Biomed. biochim. Acta 42,839-848

Reich, J.G. (1984b): Uber Selektionskriterien in metabolischen Systemen. Biomed. biochim. Acta 43, 47-55

Reich, J.G. (1985): On Optimum Properties in the Design of Metabolic and Epigenetic Systems. Biomed. biochim. Acta 44, 845-852

Reich, J.G. and Selkov, E.E. (981): Energy Metabolism of the Cell. Academic press: London

Savageau, M.A.(1975): Optimal design of feedback control by inhibition. J. molec. Evol. 5,199-222

Savageau, M.A. (1976): Biochemical Systems analysis. Addison-Wesley: London

Stouthamer, A.H. (1973): Theoretical study of the amount of ATP required for synthesis of microbial cell material. Antonie van Leeuwenhoek 39,545-565

ON THE THEORY OF NETWORKS FOR THE IMMUNE SYSTEM

Ulrich Behn [1] and J. Leo van Hemmen [2]

A generalized Lotka-Volterra equation is proposed to describe the idiotopic network of the immune system including dormant B-cells. The stability analysis of its stationary fixed points shows the possibility of cycles preserving the internal image of an antigen (memory). The Lotka-Volterra network is embedded in a hierarchical description of the immune system including adaption and learning as well as innovation by biased and random mutation, respectively.

1. INTRODUCTION

The immune system (IS), as a result of the biological evolution, protects higher organisms (which are full of interesting substances) against a plentidude of possible invadors. To do this it develops remarkable abilities /1/:

The IS can identify foreign materials. The reaction on them depends on the individual history of the organism. It is able to learn and to memorize. Thus, the IS shares an astonishing number of properties with the central nervous system (CNS) /2-5/ which makes it to an interesting subject not only for biologists (see Table 1). Obviously, the study of the IS is a challenge for interdisciplinary collaboration with the aim not only to achieve a better understanding, but also to learn from nature how to construct complex systems with highly nontrivial properties /4-6/.

Table 1. Similarities between IS and CNS at system level

macroscopic number of constituents
cells are functionally connected
system recognizes even "fuzzy" stimuli and responds appropriate to the context
functioning insensitive to fine details and damages
memory, learning from experience
early impressions are particular deep and lasting
each individual starts with "zero"
profound sense of self

Apart from this striking similarities at the system level there are important differences at the microscopic level. The cells of the IS move

1) Sektion Physik, Karl-Marx-Universität Leipzig, DDR-7010 Leipzig
2) SFB 123 Stochastische Mathematische Modelle, Universität Heidelberg, D-6900 Heidelberg

more or less freely and have a finite life time. During the whole existence of the organism there is a production of new cells, mutation and selection play an important role. In contrast to the CNS it is easier to isolate parts of the system and to study their functioning seperately, it is even possible to construct and to exploit artificial subsystems (e.g. monoclonal antibodies).

We now try to explain some major key words and to give a brief and simplified description of the constituents of the IS and how they interact.

CLONAL SELECTION. Antibodies are Y-shaped macromolecules which identify foreign material (antigens) and tag it for further treatment. 10^5 identical antibodies are attached on the surface of one B-lymphocyte. Typically there exist 10^8 different types of antibodies in the organism. They are distinguished by threedimensional structures, paratopes and epitopes, whose function can be visualized as keys and locks (Fig. 1).

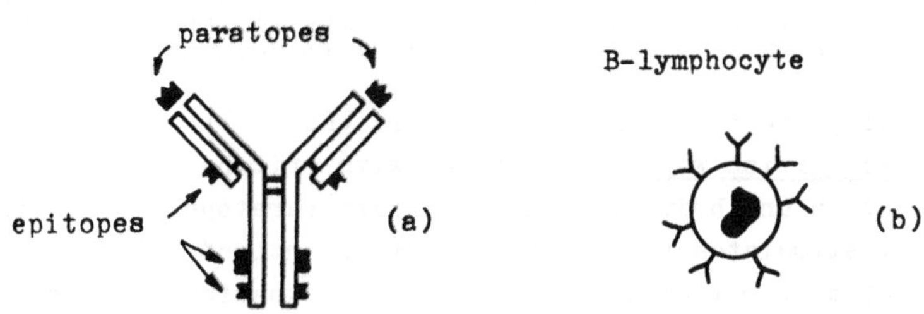

Fig. 1. Antibodies are distinguished by threedimensional complementary structures, epitopes and paratopes. The set of all epitopes characterizing an antibody of a given type is called idiotope (a). 10^5 identical antibodies are on the surface of a B-lymphocyte (b).

A B-lymphocyte is stimulated to proliferate (cloning) and to secrete free antibodies if the paratopes of its surface antibodies recognize a complementary structure. As such can serve the epitope (or even the paratope) of a different antibody or a corresponding threedimensional structure on the surface of an antigene, also called epitope. The strength of the reaction increases with the matching between the complementary structures. The paratopes of free antibodies dock at the corresponding epitopes of the antigens and thus mark them e.g. for eating by macrophages. On the other hand, a B-lymphocyte is inhibited if its epitopes are recognized by a complementary structure. The amplifying of the production of useful antibodies is called clonal selection /7/ (Fig. 2).

IDIOTOPIC NETWORK. Since the paratope of a given antibody reacts not only with the epitopes of foreign material (antigens) but also with the epitopes of antibodies of a different type, there exist a complicated network of interactions between the antibodies in one organism, the idiotopic network /2/.

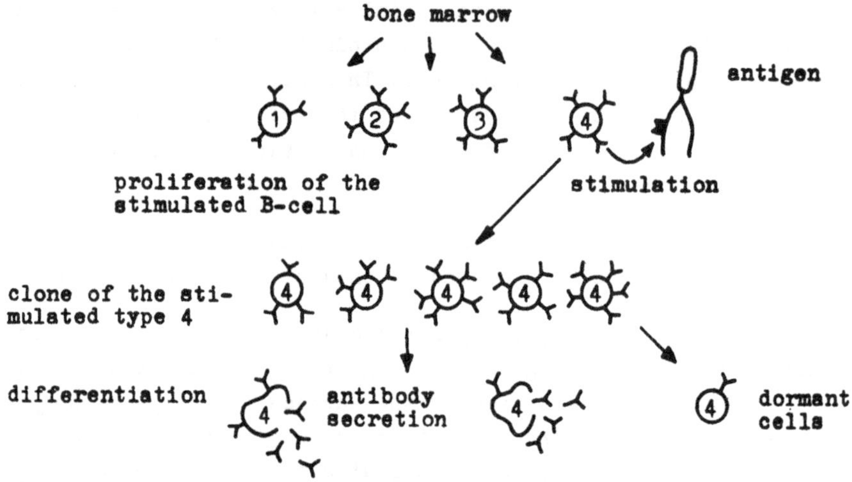

Fig. 2. Clonal selection. Only the B-lymphocyte of type 4 is stimulated to proliferate since its paratope matches with the epitope of the antigen. The stimulated type may differentiate into cells which secrete free antibodies and into dormant cells.

Typical patterns in this network are (Fig. 3):

(i) recognition waves. An antigen with epitope e_o stimulates the production of an antibody with complementary paratope p_1. Its idiotope i_1 eventually stimulates the production of an antibody with complementary (anti-idiotopic) paratope p_2 and so on. This dynamical pattern is driven by the presence of the antigen.

(ii) cycles. If in the above described wave an idiotope i_n is by chance complementary to the paratope p_1, the chain is closed to a cycle and the production of antibodies of type 1 is triggered even in the absence of the antigen. The idiotope i_n acts within this stationary pattern as an internal image of e_o (memory).

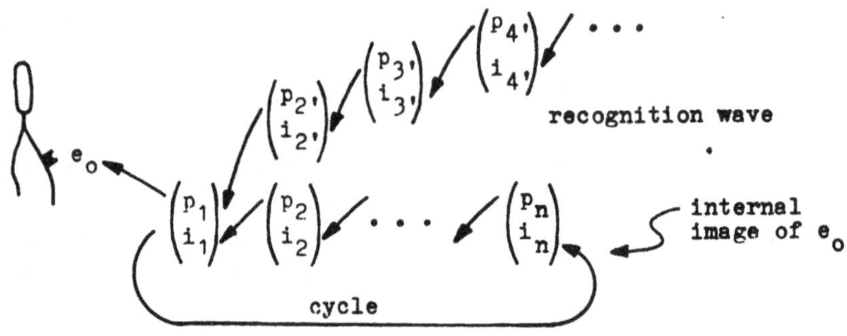

Fig. 3. Typical patterns of the idiotopic network. An antibody of type n is represented by its paratope and idiotope (p_n, i_n).

It should be mentioned that there is a second mechanism for memory: If a B-lymphocyte is stimulated by an antigene to proliferate, few of the cells of the next generation go into a dormant state. The life time of this dormant B-cells is several orders of magnitude larger than usual.

GENERATION OF DIVERSITY. Although there are 10^8 different types of antibodies at the same time this is not enough to recognize all possible invadors even if we take into account that a perfect matching is not necessary. New types are generated in the following way.
About 5% of the B-lymphocytes are replaced per day by new ones generated in the bone marrow. The new antibodies are build combining genes from a relatively small library of V, D, J, and C genes /8/.
Furthermore, stimulated B-lymphocytes reproduce themselves with a mutation rate which is five orders of magnitude larger than usual /9/. It is argued that higher order control mechanisms exist which cause some nonrandomness in the mutation.

This picture is of course a crude simplification. For instance, a whole class of cells, the T-lymphocytes which are known to play an important role in the distinction between self and non-self, is neglected as well as many other details.

2. LOTKA-VOLTERRA EQUATIONS FOR THE IDIOTOPIC NETWORK

In this Section we derive equations of motion which describe the interactions between a <u>given set</u> of constituents of the idiotopic network. Naturally, this leads to equations which are familiar from a different context, e.g. from the kinetics of autocatalytic reactions, the so-called Lotka-Volterra equations (LVE) /10, 11/ [1].

For simplicity we do not distinguish between free and surface antibodies and denote their number by x_i, where $i=1,\dots,N$ labels the type, characterized by only one epitope e_i and the paratope p_i (the B-lymphocytes are thus only implicitely dealt with). The number of antigens characterized by the epitope e_j, where $j=N+1,\dots,N+n$, is y_j.

In a simple mean field approach the probability of a collision between two of them is proportional to the products $x_i x_j$, respectively $x_i y_j$.

The strength of the reaction is proportional to the matching m_{ij} between the paratope p_i and the epitope e_j.

Thus, the stimulation of an antibody x_i is proportional to $m_{ij}x_i x_j$, respectively $m_{ij}x_i y_j$, and the inhibition is proportional to $-\varkappa m_{ji}x_i x_j$. $\varkappa$ allows for an asymmetry between stimulation and inhibition.

---

1) Several models of mathematical immunology are reviewed in /12/, cf. also /4-6, 13-18/.

A further important parameter is γ , the inverse life time of the antibodies in the absence of stimuli.

The effect of dormant B-cells is to ensure the production of antibodies of type i if there is a nonzero matching m_{ij} with the epitopes of the stimuli x_j , respectively y_j , even in the absence of x_i. This is included by adding a term $m_{ij}d_i x_j$, respectively $m_{ij}d_i y_j$, where d_i is a source strength mimicking the presence of dormant B-cells of type i .

In this way, introducing the shorthand $M_{ij} = m_{ij} - \varkappa m_{ji}$, we arrive at

$$\dot{x}_i = x_i \left(\sum_{j=1}^{N} M_{ij} x_j - \gamma \right) + d_i \sum_{j=1}^{N} m_{ij} x_j + (d_i + x_i) \sum_{j=N+1}^{N+n} m_{ij} y_j \ , \ i=1,\dots,N . \quad (1)$$

A similar set of equations holds for the antigens. (1) are generalized LVE. Setting the $d_i \equiv 0$ the model proposed in /15/ is recovered.

The matching m_{ij} measures how well the complementary structures of paratope p_i and epitope e_j (keys and locks) fit together. The m_{ij} enter the LVE (1) as parameters which could be, for example, obtained in the following way /15/. The threedimensional structures, as any information, can be encoded by binary strings i.e. sequences of 0 and 1 . Then, similar to the calculation of the Hamming distance (cf. e.g. /10/), the number of complementary bits ν is counted. If ν is below a certain threshold ν_{th} the matching is zero (no reaction). Above the threshold the matching increases with $\nu - \nu_{th}$, in the simplest version linear. The procedure can be refined allowing different lengths of the binary strings and all possible alignments.

3. MEMORY AS CYCLES IN THE LOTKA-VOLTERRA NETWORK

We now investigate the existence and the stability of simple stationary solutions (fixed points) of the above proposed LVE in the absence of antigens ($y_i \equiv 0$) to check the possibility of a memory provided by cycles in the idiotopic network.

We first consider the LVE (1) whithout taking into account the effects of dormant B-cells ($d_i \equiv 0$). This is the model originally proposed in /15/. From

$$\dot{x}_i = x_i \sum_{j=1}^{N} (M_{ij} x_j - \gamma) \quad (2)$$

we obtain the equation of motion for $s = \sum_{i=1}^{N} x_i$,

$$\dot{s} + \gamma s = \sum_{i,j=1}^{N} x_i M_{ij} x_j = (1-\varkappa) \sum_{i,j=1}^{N} x_i m_{ij} x_j \quad , \tag{3}$$

It shows (the x_i and m_{ij} are positive) that for $\varkappa \geqslant 1$ the zero fixed point $s = 0$ i.e. $\vec{x}^s = 0$ is globally stable. A nonzero fixed point $\vec{x}^s = \vec{a}$, which is determined by $M\vec{a} = \gamma \vec{1}$, can exist only for $\varkappa < 1$.

The local stability of fixed points of an equation $\dot{\vec{x}} = \vec{F}(\vec{x})$ is determined considering the dynamics of a small deviation $\vec{\varepsilon} = \vec{x} - \vec{x}^s$ which is governed by

$$\dot{\vec{\varepsilon}} = \left(\frac{\partial \vec{F}}{\partial \vec{x}}\right)_{\vec{x}=\vec{x}^s} \vec{\varepsilon} = \mathbb{F}'(\vec{x}^s)\vec{\varepsilon} \quad . \tag{4}$$

$\vec{x}^s$ is locally stable if $\vec{\varepsilon}$ dies out, i.e. if the matrix $\mathbb{F}'(\vec{x}^s)$ has only eigenvalues with negative real part.

For system (2) we find

$$\mathbb{F}'(\vec{x}^s)_{ij} = \delta_{ij}\Big(\sum_{j=1}^{N} M_{ij} x_j^s - \gamma\Big) + x_i^s M_{ij} = \begin{cases} -\gamma\,\delta_{ij} & \text{if } \vec{x}^s = 0 \\ a_i M_{ij} & \text{if } \vec{x}^s = \vec{a} \end{cases} \quad , \tag{5}$$

which shows that $\vec{x}^s = 0$ is locally stable for all $\varkappa$.

As an example for a nontrivial fixed point we consider the simplest cycle of two antibodies x_1 and x_2 characterized by the mutual matching m_{12} and m_{21} shown in Fig. 4.

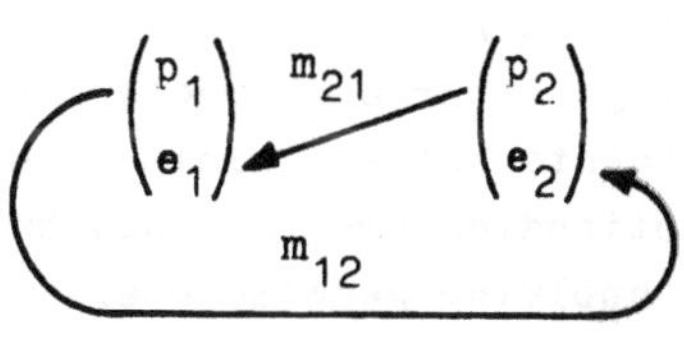

Fig. 4. Simplest cycle of two antibodies x_1 and x_2. The production of x_1 is stimulated since its paratope recognizes the epitope of x_2 and is at the same time inhibited since its epitope is recognized by the paratope of x_2. This competition gives the possibility of a stationary state.

All the other x_i and m_{ij} including m_{11} and m_{22} in (2) are put to zero. Then the nonzero fixed point,

$$\vec{a} = \gamma \left\{1/M_{21},\ 1/M_{12}\right\} \quad , \tag{6}$$

is in the positive cone if

$$\varkappa < \varkappa^0 = \min\left\{m_{12}/m_{21},\ m_{21}/m_{12}\right\} \leqslant 1 \quad . \tag{7}$$

However, since the matrix

$$\mathbb{F}'(\vec{a}) = \gamma \begin{pmatrix} 0 & M_{12}/M_{21} \\ M_{21}/M_{12} & 0 \end{pmatrix} \tag{8}$$

has the eigenvalues $\pm\gamma$, the 2-cycle is locally unstable (Fig. 5).

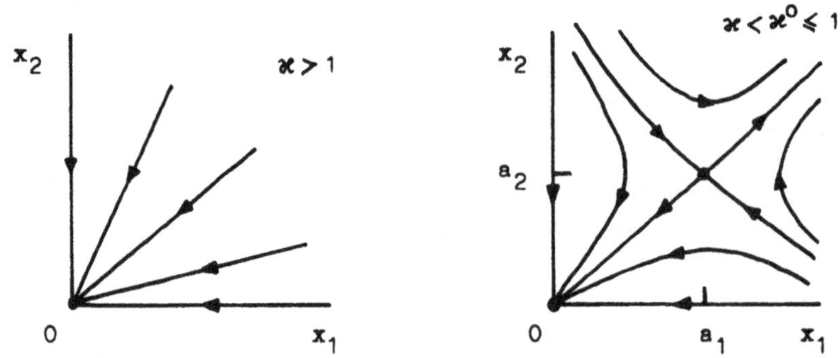

Fig. 5. Schematic flow diagrams for the case of two antibodies in the model without dormant B-cells (2). For $\varkappa > 1$ zero is the only (globally stable) fixed point. A nonzero fixed point exists for $\varkappa < 1$ and lies for $\varkappa < \varkappa^0$ in the positive cone. It is however unstable.

As a further example it can be shown that the 3-cycle characterized by $m_{12}=m_{23}=m_{31}=m$ is unstable. We argue that also higher cycles are unstable and that no memory due to cycles exists in (2).

The stability of zero and the instability of cycles make the results of a numerical simulation qualitatively reported in /15, 16/ plausible. There, the LVE (2) was integrated numerically. After a characteristic time the system is examined and all constituents below a minimal concentration are removed by hand. The removed antibodies are replaced by new ones which are generated from the old ones applying genetic operators or using a random sequence generator. Even in the absence of antigens no steady state of the network was observed but a dynamic behaviour: "something like a weather pattern".

We consider now our model which takes into account dormant B-cells. In the absence of antigens (1) reads

$$\dot{x}_i = x_i \sum_{j=1}^{N} (M_{ij}x_j - \gamma) + d_i \sum_{j=1}^{N} m_{ij}x_j \quad . \tag{9}$$

It is intuitively clear that the presence of the source term on the right hand side of (9) possibly destabilizes the zero fixed point and favours the formation of cycles.

We investigate again the 2-cycle shown in Fig. 4. Besides $\vec{x}^s = 0$ we find the nonzero fixed point

$$\vec{a} = (\gamma^2 - d_1 d_2 m_{12} m_{21}) \{ (\gamma M_{21} + d_2 m_{21} M_{12})^{-1}, (\gamma M_{12} + d_1 m_{12} M_{21})^{-1} \}. \tag{10}$$

$\mathbb{F}'(\vec{x}^s)$ for this model differs from (5) by an additional term $d_i m_{ij}$ on the right hand side. We find

$$\mathbb{F}'(0) = \begin{pmatrix} -\gamma & d_1 m_{12} \\ d_2 m_{21} & -\gamma \end{pmatrix}, \quad \mathbb{F}'(\vec{a}) = \begin{pmatrix} -d_1 m_{12} q & \gamma / q \\ \gamma q & -d_2 m_{21} / q \end{pmatrix}, \tag{11}$$

where $q = a_2/a_1$. The analysis of the (always real) eigenvalues yields that for

$$\gamma < \gamma^o = (d_1 d_2 m_{12} m_{21})^{1/2} \tag{12}$$

the 2-cycle is locally stable and the zero fixed point is unstable. For $\gamma > \gamma^o$ the opposite is true (Fig. 6). The conditions that $\vec{a}$ lies in

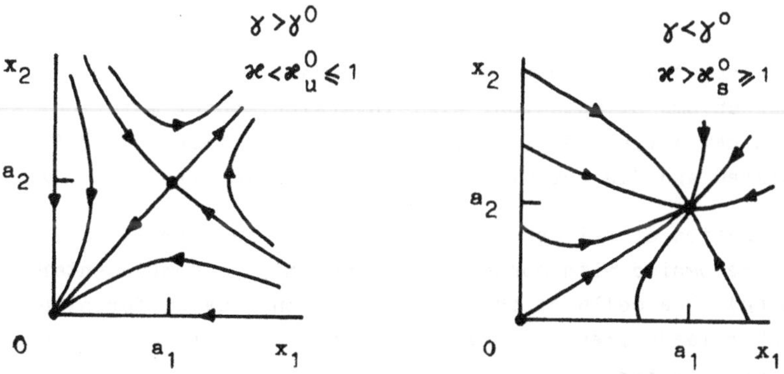

Fig. 6. Schematic flow diagrams for the case of two antibodies in the model which includes dormant B-cells (9). there exists a nonzero fixed point which changes for $\gamma = \gamma^o$ its stability. For $\varkappa_u^o < \varkappa < \varkappa_s^o$ the fixed point is not in the positive cone. The stable cycle can serve as a memory.

the positive cone are for the stable, respectively the unstable, cycle

$$\varkappa > \varkappa_s^o = \max\{\varkappa_{12}, \varkappa_{21}\}, \text{ and } \varkappa < \varkappa_u^o = \min\{\varkappa_{12}, \varkappa_{21}\}, \tag{13}$$

where $\varkappa_{ij} = (\gamma m_{ij} + d_i m_{ij} m_{ji})(\gamma m_{ji} + d_i m_{ij}^2)^{-1}$. In the symmetric case ($m_{12}=m_{21}$) we have $\varkappa_s^o = \varkappa_u^o = 1$.

The linear stability analysis shows in this way that there exist only in the presence of dormant B-cells a parameter region in which the simplest cycle of two antibodies is stable. The stable cycle provides a stationary nonzero number of antibodies of the involved types, these antibodies do not die out, they are memorized. Antigens with an epitope similar to the epitopes of the involved antibodies are immediately attacked. Since the matching need not to be perfect the memory is associative.

4. INNOVATION, ADAPTIVE LEARNING, AND MEMORY IN A HIERARCHICAL SCHEME

In the previous Sections we analyzed the LVE describing a given set of constituents of the idiotopic network. We know however, as briefly desribed in Section 1, that the list of variables and parameters of these LVE is dynamic. Therefore the LVE have to be embedded into a hierarchical scheme which governs the generation of new variables and the dynamics of the parameters. This scheme consists essentially in the following.

(i) To describe the renewal of B-lymphocytes from the bone marrow we inject at randomly chosen instants new antibodies whose paratopes and epitopes are generated at random or applying genetic operators which describe typical mechanisms of mutation, e.g. inversion, point mutation, and crossover. These new antibodies (innovation) replace those antibodies which are not stimulated and die out after a characteristic life time $1/\gamma$.

The proliferation of B-lymphocytes of type i is stimulated if its paratopes p_i recognize with nonzero matching m_{ij} a complementary epitope e_j (cloning). The cells of the new generations may differentiate into those which release free antibodies and into dormant cells with a considerable longer life time.

(ii) To describe the enhanced mutation during the cloning of stimulated B-cells of sort i we inject new antibodies, whose paratopes are mutations of p_i, at a rate which increases with $m_{ij}x_i x_j$, respectively with $m_{ij}x_i y_j$. Thus, we generate new antibodies centered about the stimulated type. It is likely that the matching with the stimulating epitope could be improved in this way.
A possible higher order control mechanism can be simulated introducing a Monte-Carlo dynamics of the paratopes: A mutation $p_i \rightarrow p_k$ is accepted if the matching with the stimulating epitope e_j increases. Thus

$$H(e_j) = -\sum_{j=1}^{N} m_{jj}^{2} = \min! \qquad (14)$$

acts as a 'teleological principle' which ensures an adaption of the paratopes to the stimulating epitope (adaptive learning).
Writing $m_{ij} = \langle p_i | e_j \rangle$ (whatever is the prescription to calculate the matching between epitope and paratope) elucidates the similarity with the description of neural networks. Here, however, we deal with a dynamics of the patterns.

(iii) To describe the appearance of dormant cells of the stimulated type i we insert a nonzero d_i into the LVE if $m_{ij}x_i x_j$, respectively $m_{ij}x_i y_j$, exceeds some threshold. Above the threshold we allow the formation of stable cycles and below the threshold we allow the corresponding species to die out (we only mention that this effect could also be achieved introducing higher order nonlinearities in the LVE).
Starting from the virgin state (where all $d_i \equiv 0$) the organism acquires in the course of life a set of nonzero $\{d_i\}$ which reflects the individual history (memory). In other words: Due to the nonzero $\{d_i\}$ there is some symmetry breaking of the virgin state.
Taking into account that also the dormant cells have a longer but finite life time we conclude that only the formation of cycles (which needs some fortune) makes an information unforgettable. Indeed, to ensure this, one repeats for instance a vaccination.
Therefore, in our understanding, the two mechanisms for memory do not play an alternative but a synergistic role.

5. CONCLUDING REMARK

We have seen that the nontrivial and efficient behaviour of the IS results from a synergism of different strategies. In a different context, such a point of view is advocated also by other authors of this conference.

Forthcoming investigations of our scheme should proceed to analyze properties of small subsystems, e.g. the dynamics due to an antigen in the presence of a cycle preserving an internal image of this antigen. Only the experience with small subsystems makes a stochastic simulation of larger systems feasible, which could e.g. simulate the reaction of the virgin state to the exposure of an antigen, the stimulation of complementary antibodies, the appearance of dormant cells, and the formation of cycles.

The authors acknowledge valuable dicussions with Ingrid Behn. Thanks are also due to Lutz Schimansky-Geier who made Refs. 13 and 14 available.

REFERENCES

/1/ An excellent introduction gives e.g.: Spektrum der Wissenschaft, Immunsystem, Einf. von G.Köhler und K.Eichmann, Spektrum der Wissenschaft Verlagsgesellschaft, Heidelberg 1987.

/2/ N.K.Jerne, Sci.Amer. 229/1(1973)52; Ref. 1, p54.

/3/ A.J.Cunningham, in: The Immune System I, Eds. Ch.M.Steinberg and I.Lefkovits, S.Karger, Basel 1981.

/4/ G.W.Hoffmann, J.Theor.Biology 17(1986)33.

/5/ G.W.Hoffmann, M.W.Benson, G.M.Bree, and P.E.Kinahan, Physica 22D (1986)233.

/6/ G.W.Hoffmann, in: Computer Simulation in Brain Science, Ed. R.Coterill, Cambridge University Press, Cambridge 1987.

/7/ F.M.Burnet, Ref. 1, p12.

/8/ S.Tonegawa, Ref. 1, p78.

/9/ G.Köhler, Ref. 1, p8.

/10/ W.Ebeling und R.Feistel, Physik der Selbstorganisation und Evolution, Akademie-Verlag 1982.

/11/ M.Peschel and W.Mende, The Predator-Prey Model: Do We live in a Volterra World, Akademie-Verlag, Berlin, and Springer, Wien, New York 1986.

/12/ Л.Н.Белых, Г.И.Марчук, Р.В.Петров, в сб.: Математические модели в иммунологии и медицине, сб. статей под ред. Г.И.Марчука и Л.Н.Белых, мир, москва 1986.

/13/ Ю.М.Романовский, Н.В.Степанова, Д.С.Чернавский, Математическая биофизика, наука, москва 1984.

/14/ A.S.Perelson, Mathematical Immunology, in: Mathematical Models In Molecular and Cellular Biology, Ed. L.A.Segel, Cambridge University Press, Cambridge 1980.

/15/ J.D.Farmer, N.H.Packard, and A.S.Perelson, Physica 22D(1986)187.

/16/ J.D.Farmer, S.A.Kauffman, N.H.Packard, and A.S.Perelson, Conf.Proc. "Perspectives in Theoretical Biology and Medicine", National Institute for Health, Bethesda, Maryland 1986.

/17/ G.Weisbuch and H.Atlan, J.Phys. A21(1988)L189.

/18/ I.Dayan, D.Stauffer, and S.Havlin, J.Phys. A21(1988)L2473.

TIME HIERARCHY IN ENZYMATIC REACTION NETWORKS AS DERIVED FROM AN EXTREMUM PRINCIPLE

Stefan Schuster[1)]

1. Introduction

The myriads of chemical reactions simultaneously proceeding in living cells can be regarded as networks with vertices and arcs representing (bio)chemical species (reactants) and (bio)chemical reactions, respectively. In general, these networks are more complicated than graphs as defined in graph theory in that one (directed) arc can join more than two vertices.

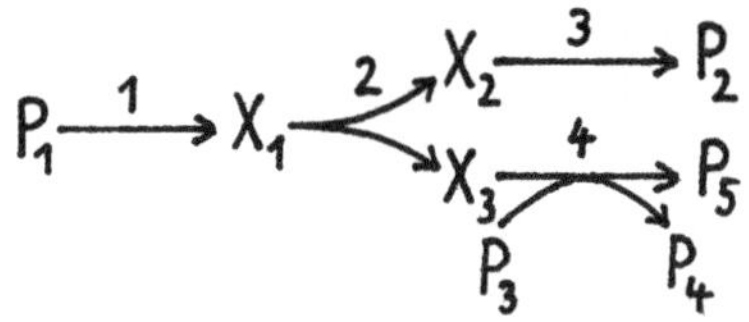

(*)

This scheme depicted in the way being usual in biochemistry may serve as an example.

It is an essential feature of biochemical networks that the reactions involved are catalyzed by enzymes. Unlike physico-chemical properties as equilibrium constants of reactions, the kinetic parameters of enzymes have changed during evolution. It is often argued that, by these alterations, biological reaction networks have been shifted towards (at least local) optimal states /3,4,10-12,16/. The investigation of optimum properties of biological systems is important for the design of biotechnological processes as well. In either regard, optimization can be formalized by means of an extremum principle

$$\text{maximize } \Phi(p) \tag{1}$$

subject to some appropriate side condition(s), where $\Phi(p)$ is a real-valued function of the vector p encompassing the alterable enzymatic parameters /7,10,11,16/.

Extremum principles represent a very fundamental and compact formalization of natural laws and can render the same to the optimality concept in biology. In our opinion, they even offer the possibility to disentangle this concept from any teleological association. Extremum principles underlying evolutionary adaptation should, as far as they cannot be derived from physical laws, considered as first principles not requiring any teleological substantiation. Nevertheless, they can often be interpreted in biological terms (efficiency, homoeostasis, controllability, etc.).

---

1) Humboldt-Universität zu Berlin, Sektion Biologie, Bereich Biophysik, Invalidenstr. 42, BERLIN 1040, DDR

The crucial problem is to find the concrete objective functions $\Phi(p)$. In several approaches, they involve steady-state reaction rates (termed "fluxes" henceforth) /6; 7; 8,p.442; 10; 16/. However, as Reich points out /10/, the results obtained from these principles disagree with real biochemical systems inasmuch as they do not show time hierarchy, i.e. the separation of time constants which is a conspicuous feature of living matter at any level of organization /1,4,9,12/.
On the other hand, approaches using objective functions concerning stability of steady states and insensitivity to parameter changes in systems with special feedback regulations do lead to time hierarchy /3-5, 12/. Indeed, not all of these investigations start from an extremum principle (1) but one can easily reformulate the criteria in such a way.
Recently, we have investigated an objective function concerning the local asymptotic stability of steady states and have applied it to unbranched reaction chains without feedback inhibition /13/. In the present contribution, this approach is extended to reaction networks with arbitrary stoichiometry and with a very general rate law comprising all reversible enzyme kinetics. Since the biological function of an enzymatic network subsisting in steady state is in any case related to matter transformation, some fluxes must enter the used side conditions (if not the extremum principle itself). Throughout we use a side condition fixing all fluxes.

2. Basic Equations

In addition to usual notations of matrix algebra, we employ the following. 0_i and $0_{i,j}$ $(i,j = 1,2,\dots)$ denote the i-dimensional null vector and the $i \times j$ null matrix, respectively. If all the components of an i-vector Y are positive, we write $Y > 0_i$. (diag Y) stands for the diagonal matrix containing the components of a vector Y as diagonal elements. Y_Z denotes the matrix of partial derivatives $(\partial Y_i/\partial Z_j)$ with Y_i and Z_j being the components of Y and Z, respectively.
In spite of the highly organized ultra-structure of living cells, it is assumed in the vast majority of models in biochemistry that all concentrations are spatially homogeneous in each considered compartment. Following this assumption and excluding explicit time dependence, one can describe the temporal behaviour of concentrations by the O.D.E. system

$$\dot{X} = C\,V(X) \tag{2}$$

where X, C, and V are the vector of concentrations X_i $(i = 1,\dots,n)$, the stoichiometric matrix and the vector of net reaction rates v_j $(j = 1,\dots,r)$ /2,4/. The sign of v_j depends on the orientation of the corresponding reaction (arc). Concentrations of one and the same substance in different compartments have to be designated by different components of X.

In many kinetic models of biochemical networks, the concentrations of some reactants (e.g. substrates, products, or cofactors) are deemed to be time-invariant because of large supply or regulation of infusion or effusion. Following Clarke /2/, we term these reactants "external species". Their concentrations are denoted by P_i ($i = 1,\dots,m$) and are not incorporated into the vector X. For simplicity's sake, let X_i and P_i denote concentrations as well as the corresponding species themselves. Be c the rank of C. If $c < n$, there exist n-c independent conservation conditions which can be compactly written as

$$B\,X(t) = K \quad \text{for all } t \tag{3}$$

where B is an $(n-c) \times n$ matrix fulfilling

$$B\,C = 0_{n-c,r} \tag{4}$$

and having rank n-c (cf. /2/). K denotes an (n-c)dimensional vector of constants.

For the rate laws $v_j(X)$, we use the general expression

$$v_j(X) = G_j(X)\left[-\ln\left(\prod_{i=1}^{n} X_i^{c_{ij}}/\tilde{q}_j\right)\right] \tag{5}$$

where

$$\tilde{q}_j = q_j \Big/ \prod_{i=1}^{m} P_i^{e_{ij}} \tag{6}$$

with q_j denoting the equilibrium constant of reaction j. c_{ij} (e_{ij}) are the stoichiometric coefficients of X_i (P_i) in reaction j (accordingly, c_{ij} are the elements of C). Apart from two plausible restrictions, $G_j(X)$ is an arbitrary real-valued function. These restrictions (which are satisfied by all enzyme kinetics) are

$$G_j(X) > 0 \quad \text{for any } X > 0_n;\ j = 1,\dots,r \tag{7}$$

$$\left|\left.\frac{\partial G_j}{\partial X_k}\right|_{\bar{X}}\right| < \infty \quad \text{if both } \bar{X} \text{ and } G_j(X) \text{ are finite; } j = 1,\dots,r;\ k = 1,\dots,n. \tag{8}$$

Let the expression in square brackets in (5) be abbreviated by A_j. Throughout, we will assume $X > 0_n$ and $0 < \tilde{q}_j < \infty$ for all j so that A_j always exists. It represents, apart from a constant factor, the affinity of reaction j in ideal gases or solutions (cf./8,p.34/). Although living cells do not contain ideal solutions, all known rate laws of reversible enzymatic reactions (steady-state as well as equilibrium models) can be described by (5 - 8). This becomes conspicuous if one writes (5) as

$$v_j(X) = F_j(X)\left[\tilde{q}_j \prod_{i=1}^{n} X_i^{c_{ij}^-} - \prod_{i=1}^{n} X_i^{c_{ij}^+}\right] \tag{9}$$

where

$$c_{ij}^- = \begin{cases} -c_{ij} & \text{if } c_{ij} < 0 \\ 0 & \text{if } c_{ij} \geq 0 \end{cases} \tag{10}$$

and

$$c_{ij}^+ = c_{ij} + c_{ij}^- . \tag{11}$$

The transformation from (5) to (9) is achieved by defining $F_j(X)$ in an obvious way with the only difficulty that a discontinuity across the manifold $\prod_{i=1}^{n} X_i^{c_{ij}} = \tilde{q}_j$ has to be removed /14,15/. The kinetics (9) comprises, for example, the reversible Michaelis-Menten kinetics

$$v_j(X) = \frac{V^+X_1/K^+ - V^-X_2/K^-}{1 + X_1/K^+ + X_2/K^-} \tag{12}$$

of the reaction $X_1 \longrightarrow X_2$ (cf. /12,p.49/) as can be seen by choosing

$$F_j(X) = \frac{V^-/K^-}{1 + X_1/K^+ + X_2/K^-} . \tag{13}$$

The "thermodynamic" notation (5) has the advantage to be representable as a matrix equation

$$V(X) = [\operatorname{diag} G(X)](\ln \tilde{q} - C^T \ln X) \tag{14}$$

where $G(X)$ and $\tilde{q}$ denote the vectors

$$G(X) = (G_1(X), G_2(X), \ldots, G_r(X))^T \tag{15}$$

and

$$\tilde{q} = (\tilde{q}_1, \tilde{q}_2, \ldots, \tilde{q}_r)^T, \tag{16}$$

respectively. The logarithmic function of a vector is to be interpreted as the vector of the logarithms of the corresponding components.
As $G_j(X)$ is assumed to have no zeroes, we have

$$v_j(X) = 0 \quad \text{if and only if} \quad \prod_{i=1}^{n} X_i^{c_{ij}} = \tilde{q}_j \tag{17}$$

which is the well-known law of mass action. Since the usual mass action kinetics

$$v_j(X) = \vec{k}_j \prod_{i=1}^{n} X_i^{c_{ij}^-} - \overleftarrow{k}_j \prod_{i=1}^{n} X_i^{c_{ij}^+} \tag{18}$$

is a special case of kinetics (5) provided that the rate constants $\vec{k}_j$ and $\overleftarrow{k}_j$ of forward and reverse reactions, respectively, do not vanish, we term the function (5) "generalized mass action kinetics".
In steady states, (2) reduces to

$$C\,V(X) = 0_n . \tag{19}$$

This equation system has, with respect to V, an (r-c)dimensional solution space. Therefore, the side condition about fixed fluxes can be written as

$$v_j = \text{const.} \quad \forall j \in J \tag{20}$$

where J is a set of r-c indices for which the fluxes v_j can be given arbitrarily before solving (19). We will term such a collection of fluxes a complete set of independent fluxes. The network (*) given in the introduction is characterized by $r-c=2$, that is, one can choose two independent fluxes, e.g. the unordered pairs $\{v_1,v_3\}$, $\{v_1,v_4\}$, or $\{v_2,v_4\}$. The pair $\{v_1,v_2\}$, however, is not possible.
V has to be given by (20) in such a way that eq. (19) has a solution for X. Using (14), it can be shown that all vectors V fulfilling this condition lie in a pointed convex polyhedral cone /14/ which we term "flux cone".
In the extremum problem considered in this paper, the functions $G_j(X)$ are variable since they express those enzymatic properties which can be changed. As we restrict the analysis to steady states, we can calculate $G_j(X)$ only for steady state concentration vectors X^s:

$$G^s = (G_1^s,\dots,G_r^s) = G(X^s). \tag{21}$$

3. Minimizing the Largest Time Constant

Stationary states are observed in enzymatic systems very frequently though not being the only asymptotic time behaviour relevant to such systems. Whenever steady states have functional importance, they have to be asymptotically stable. As is well known, this requirement is fulfilled if all the eigenvalues λ_i of the Jacobian matrix

$$M = C\,V_X \tag{22}$$

calculated at the considered steady state have negative real parts. Yet, as R. Rosen has pointed out /3,p.106/, the return of a biological system to optimal performance following perturbation must usually be rapid since every such system is subject to permanent environmental fluctuations. Therefore, the "asymptotic" aspect of asymptotic stability becomes unsatisfactory.
In general, the relaxation toward steady states is controlled by the largest of the real parts of the eigenvalues λ_i. It is easy to show that each conservation condition causes one eigenvalue λ_i to vanish (cf. formula (32a) or /14/). Thus, only the remaining c eigenvalues need to be considered if one admits only perturbations which do not violate the conservation conditions as it is usually done in biochemical models. Numbering the λ_i such that

$$\operatorname{Re}\lambda_1 \le \operatorname{Re}\lambda_2 \le \dots \le \operatorname{Re}\lambda_n, \tag{23}$$

we can formalize the criterion for steady states to be as stable as possible with all fluxes being constant in the form

$$\text{minimize}\quad \tau_c = -1/\mathrm{Re}\,\lambda_c \tag{24}$$

subject to (20). τ_c is the largest relevant time constant or "time-scale" of relaxation.

Differentiation of (3) at some X^s with respect to some concentration X_k yields

$$\frac{\partial v_j}{\partial X_k} = \frac{\partial G_j}{\partial X_k} A_j - G_j^s \frac{c_{kj}}{X_k^s} \tag{25}$$

so that the Jacobian M can be written as

$$M = C\,(\mathrm{diag}\,A)\,G_X - C\,(\mathrm{diag}\,G^s)\,C^T\,(\mathrm{diag}\,1/X^s). \tag{26}$$

A vector G^s for which τ_c equals zero is surely a solution of the programming problem (24,20). τ_c can vanish only if all $\mathrm{Re}\,\lambda_i$ $(i = 1,\ldots,c)$ tend to $-\infty$ and, hence, if some elements of M diverge. Since we exclude vanishing and, of course, diverging concentrations and due to assumption (8), entries of M can diverge only if some G_j^s do so, say, for exactly p indices j. We number the reactions such that

$$G_j^s \rightarrow \infty \quad \text{for } j = 1,\ldots,p \tag{27}$$

and subdivide C as follows:

$$C = (\,S \quad R\,) \tag{28}$$

with S being an $n \times p$ matrix. Analogously, we partition G^s and A:

$$G^s = \begin{pmatrix} G^{s\prime} \\ G^{s\prime\prime} \end{pmatrix} \tag{29}$$

$$A = \begin{pmatrix} A' \\ A'' \end{pmatrix} \tag{30}$$

where $G^{s\prime}$ and A' are p-vectors.

It is now convenient to perform a variable transformation

$$\begin{pmatrix} \hat{Y} \\ \bar{Y} \end{pmatrix} = \begin{pmatrix} B \\ D \end{pmatrix} X \tag{31}$$

with $\dim(\hat{Y}) = n-c$, $\dim(\bar{Y}) = c$, and D being a $c \times n$ matrix chosen such that $\begin{pmatrix} B \\ D \end{pmatrix}$ is regular. Due to (4), eq. (2) then transforms to

$$\dot{\hat{Y}} = 0_{n-c} \tag{32a}$$

$$\dot{\bar{Y}} = D\,C\,V. \tag{32b}$$

Using the decompositions (28 - 30) and the definitions

$$\mu = (\min_{j=1,\ldots,p} G_j^s)^{-1} \tag{33}$$

$$g' = \mu\,G', \tag{34}$$

(32b) can be rewritten as

$$\mu \dot{\bar{Y}} = D\,S\,(\mathrm{diag}\, g')\,A' + \mu\, D\,R\,(\mathrm{diag}\, G'')\,A''. \tag{35}$$

(33) implies that the limit (27) is equivalent to $\mu \longrightarrow 0$. In this limit, (35) reads, for the time-scale $t' = t/\mu$,

$$\frac{d\bar{Y}}{dt'} = D\,S\,(\mathrm{diag}\, g')\,A' \tag{36}$$

which is just the adjoint system of the singularly perturbed O.D.E. system (32a,35) (cf. /1/). By inserting (28) into (4) one obtains

$$B\,S = 0_{n-c,p}. \tag{37}$$

Thus, one can conclude from the regularity of $\begin{pmatrix} B \\ D \end{pmatrix}$ that every singular point of (36) (if any) fulfils

$$S\,(\mathrm{diag}\, g')\,A' = 0_n. \tag{38}$$

In order that the rates v_j $(j = 1,\ldots,p)$ remain finite in the limit (27), the affinities of the corresponding reactions have to vanish:

$$\sum_{i=1}^{n} c_{ij} \ln X_i = \tilde{q}_j, \quad j = 1,\ldots,p. \tag{39}$$

Since, for arbitrary values of $\tilde{q}_j$, this equation system can in general not be solved for $\ln X_i$ $(i = 1,\ldots,n)$ if $p > s = \mathrm{rank}(S)$, we will assume

$$p = s. \tag{40}$$

This assumption will be amplified in section 4. By virtue of (40), all the columns of S are linearly independent so that (38) gives $(\mathrm{diag}\, g')\,A' = 0_p$ which leads to

$$A' = 0_p \tag{41}$$

since $(\mathrm{diag}\, g')$ is regular owing to $g_j' > 0$ for $j = 1,\ldots,p$ (cf. (33,34)). Eq. (41) is another notation of (39) and means that all reactions with indices $j = 1,\ldots,p$ are in thermodynamic equilibrium. Strictly speaking, this holds true only in time scale $t' = t/\mu$ or, in other words, with respect to the normalized fluxes $\tilde{v}_j = \mu v_j$ $(j = 1,\ldots,p)$. The fluxes v_j, however, are in general finite because of (20).
Using the Lyapunov function

$$L(X) = \sum_{i=1}^{n} (X_i \ln X_i + a_i X_i) + b \tag{42}$$

where a_i and b are constants chosen appropriately, one can prove for any network endowed with generalized mass action kinetics (5) that in the equilibrium state given by $A' = 0_p$ the concentration vector X^s is, for given conservation quantities of the fast subsystem

$$\dot{X} = S\,(\mathrm{diag}\, G')\,A', \tag{43}$$

uniquely determined and that X^s is globally asymptotically stable relative to all vectors $X > 0_n$ which fulfil these very conservation conditions /14,15/.
For X^s, one can write M as

$$M = S\,(\mathrm{diag}\,A')\,G'_X + R\,(\mathrm{diag}\,A'')\,G''_X - \frac{1}{\mu}\,S\,(\mathrm{diag}\,g^{s\prime})\,S^T\,(\mathrm{diag}\,1/X^s) -$$
$$- R\,(\mathrm{diag}\,G^{s\prime\prime})\,R^T\,(\mathrm{diag}\,1/X^s). \qquad (44)$$

Now consider the matrix M' defined by

$$M' = \mu M(\mu). \qquad (45)$$

In the limit (27), we have

$$M' \longrightarrow M'^{o} = -S\,(\mathrm{diag}\,g^{s\prime})\,S^T\,(\mathrm{diag}\,1/X^s) \qquad (46)$$

if we assume

$$\mu\,(\mathrm{diag}\,A')\,G'_X \longrightarrow 0_{c,n} \quad \text{as } \mu \longrightarrow 0. \qquad (47)$$

This is not a very restrictive assumption since $\mu \longrightarrow 0$ implies $A' \longrightarrow 0_p$. Thus the limit (47) means that the derivatives $\partial G'_j/\partial X_k$ at X^s do not diverge faster than $1/\mu = \min_j G_j^{s\prime}$. Due to a theorem of matrix algebra (Theorem 5 in /17,p.129/), $S\,(\mathrm{diag}\,g^{s\prime})\,S^T$ is positive semi-definite with rank $s = \mathrm{rank}(S)$. As we have assumed $X > 0_n$, the matrix $(\mathrm{diag}\,1/X^s)$ is positive definite so that M has rank s, too, and is, owing to another theorem about Hermitian matrices /17,p.198/, negative semi-definite. Thus the matrix M'^{o} has s negative real eigenvalues and zero as eigenvalue of multiplicity n-s. Consequently, s characteristic roots of $M = M'/\mu$ tend to $-\infty$ as $\mu \longrightarrow 0$. $\tau_c \longrightarrow 0$ is then possible if and only if $s \geq c$. Since rank(S) cannot be greater than rank(C) (cf. decomposition (28)), one can conclude, using assumption (40), that in the optimum state

$$p = s = c. \qquad (48)$$

Thus the values G_j^s belonging to c reactions for which the corresponding columns in C are independent have to diverge. This implies that (37) is even equivalent to (4) so that the conservation conditions of the whole reaction system and of the fast subsystem coincide. Thus the steady state X^s is, for given vector K of conservation quantities, unique and globally asymptotically stable relative to all X with $X > 0_n$ and $BX = K$. The values G_j^s $(j = r-c+1,\dots,r)$ have to be chosen in such a way that (20) is fulfilled. This is always possible if the vector V given by (20) lies in the flux cone.

4. Discussion

The result obtained from the extremum problem (24,20) can be formulated verbally as follows. In order that the relaxation towards any steady state proceed as fast as possible, $c = \mathrm{rank}(C)$ reactions for which the corresponding columns in the stoichiometric matrix C are linearly independent have to be as fast as possible. If they were infinitely fast, i.e., if their functions $G_j(X)$ had infinite values for the steady-state vector X^s (which is, of course, not possible in reality), all time constants of relaxation would vanish.

The present analysis applies to any reaction network endowed with the generalized mass action kinetics (5) and fulfilling five conditions explained in what follows. First, it has been necessary to consider all reactions to be reversible ($0 < \tilde{q}_j < \infty$). In order to simplify kinetic models, one often employs the irreversibility assumption but, from a thermodynamic point of view, any chemical reaction is reversible.

Further, we have excluded vanishing concentrations whereby we have circumvented some "pathological" cases which are considered in /15/.

Third, it has been assumed that the functions $G_j(X)$ which express both the catalytic power and the kinetic nonlinearities (co-operativity, allosteric properties, etc.) of the individual enzymes have non-diverging derivatives with respect to all concentrations if neither any concentration nor the function value $G_j(X)$ diverge. Although this assumption is fulfilled by all enzymatic rate laws, it is well known that many enzymes with sigmoidal kinetics operate just in the region of steepest slope of this kinetics. Thus it is worth investigating whether this feature can be an alternative strategy for diminishing the time constants of relaxation.

For concentration vectors X^s with diverging G^s values, also the derivatives $\partial G_j/\partial X_k$ are allowed to diverge. As stated in (47), these derivatives are, however, assumed not to be large of order greater than G_j^s. This assumption deserves the same investigation as the third one.

The fifth premise is given by (40). Actually, it does not always follow from (39) since the latter equation system can sometimes be redundant, viz., if the apparent equilibrium constants $\tilde{q}_j$ fulfil certain conditions (cf. /15/). Nevertheless, since we have found a solution with $\tau_c = 0$ under condition (40), it is unnecessary to seek for a solution violating (40) because it requires metabolic effort (for instance, by producing large enzyme concentrations) to make enzymes very fast.

If $c < r$, the solution is not unique since there exist several possibilities to arrange the columns of C in such a way that S contains c linearly independent columns. The slow reactions must correspond to a complete set of independent fluxes.

If all reactions are endowed with a generalized mass action kinetics (5), the property to be fast implies the phenomenon to subsist in quasi-equilibrium. The limit (27) has to be interpreted as a mathematical idealization of very fast reactions. This approximation is not as rough as it appears at first sight since it is anyway irrelevant to the system's temporal behaviour how fast quasi-equilibrium reactions actually are.

The obtained result shows qualitative accordance with real metabolic pathways and enzymatic transport systems. In most of them, the rank of the stoichiometric matrix is only a little smaller than the number of reactions so that the optimization of local stability leads to the result that there are only few slow, rate-limiting reactions and a great number of fast reactions. This is in agreement with current ideas of time hierarchy /5/ and with the kinetic properties of many real networks. In many unbranched reaction chains (having one independent flux only), one rather slow reaction step exists which is called rate-limiting step. However, the distinct time hierarchy obtained from (24,20) is, to our eyes, somewhat too extreme. It can be rendered more realistic if a side condition concerning enzyme parameters is included. In reality, enzymes cannot be infinitely fast since their catalytic capacities are limited by, for instance, diffusional resistance /7/, and their concentrations cannot diverge, either. In /16,6/ a side condition fixing a linear combination of enzyme parameters were included into programming problems related to the maximization of fluxes.

In /13,14/ we have followed the idea developed in /6/ to take into account a side condition about the sum of intermediate concentrations. Since the osmotic balance of the cell is of great biological importance, it seems reasonable to keep the total osmolarity of the reaction network under consideration constant on optimizing stability. As the concentrations of enzymes are mostly much smaller than those of reactants, one can neglect the former and formulate the side condition in a first approximation as

$$\sum_{i=1}^{n} X_i = \text{const.} \tag{49}$$

In general, the programming problem (24,20,49) cannot be solved analytically. In /13,14/ results of numerical computations for an unbranched chain with linear kinetics have been shown. By including (49), the time hierarchy in enzymatic chains becomes more gradated. Two adjacent reactions are slow, some reactions are much faster but finite, and some reactions subsist in equilibrium.

In networks optimal with respect to (24,20), the only attractor is a unique stable steady state. For systems with finite values of G_j^s, several attractors (even of different dimensions) may co-exist. Thus the asymptotic dynamical behaviour can be simplified by suitable separation of the values of kinetic functions, i.e., by time hierarchy. This point has been stressed earlier /4,5,12/. In contrast to these papers, the present analysis is not restricted to systems with special regulatory feedback patterns.

Since the real parts of c eigenvalues of the Jacobian M tend to $-\infty$ in the limit (27) and the spectrum of M depends continuously on the functions $G_j(X)$, the simplification of attractors to a unique steady state must occur even at finite G_j^s values.

Literature

/1/ Battelli, F.; Lazzari, C.: On the Pseudo-Steady-State Approximation and Tikhonov Theorem for General Enzyme Systems. Math. Biosci. 75 (1985) 229 - 246.

/2/ Clarke, B.L.: Stability of Complex Reaction Networks. In: Prigogine, I.; Rice, S.A. (eds.): Advances in Chemical Physics, vol. 43, p. 1 - 216. John Wiley & Sons, New York 1980.

/3/ Dibrov, B.F.; Zhabotinsky, A.M.; Kholodenko, B.N.: Dynamic Stability of Steady States and Static Stabilization in Unbranched Metabolic Pathways. J. Math. Biol. 15 (1982) 51 - 64.

/4/ Heinrich, R.; Rapoport, S.; Rapoport, T.A.: Metabolic Regulation and Mathematical Models. Prog. Biophys. Molec. Biol. 32 (1977) 1 - 82.

/5/ Heinrich, R.; Sonntag, I.: Dynamics of Nonlinear Biochemical Systems and the Evolutionary Significance of Time Hierarchy. BioSystems 15 (1982) 301 - 316.

/6/ Heinrich, R.; Holzhütter, H.G.; Schuster, S.: A Theoretical Approach to the Evolution and Structural Design of Enzymatic Networks; Linear Enzymatic Chains, Branched Pathways and Glycolysis of Erythrocytes. Bull. Math. Biol. 49 (1987) 539 - 595.

/7/ Keleti, T.; Welch, G.R.: The Evolution of Enzyme Kinetic Power. Biochem. J. 223 (1984) 299 - 303.

/8/ Nicolis, G.; Prigogine, I.: Self-Organization in Nonequilibrium Systems. John Wiley & Sons, New York 1977.

/9/ Reich, J.G.: Time Hierarchy, Equilibrium and Non-Equilibrium in Metabolic Systems. BioSystems 7 (1975) 39 - 50.

/10/ Reich, J.G.: Zur Ökonomie im Proteinhaushalt der lebenden Zelle. Biomed. Biochim. Acta 42 (1983) 839 - 848.

/11/ Rosen, R.: Optimality Principles in Biology. Butterworths, London 1967.

/12/ Savageau, M.A.: Biochemical Systems Analysis. Addison Wesley, Reading (Mass.), 1976.

/13/ Schuster, S.; Heinrich, R.: Time Hierarchy in Enzymatic Reaction Chains Resulting from Optimality Principles. J. theor. Biol. 129 (1987) 189 - 209.

/14/ Schuster, S.: Thesis. Humboldt University Berlin, 1988.

/15/ Schuster, S.; Schuster, R.: A Generalization of Wegscheider's Condition. Implications for Properties of Steady States and for Quasi-Steady-State Approximation. J. Math. Chem., in the press

/16/ Waley, S.G.: A Note on the Kinetics of Multi-Enzyme Systems. Biochem. J. 91 (1964) 514 - 517.

/17/ Zurmühl, R.: Matrizen und ihre technischen Anwendungen. Springer, Berlin 1964.

A general dynamic network model of evolutionary change - applied to processes of development of science

E. Bruckner, A. Scharnhorst [1]

1. Introduction

Discrete Markov processes on networks (generalized birth and death processes) allow the description of evolutionary processes in a rather general (formal) way.
The aim of the present paper results from an idea of Werner Ebeling of a general model, (Ebeling, Feistel 1982; Bruckner, Ebeling, Scharnhorst 1988) which contains earlier developed models as special cases and allows the opening up of new application areas (Ebeling 1984, 1987). Two examples in this regard concerning the process of creation of new technologies in an industry and manpower growth processes of fields of research in science have been presented in more detail elsewhere (Jimenez Montano, Ebeling 1980; Bruckner, Ebeling, Scharnhorst 1987).
The mathematical structure of the stochastic network model which will be represented here has been developed mainly by Ebeling and his research group and is based on earlier more special models of the birth and death type (Ebeling, Feistel 1977; Ebeling, Sonntag, Schimansky-Geier 1981). The development of the model was further influenced by the work on stochastic modelling of social processes (West 1976; Walls 1976; Weidlich, Haag 1983; Mosekilde, Rasmussen 1983; Kwasnicka, Galar, Kwasnicki 1983; Allen, Engelen, Sanglier 1984; Wunderlin, Haken 1984). Especially we have to mention the models of biological and chemical birth and death processes (Bartholomay 1958; McQuarrie 1967; Nicolis, Prigogine 1977), the models of prebiological evolution (Eigen, Schuster 1979) and of ecological processes (Allen, Ebeling 1983).
The general idea consists mainly in the following:
In many natural as well as social systems evolutionary phenomena are observed which are based on simple elementary processes like self-reproduction, decline and exchange. Instead speaking of species because of the very general nature of such processes as a corresponding general concept concerning the units of elementary processes a field concept may be introduced where a field is representing all elements of a given type.
(i) In all those evolutionary processes the appearance of new fields (chemical sorts, biological species, scientific ideas

1) Institute of Theory, History and Organisation of Science of the Academy of Sciences of the GDR, Prenzlauer Promenade 146-152, Berlin, 1100, GDR

etc.) plays an essential role. The number of potential fields which may be created by mutations or alterations of the old ones is very large (practically infinite).

(ii) In the game of evolution the occupation of new fields starts with a rather small number of representatives. This causes strong stochastic influences as e.g. delay of growth, neutral drift, "unmotivated" fast growth, "tunneling" through barriers, disappearance of new better fields.

(iii) The behavior of new fields can be described only by stochastic models, on the other hand established fields, which are populated already with a larger number of representatives, may be described by deterministic models.

The structure of the couplings between the fields may be represented by graph-theoretical concepts (Ebeling, Sonntag 1986; Rasmussen, Mosekilde, Engelbrecht 1988). The graph or the corresponding matrices reflect the physics, biology, ecology or the sociology of the special problem.

In order to demonstrate the usefulness of the model for applications we studied a number of non-linear growth properties of scientific communities. In this context several simulation experiments were carried out examples of which we present in section 3.

2. The model

For the establishment of a stochastic birth, death and transition model for many interacting fields one assumes that elements of z different types are present in the system. The number of types may be very large or even infinite. In the stochastic description each type of elements i=1,2,...z according to their discrete nature is described by integers $N_i > 0$. A given N_i means that the field of type i is occupied by a population consisting of N_i representatives. The occupation numbers N_i are functions of time, i.e. $N_i = N_i(t)$. A complete set of occupation numbers $N_1, N_2, \ldots, N_z$ at a fixed time characterizes the occupation state of the system. Due to the large number of the potential set of the elements 1,2,3...z in typical cases most of the occupation numbers have the value zero (Ebeling, Sonntag 1986). The state of the system at the time t is described by the probability distribution of the occupation numbers $P(N_1, N_2, .N_i, N_j .., N_z, t)$.

We consider the four fundamental processes of evolutionary behavior self-reproduction, decline, transitions between the

fields and input from external sources or spontaneous generation:
1. Self-reproduction: The fields are assumed to produce elements of their own type, where the processes identical self-reproduction as well as error reproduction occur. The failure rate shall be assumed to be kept small by some kind of quality control.
2. Decline: The elements are assumed to contribute in an active manner to their fields only for a limited time. At any time they may leave or be forced to leave the system.
3. Transitions: The fields are assumed to be able to exchange elements. This may be connected with competition and selection.
4. Input: The fields may be populated by a process of inflow (infection) from outside or by spontaneous generation.
In the stochastic description those fundamental processes correspond to the following elementary processes with different transition probabilities.
For identical self-reproduction of an element of kind i the transition probability is given by a quadratic function of the occupation numbers

$$W\,(N_i + 1 \mid N_i) = A_i^{0} N_i + A_i^{1} N_i N_i + B_{ij} N_i N_j \qquad (1a),$$

for error reproduction (mutation) of an element i by a linear law

$$W\,(N_i + 1, N_j \mid N_i, N_j) = M_{ij} N_j \qquad (1b),$$

for decline by

$$W\,(N_i - 1 \mid N_i) = D_i^{0} N_i + D_i^{1} N_i N_i + D_i^{2} N_i N_i N_i + C_{ij} N_i N_j \quad (1c),$$

and for exchange by

$$W\,(N_i + 1, N_j - 1 \mid N_i, N_j) = A_{ij}^{0} N_j + A_{ij}^{1} N_i N_j \qquad (1d).$$

The occupation of a field i by an inflow from outside or by spontaneous generation of an element has the constant probability

$$W\,(N_i + 1 \mid N_i) = \Phi_i \qquad (1e).$$

All coefficients in equations (1a - 1e) should have non-negative values. We assume that during elementary processes only one or at most two complementary occupation numbers can change.
The inflow into the system Φ_i which should be different from zero for at least one element guarantees that the system cannot be absorbed by the empty state with all $N_i = 0$.

3. Spezialization to the Science System and Simulations

Besides economic and technological systems also the science system shows a complex exchange behavior in relation to its members. The specification to that system requires an identification of the elementary processes and an appropriate

parameter estimation.
To establish a scientometrical meaning of the underlying equations above all the four fundamental processes of evolutionary behavior have to be determined which we propose to be as follows:

1. Self-reproduction: Students and young scientists join the field of research they want to, and are allowed to, start working in. Their choice will be mainly influenced by the education process which is based on social needs as well as on individual interests and represented within the science system itself e.g. by scientific schools. Actually the creation of schools within a scientific culture is a well known phenomenon (Bruckner, Scharnhorst 1986).
2. Decline: Scientists are active in science for a limited number of years. Then, for different reasons, but mainly for the reason of age, they stop working and leave the science system.
3. Transitions: Scientists turn to other fields of research for various reasons or open up new ones themselves. This exchange process of scientists between research fields is known in the scientometrical literature under the concept of field mobility (Vlachy 1981; Pao, McCreery 1986). According to that concept the change of subject of a scientist is to be considered as a migration process from one research field to another.
4. Input: In the historic process of development of science the education of disciples, e.g. within the transition to another social order, may be occasionally interrupted. Then the development of science doesn't come to an end, but a specific kind of rational behavior will be generated ever again from the determinants of social life.

Non-linear dynamic phenomena in migratory systems within the last years have been investigated by Weidlich, Haag, Reiner, Sturis, Mosekilde and others.
Thus the model describes the growth of research fields influenced by self-reproduction, decline and field mobility processes, e.g. the coupled growth of n subfields of a scientific discipline. Concepts closely related to research field or subfield would be problem field, research area, specialty and others. As most of these concepts are theoretically disputed about, it is worth noting that what we need is, in some way or another, a definition and empirical determination of the units to which the fundamental processes have to be applied.

To describe coupled growth processes of subfields in science we are using one of the relevant scientometric indicators, the number of the scientists themselves (Gilbert 1978). We therefore will identify N_i with the number of scientists in a field i. Since there are so far very few evolutionary approaches in scientometrics the simulation experiments had been oriented to refind within the framework of an evolutionary model typical regularities and features of growth of scientific communities. The growth properties of scientific communities concerning manpower, publications or citations have been investigated for a long time. As a result a general S-shaped growth law of scientific communities with a delayed growth phase, a rapid growth phase and a saturation phase were established (comp. e.g. Rose 1967, see Fig. 1a). A similar growth behavior could be reproduced by our simulation experiments (see Fig. 1b).

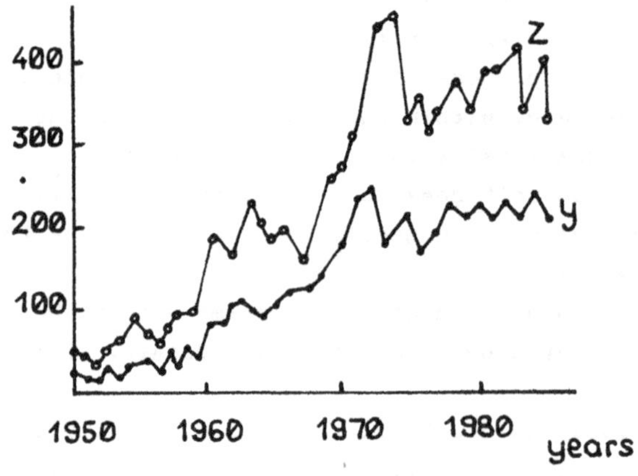

Figure 1a: Example of a fluctuating S-shaped growth law of scientific communities with a delayed growth phase, a rapid growth phase and a saturation phase. Growth of authors (y) and publications (z), research field: nuclear physics. Adapted after source: Trofimenko 1987.

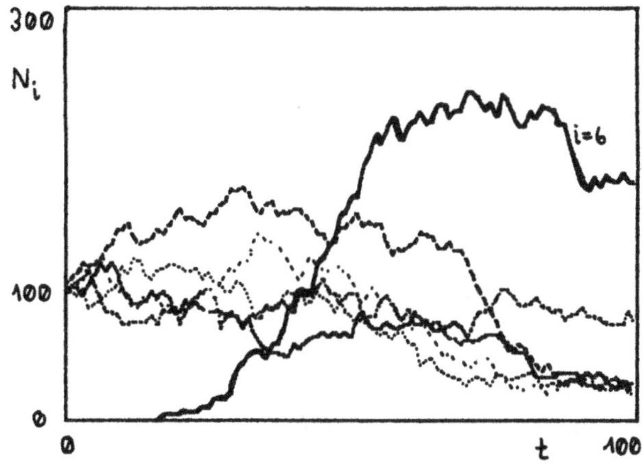

<u>Figure 1b</u>: Selected simulation curve of 6 fields.
Parameters: $A_i^o = \{ .065, .066, .067, .068, .069, .1 \}$ $i=1..6$, $D_i^o = .05 \ \forall \ i$, $D_i^1 = .0001 \ \forall \ i \neq 6$, $D_6^1 = .0004$, $A_{ij}^o = .0005 \ \forall \ i,j$, $Im = .005$, initial conditions: $N_i(0) = 100 \ \forall \ i=1..5$, $N_6(0) = 0$.

Concerning the field mobility process in terms of the model one has to distinguish between two different phenomena: the simple, non-cooperative exchange or field mobility in the narrower sense and a field mobility behavior due to a cooperative process. In order to model mainly the imitation effect of cooperative exchange (Jimenez Montano, Ebeling 1980; Bruckner, Ebeling, Scharnhorst 1987) the mutual directed exchange rate A_{ij}^1 has been approximated by the special assumption

$$A_{ij}^1 = Im * A_i^o \qquad (2),$$

where the constant (Im) is an abbreviation for IMitation.
If a new, attractive field is created, a strong influx of scientists from the surrounding fields will be observed. By imitation the crowding people are adapting to the pattern created by the new field. The high valued field thus may be occupied temporarily far beyond its saturation point. In this case of overshooting the arriving elements at last will have to leave it again by decline (see Fig. 2b). In science the overshooting may be interpreted as fashion effect. The appearance of fashion in science has been documented by many authors (De Solla Price 1961, Hagstrom 1974).

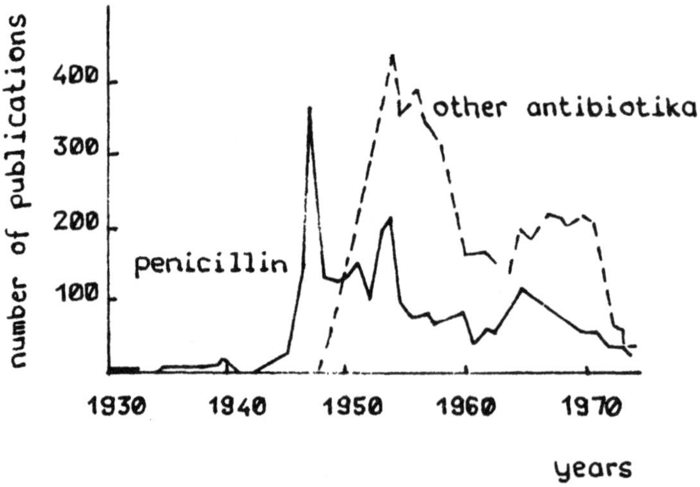

Figure 2a: Growth of publications, research fields: penicillin and antibiotica research. Adapted after Source: Wolf 1987.

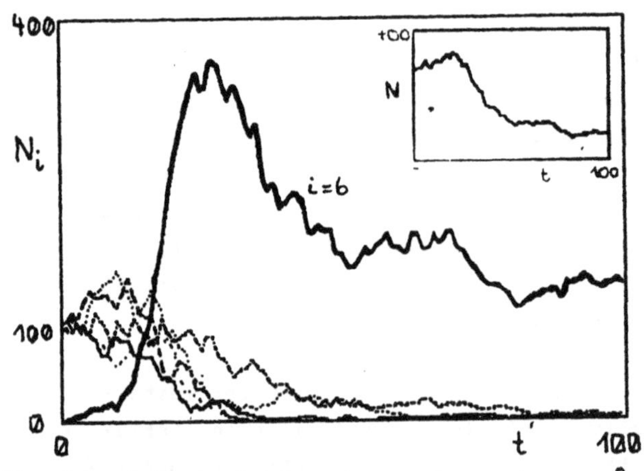

Figure 2b: Selected simulation curve. Parameters: A^{o}_{ij} = .0005 $\forall$ i,j , Im = .01 , for the other parameters see Fig. 1b, in the window total number of scientists $N = \sum_i N_i$.

Literature

Allen, P.M.; W. Ebeling: Evolution and the stochastic description of simple ecosystems. BioSystems 16(1983),113-126.

Allen, P.M.; G. Engelen; M. Sanglier: Self-organizing dynamic models of human systems. In: E. Frehland (Ed.), Synergetics - from microscopic to macroscopic order. Berlin (West) et.al., 1984,p.150-171.

Bartholomay, A.F.: On the linear birth and death processes of biology as Markov chains. Bull. Math. Biology 20(1958),97.

Bruckner, E.; W. Ebeling; A. Scharnhorst: The application of evolution models in scientometrics (to appear). Scientometrics (1987).

Bruckner, E.; W. Ebeling; A. Scharnhorst: Stochastic dynamics of instabilities in evolutionary systems (submitted). System Dynamics Review (1988).

Bruckner, E.; A. Scharnhorst: Bemerkungen zum Problemkreis einer wissenschaftswissenschaftlichen Interpretation der Fisher-Eigen-Gleichung, dargestellt an Hand wissenschaftshistorischer Zeugnisse (in German). Wissenschaftliche Zeitschrift der Humboldt-Universität zu Berlin, Math.-Nat. R. 35(1986)5,481-493.

Ebeling, W.: Die Stellung der Physik im System der Wissenschaften. Kritik des Physikalismus (in German). Deutsche Zeitschrift für Philosophie, 32(1984)1,33-40.

Ebeling, W.: On stochastic models for human conduct in the evolution of science and technology. In: I.Prigogine, M.Sanglier (Eds.), Laws of nature and human conduct. Brussels, 1987,p.77-79.

Ebeling, W.; R. Feistel: Stochastic theory of molecular replication processes with selection character. Annalen der Physik 34(1977),81.

Ebeling, W.; I. Sonntag; L. Schimansky-Geier: On the evolution of biological macromolecules. II. Catalytic networks. Studia biophysica 84(1981)87.

Ebeling, W.;R. Feistel: Physik der Selbstorganisation und Evolution. Berlin, 1982.

Ebeling, W.;I. Sonntag: The stochastic description of evolutionary processes in underoccupied systems. BioSystems 19(1986),91-100.

Eigen, M.;P. Schuster: The hypercycle. Berlin(West) et.al., 1979.

Gilbert, G.N.: Measuring the growth of science, A review of indicators of scientific growth. Scientometrics 1(1978)1,3-9.

Hagstrom, W. O.: Segmentierung als eine Form strukturellen Wandels in der Wissenschaft. In: P. Weingart (Ed.), Wissenschaftssoziologie I. Frankfurt a.M., 1974.

Jimenez Montano, M.A.; W. Ebeling: A stochastic evolutionary model of technological change. Collective Phenomena 3(1980),107-114.

Kwasnicka, H.;R. Galar;W. Kwasnicki: Technological substitution forecasting with a model based on biological analogy. Technological Forecasting and Social Change 23(1983),41-53.

McQuarrie, D.A.: Stochastic approach to chemical kinetics. London, 1967.

Mosekilde, E.; S. Rasmussen: Random processes in system dynamics. Dynamica 9I(1983),33-39.

Mosekilde, E.; J. Aracil; P. M. Allen: Instabilities and chaos in non-linear dynamic systems. System Dynamics Review (1988).

Nicolis, G.; I. Prigogine: Self-organisation in non-equilibrium systems. New York, 1977.

Pao, M.L.; L. McCreery : Markov chains theory in the detection of research activities. Czechoslovak Journal of Physics B36(1986)1, 111-114.

Peschel, M.; W. Mende: The Predator-Prey model. Do we live in a Volterra world?. Berlin, 1986.

De Solla Price, D. J.: Science since Babylon. New Haven, 1961.

Rasmussen, S.; E. Mosekilde; J. Engelbrecht: Time of emergence and dynamics of cooperative gene networks. System Dynamics Review (1988).

Reiner, R.; W. Weidlich : Chaotic and regular dynamics in migratory systems. Proceedings of the 2nd European Simulation Congress. Simulation Councils Inc.: Antwerpen, 1986.

Reiner, R.; W. Weidlich ; M. Munz: Migratory dynamics of interacting subpopulations - regular and chaotic behavior. System Dynamics Review (1987).

Rose, S.: The S-curve considered. Technology and Society 4(1967),33-39.

Sturis, J.;E. Mosekilde: Bifurcation sequence in a simple model of migratory dynamics. System Dynamics Review (1988).

Trofimenko, A.P: Nuclear physics in the last 50 years. Scientometrics 11(19787),231 -250.

Vlachy, J.: Mobility in physics - a bibliography of occupational, geographic and field mobility of physicists. Czechoslovak Journal of Physics B31(1981)6,669-674.

Walls, D.F.: Non-equilibrium phase transitions in sociology. Collective Phenomena 2(1976),125-130.

Weidlich, W.;G. Haag: Concepts and models of quantitative sociology. Berlin(West) et.al., 1983.

West, B.J.: Nonlinear models of population growth with diffusion. Collective Phenomena 2(1976),111-118

Wolf, J.: Über die Schwierigkeit, das Entstehen einer neuen Forschungsrichtung zu prognostizieren. In: Kolloquien, ITW der AdW der DDR, Heft 59. Berlin, 1987.

Wunderlin, A.;H. Haken : Some applications of basic ideas and models of synergetics to sociology. In: Frehland, E. (Ed.): Synergetics - from microscopic to macroscopic order. Berlin(West) et.al., 1984 p.174-182.

COMBINATORIAL OPTIMIZATION BY SELECTION PRESSURE CONTROLLED REPLICATOR NETWORKS

Hans-Michael Voigt
Ivan Santibanez-Koref

Academy of Sciences of the GDR
Centre for Scientific Instrumentation (ZWG)
Rudower Chaussee 6, Berlin-Adlershof, 1199

Keywords

Neural Networks, Replicator Networks, Biological Evolution, Natural Selection, Combinatorial Optimization, Travelling Salesman Problem, Diversified Replication, Selection Pressure Control

Introduction

Following **Darwin's** famous work "On the Origin of Species", evolution processes of living nature can be characterized by ***replication, mutation*** and ***selection.*** Natural selection means the the evolution of species to ever higher stages with respect to function and structure. This evolution implies the application of natural selection mechanisms for optimization purposes.

For the description of evolutionary processes a large variety of models has been established. One of the most fundamental is the ***Lotka-Volterra-Equation***. The transformation of this equation to the unit simplex yields the so called ***replicator equation***

$$\dot{x}_i = x_i\big(f_i(x) - \Phi(x)\big)$$

$$x'_i = x_i \frac{f_i(x)}{\Phi(x)}$$

for ***overlapping*** and ***non-overlapping population generations*** which is defined on the probability simplex

$$S_n = \left\{(x_1,\dots,x_n) : x_i \geq 0, \sum_i x_i = 1\right\}.$$

This equation reflects replication and selection. Mutation terms may be added. It is worth to note that this equation plays an essential role in the description of the evolution of ***macromolecules***, the evolution of ***alleles*** in a ***gene pool***, the evolution of species in ***animal populations***, and evolution processes in ***large scale systems***.

In terms of genetics, x_i means the proportion of allele i in the gene pool, $f_i(x)$ the mean fitness of alleles i, and $\Phi(x)$ the mean fitness of the total gene pool. For linear fitness functions $f_i(x)$.

$$f_i(x) = \sum_j G_{ij} x_j = (Gx)_i$$

with real, symmetric, non-negative interaction matrices G this is the well-known ***Fisher-Wright-Haldane-Model*** of ***population genetics***.

Stable structures of a population or gene pool are given by stable attractors, in the most simple case by stable fixed points.

Underlying a homogeneous potential function $U(x)$ of degree s and using as fitness functions $f_i(x)$ the Euclidean gradients

$$f_i(x) = \frac{\partial U(x)}{\partial x_i}$$

we have for the mean total fitness $\Phi(x)$ the relation

$$\Phi(x) = sU(x).$$

In this case a ***maximum principle*** in the sense of Shahshahani holds, and the increase rate of the mean fitness of the total gene pool

$$\dot{\Phi}(x) \geq 0 \quad , \quad \Phi' \geq \Phi,$$

respectively, is non-negative. This is the fundamental theorem of population genetics.

Conversely, we have with the above given settings for the ***inverse replicator equation***

$$\dot{x}_i = x_i \left(\frac{1}{f_i(x)} - \bar{\Phi}(x) \right)$$

$$x'_i = x_i \frac{\left(\frac{1}{f_i(x)} \right)}{\bar{\Phi}(x)}$$

a ***minimum principle***.

Diversified Replication

If we assume that evolution proceeds not only for a single gene locus, as in the above case, but for m different connected loci, then a ***diversified replicator equation***

$$\dot{x}_{ik} = x_{ik}\left(f_{ik}(x) - \Phi_i(x)\right)$$

$$x'_{ik} = x_{ik}\frac{f_{ik}(x)}{\Phi_i(x)}$$

which is defined on

$$S^i_m = \left\{(x_{i1}, \ldots, x_{im}) : x_{ik} \geq 0, \sum_k x_{ik} = 1\right\}$$

may be used as an appropriate model. Here x_{ik} is the proportion of alleles i at gene locus k, $f_{ik}(x)$ the mean fitness of alleles i at locus k, $\Phi_i(x)$ the mean fitness of alleles i, and

$$\Phi(x) = \sum_i \Phi_i(x)$$

the mean fitness of the total gene pool with $i = 1, \ldots, n$ and $k = 1, \ldots, m$. As in the single locus model for homogeneous potential functions $U(x)$ and Euclidean gradients

$$f_{ik} = \frac{\partial U(x)}{\partial x_{ik}}$$

as fitness functions the relation

$$\Phi(x) = sU(x)$$

holds, and a ***maximum principle*** in the sense of Shahshahani can be shown. The increase rate of the mean fitness of the total gene pool is also non-negative. That's the fundamental theorem for diversified replication.

In much the same way as in the one locus model an ***inverse diversified replicator equation*** can be derived for which a ***minimum principle*** holds.

The application of diversified replication to combinatorial optimization problems will be demonstrated by the travelling salesman problem. The approach was equally used for the graph partitioning problem, the module placement problem, the mapping problem of processes to processors for multi-processor systems etc.

The Travelling Salesman Problem

In case of the travelling salesman problem the potential function is quite clear. If G_{ij} represents the distance between city i and city j we have

$$U=\sum_{k=1}^{n}\left(C_{kk+1}+C_{kk}\right)\rightarrow \min \quad , \quad C_{nn+1}=C_{n1}$$

with

$$C_{kl}=\sum_{i}x_{ik}\sum_{j}G_{ij}x_{jl}.$$

The Euclidean gradients are given by

$$\frac{\partial U}{\partial x_{ik}}=\left(Gx_{.k-1}\right)_i+\left(Gx_{.k}\right)_i+\left(Gx_{.k+1}\right)_i.$$

Furthermore we have to consider the constraints

$$X_k=\sum_{i}x_{ik}=1.$$

Using the ***inverse diversified replicator equation*** and introducing a ***selection pressure control*** u we have as fitness functions $f_{ik}(x)$.

$$f_{ik}(x)=\frac{\dfrac{1}{\sum_j G_{ij}\left(x_{jk-1}+x_{jk}+x_{jk+1}\right)}+ux_{ik}}{X_k} \quad \text{for} \quad u\geq 0$$

$$f_{ik}(x)=\frac{\dfrac{1}{\sum_j G_{ij}\left(x_{jk-1}+x_{jk}+x_{jk+1}\right)}-u\left(1-x_{ik}\right)}{X_k} \quad \text{for} \quad u<0$$

x_{ik} is the probability with which city i is at the k-th position of the salesman's tour. It should be noted that we assumed a number of other possible fitness functions. The best results were obtained for the travelling salesman problem with the fitness function according to the ***inverse diversified replicator equation***.

Replication and ***selection*** are given by the ***recurrence equation***

$$x'_{ik} = x_{ik} \frac{f_{ik}(x)}{\Phi_i}.$$

Mutations are introduced by a slight random perturbation for each new generation

$$x_{ik} := \frac{x_{ik} + \mu y_{ik}}{1 + \mu \sum_i y_{ii}}$$

where the y_{ik} are uniformly distributed random numbers in (0,1) and μ is the ***mutation rate***.

The evolution process works as follows:

1	***Start*** with a uniform distribution of the x_{ik}
2	Set the selection pressure u sufficiently low
3	Disturb the x_{ik} slightly (***mutation***)
4	Iterate the recurrence equation (***replication*** and ***selection***)
5	If the probabilities x_{ik} are stabilized go to 6, else go to 3
6	If the assignments x_{ik} are sufficiently crisp then ***Stop***
7	Increase the selection pressure slightly and go to 3

Some Results

Neural Networks (Hopfield & Tank)

Wilson & Pawley used the original function and parameter set of Hopfield & Tank to compute the Hopfield & Tank 10-city TSP-example. The simulation failed with the following results for 100 runs:
15 tours converged within 1000 iterations to valid tours (no one was

optimal)

45 were frozen in configurations not corresponding to valid tours

40 runs did not converge within 1000 iterations

With ***replicator networks*** the optimal solution was always found at u=-.1 and a mutation rate of .00001 for 20 runs within 50 ... 80 iterations.

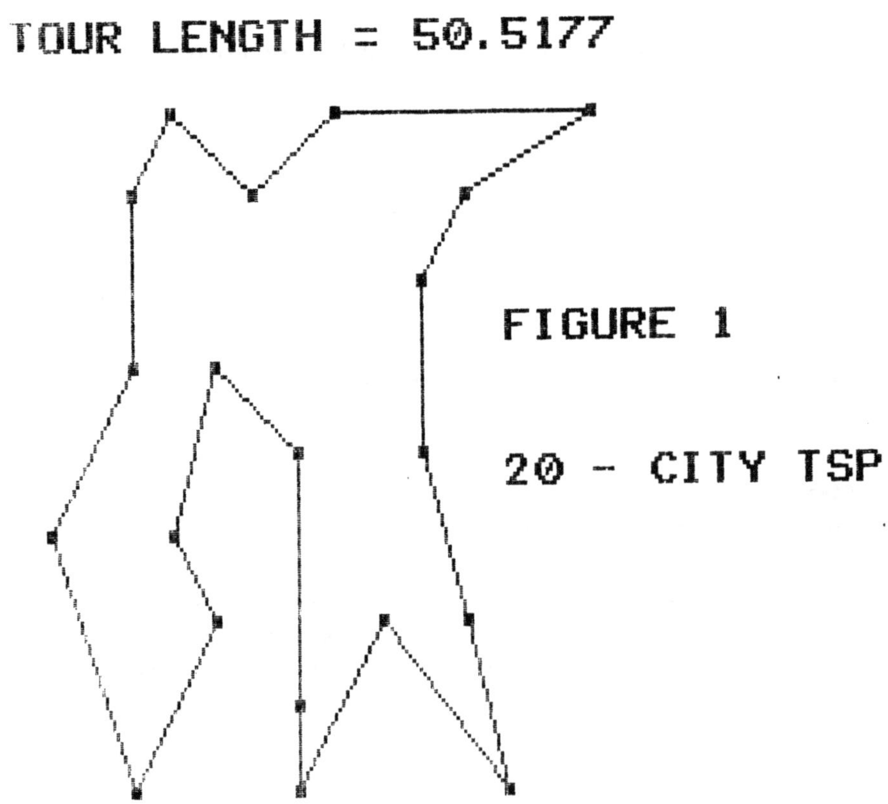

Figure 1. Best tour for a 20-city travelling salesman problem

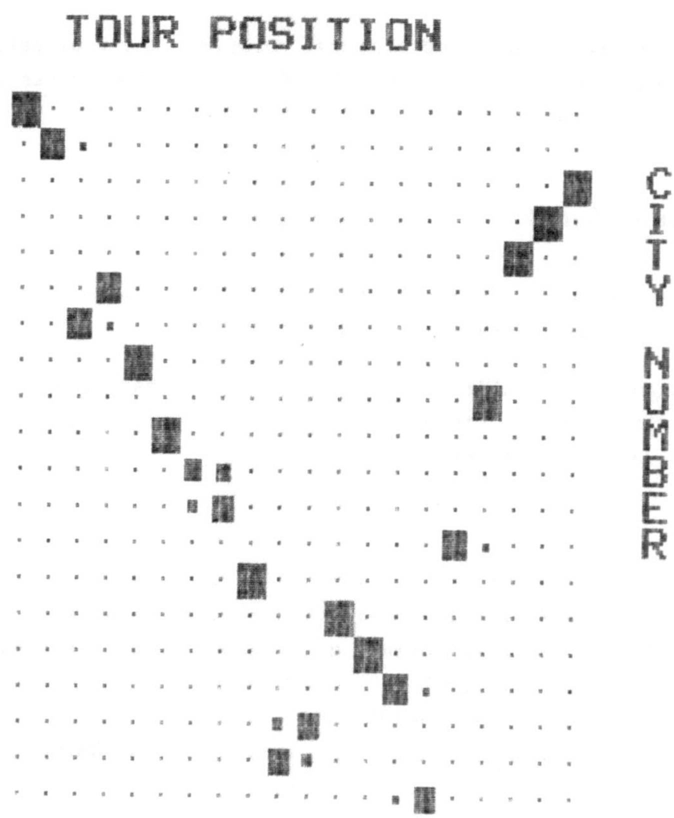

Figure 2. Assignment of cities to tour positions for the 20-city TSP

Boltzmann Machines

Aarts & Korst used for the solution of the Hopfield & Tank 10-city problem 5 min and for the 30-city problem 60 min CPU-time of a VAX 11/780.

With the ***replicator network*** approach the 10-city problem took 5 min and the 30-city problem 180 min computing time of a PC/XT-Compatible (8088 without arithmetic coprocessor). Compared to the VAX 11/780 this is only a fraction of computing time.

In Figure 1 there is shown a 20-city problem which was computed with 318 iterations. The tour is the minimal one. Assignments of cities to tour positions are shown in Figure 2.

Conclusions

In case of the ***travelling salesman problem*** the replicator network approach is superior to the Hopfield & Tank neural networks and to the Boltzmann machine approach.

Acknowledgment

We have constantly benefited from extensive discussions with M.Peschel from the Academy of Sciences of the GDR.

Discussion with H.Mühlenbein from the Gesellschaft für Mathematik und Datenverarbeitung about his experiences with replicator network algorithms were very stimulating.

References

Aarts E.H.L. & J.H.M. Korst Solving Travelling Salesman Problems with Massively Parallel Networks Based on the Boltzmann Machine. European Journal of Operations Research

Brady R.M. Nature 317, 804-806(1985)

Darwin Ch. On the Origin of Species (1859) (Reprint Harvard University Press 1964, Knoener 1906)

Durbin R. & D. Willshaw Nature 326, 689-691(1987)

Ewens W.J. Mathematical Population Genetics (Springer 1979)

Ebeling W. & R. Feistel Physik der Selbstorganisation und Evolution (Akademie-Verlag 1982)

Eigen M. & P. Schuster The Hypercycle (Springer 1979)

Fisher R.A. The Genetical Theory of Natural Selection (Clarendon Press 1930)

Garey MR. & D.S. Johnson Computers and Intractability (Freeman 1979)

Hadeler K.P. Mathematik fuer Biologen (Springer 1974)

Hofbauer J. & K. Sigmund Evolutionstheorie und dynamische Systeme (Parey 1984)

Hopfield J.J. & D.W. Tank Biol. Cybern. 52,141-152 (1985)

Kirkpatrick S., C.D. Gelatt & M.P. Vecchi Science 220,671-680 (1983)

Lotka A.J. Proc. N.A.S. 6,410-415(1920)

Maynard Smith J. Evolutionary Game Theory (Cambridge University Press 1982)

Mühlenbein H., M. Gorges-Schleuter & O. Krämer Parallel Computing 4,269-279(1987)

Papadimetriou C.H. & K. Steiglitz Combinatorial Optimization (Prentice-Hall 1982)

Peschel M. & W. Mende Predator-Prey-Models (Akademie-Verlag & Springer 1986)

Shahshahani S. Memoirs AMS 211 (1979)

Sigmund K. Mathematical Research 23, 63-71 (Akademie-Verlag 1985)

Svireshev Yu.M. & D.O. Logofet Stability of Biological Communities (Mir Publishers 1983)

Volterra V. Lecons sur la theorie mathematique de la lutte pour la vie (Gauthiers-Villars 1931)

Voigt H.-M. Evolution und Optimierung. Diss. B (Habilitation) (Acad. Sci. GDR 1986)

Voigt H.-M. Lect. Notes in Economics and Mathematical Systems 273, 117-125 (Springer 1986)

Voigt H.-M. (Ed.) Structure Formation Based on Self-Organisation Principles with Applications to Electronics Design (Acad. Sci. GDR, Inst. for Informatics, Report 12, 1985)

Voigt H.-M. Population Genetics and Combinatorial Optimization. Proc. Int. Tagung Opt. und Anwendungen,53-56 (Eisenach, Nov.1986)

Voigt H.-M. Wiss. Z. TH Ilmenau 2,117-132(1985)

Voigt H.-M. Report R-MATH-01/83,242-249 (Acad. Sci. GDR, Inst. for Mathematics 1982)

Voigt H.-M. Mathematical Research 23,228-231 (Akademie-Verlag 1985)

Voigt H.-M. Optimization by Selection Pressure Controlled replicator Networks. Systems Anal. Mod. Sim. (to appear)

Voigt H.-M. & I. Santibanez-Koref Mathematical Research 46,274-277 (Akademie-Verlag 1988)

Voigt H.-M. Evolution and Optimization: An Introduction to Solving Complex Problems by Replicator Networks (Akademie-Verlag 1989)

Wilson G.V. & G.S. Pawley On the Stability of the Travelling Salesman Problem Algorithm of Hopfield and Tank. Univ. of Edinburgh, Dep. of Physics

Zeeman E.C. Lect. Notes in Mathematics 819, 249-270 (Springer 1980)

Thermodynamical and Biological Optimization

T. Boseniuk[1]

1. Introduction

For a long time optimization has been a domain of mathematicians. By the help of mathematical methods many algorithms for the solution of several optimization problems has been found./1/

In recent time a growing interest of scientists from physics and biology in optimization problems can be stated /2,3,4,5/. This interest is based on analogies between optimization and natural processes. There are at least two of such analogies: In statistical physics each system has several states $\{q_i\}$. These states occur with different probabilities. The probability only depends on the energy E of the state. It is:

$$p(\{q_i\}) = const.*exp(e(\{q_i\})/T) \qquad (1)$$

Here T is the temperature of the system. At zero temperature only the state with lowest (optimal) energy $E=E_{min}$ occurs. In biology the analogy is more literally. One result of evolution was and is the optimization of the genetic code. But the problem here is much more sophisticated than in the case of optimization or in statistical physics so that we will use a very simple model of evolution. Before discussing the analogies in more detail let us explain the problems investigated here.

2. The Travelling Salesman Problem

Among the discrete optimization problems there exist a class which is very hard to solve - the class of NP-complete problems. In few words: that are problems which need a very expensive computational effort. For the exact solution this effort is at least proportional to the exponent of the system size. But even the time for the de-

1 Humbodt-Universität zu Berlin, Sektion Physik, Bereich 04
Invalidenstraße 42, Berlin 1040, DDR

termination of a near optimal solution grows rapidly with the system size. Among the
class of NP-complete problems there are examples of high technical importance - e.g. the problems of chip design. In statistical physics the determination of the ground state of spin glasses belongs to the class of NP-complete problems. Our investigations were made for two different Travelling Salesman Problems (TSP). A TSP can be stated very easy. A set of cities {i} with a cost matrix d_{ij} is given. The problem is to find the shortest closed tour which connects all cities. For a n=100^{156} city TSP there exist (n-1)!/2 (about 10) different tours. Although not all of these tours must be compared the determination of the shortest tour remains NP-complete. A typical property of NP-complete problems is the effect of frustration. That means for all single elements (the cities in the case of TSP) it is not possible to optimize all local conditions at the same time. In the case of TSP for each city it is optimal to be connected with its two nearest neighbours. Actually this is not possible for all cities because the nearest neighbours of city A usually have other nearest neighbours than A. The complexity of a TSP of course also depends on the structure of the matrix d_{ij} . Usually the d_{ij} are geometrical distances. Let us first assume that each city represents a point of a lattice with lattice constant 1. Than the shortest tour can be determined very easy (Fig. 1 shows some examples for a 100 city lattice).

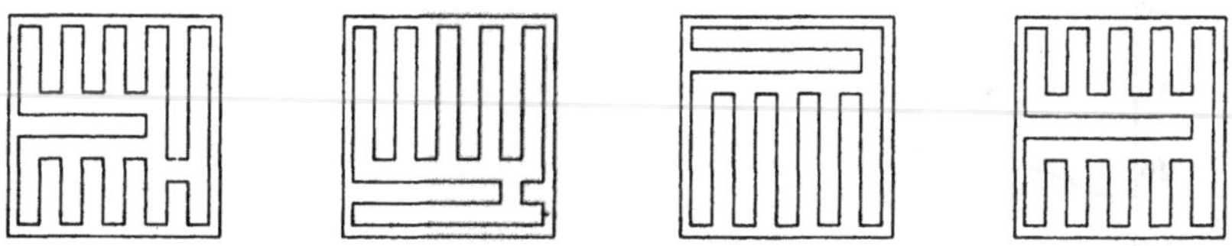

Fig. 1: Different solutions for the laatice problem

Correctly one of the optimal tours is determined, because there exist many of it. The length of such an optimal tour is equal to the number of cities n=100. After normalization l=L/n one obtains l=1.0. In this case no NP-completeness can be found; again the effect of frustration is vanished. If the cities are randomly and uniformly distributed within a 10*10 square the problem becomes more difficult. As in the fundamental work of KIRKPATRICK /4/ we have used the Manhattan-distance for the calculations but have plotted the direct (Euclidian) connections. Fig. 2 shows some near optimal tours again for a 100-city problem.

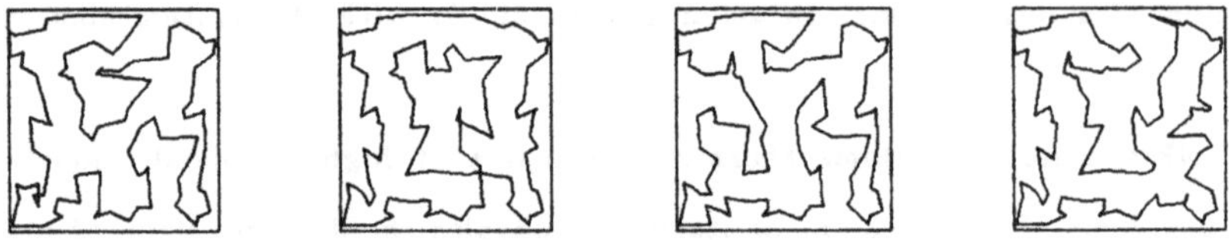

Fig. 2: Near optimal solutions for the geometric TSP

The tours are computed by the help of the methods described in chapter 6. As before we have used the normalized lengths l=L/n. One finds that the lengths only differ by about 1 per cent from each other (see fig. 4). In addition it can be shown that the different tours are relatively similar to each other. To determine the similarity of two tours one can use the measure of Hamming distance. In the case of tours this is simply the number of connections which is different in both tours. Fig. 3a shows the time development of the mean Hamming distance during evolution. Therefore 20 independent runs were carried out and each 10 life cycles (see chapter 6) the mean Hamming distance between the best tours of each run was computed. The x-coordinate presents the normalized tour length. The mean Hamming distance Hd converges to a value of about 15 for the 100 city TSP.

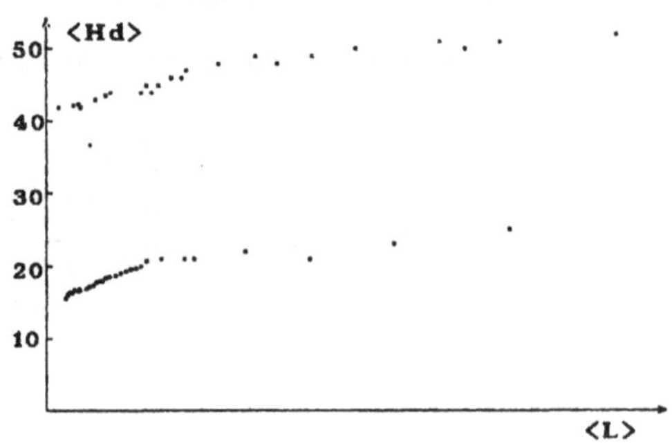

Fig. 3: Mean Hamming distance during evolution

a) geometric TSP b) ROM-TSP

Another possibility is the use of a matrix which elements are not distances. For example the d_{ij} might be given as random numbers /6/. We have also investigated a 100-city problem of this type. In our example we have used the ROM-bytes of the Computer (Sinclair Spectrum) to be the d_{ij}:

$$d_{ij} = \begin{cases} \text{Peek}(100*i+j) \text{ for } i>j \\ \text{Peek}(100*j+i) \text{ for } j>i \end{cases} \quad (2)$$

By this way the symmetry $d_{ij} = d_{ji}$ is guaranteed. It should be noted here that no triangle inequality yields.

Computing near optimal tours by the same methods as in the geometrical case one finds a greater scattering of lengths (see Tab. 1) and a highei diversity among the different tours. Fig. 3b shows the time development of mean Hamming-distance for the ROM-TSP. It converges to a value of about 40. We want to interpret the differences in the mean Hamming distances in such a way that the problem with ROM-matrix is harder to solve. In this case the optimal solution can be found within a sphere of radius 40 while in the case of the geometric problem this radius is about 15. Before discussing the idea of thermodynamical and biological strategy a simple greedy strategy should be explained. This strategy starts with a random city. Beginning with this starting city the procedure always looks for the nearest neighbour of the last city which is still not involved in the tour until all cities are connected. The last city is connected with the starting one. In the lattice case the greedy algorithm is able to find an optimal tour. In the two other cases a greedy tour is still far from optimum. But it can be improved by a simple random gradient search. Therefore the tour must be changed a little bit. The best way to do such changes is the reversing a part of the tour. Therefore the tour is cut at two cities and one part of the tour is reversed. By this way it length is changed by ΔL. If ΔL is negative the old tour is replaced by the new one otherwise not. This reversing a part of the tour operation will also be used in the th ermodynamic and biological algorithm we will discuss now.

3. The Thermodynamic Strategy

As already said in the introduction the state a system can be found in at zero temperature is those with minimal energy. But already from experience it is known that also at very low temperatures states with higher energy occur. The state of a real system does not only depend on its present temperature but also on its history.

Smiths have known this fact already for several centuries. To improve the quality of their products they anneal it. That means they heat it and cool it down very slowly. Good quality means that the material has a near lattice structure - a structure with low (near ground state) energy. The idea of KIRKPATRICK /5/ and CZERNY was to simulate the annealing of the system which should be optimized. Therefore the parameter which should be minimized (the length of the tour L) has to be identified with the physical energy. The variables of the optimization problem (the arrangement of cities) play the role of physical coordinates and moments. By the help of this assumptions it is possible to simulate a TSP at a certain temperature. The algorithm for the simulation of the thermodynamical properties of physical systems was developed by METROPOLIS et al. It starts with with any state; in the case of TSP that means with any allowed tour. Following the state is changed a little bit randomly; for example by reversi ng a part of the tour. this change is connected with a change of energy (length) ΔE. Now the old state is replaced by the new one with the probability:

$$P(\{q_i\}' \leftarrow \{q_i\}) = \begin{cases} 1 & \text{if } \Delta E < 0 \\ \exp(-\Delta E/T) & \text{if } \Delta E > 0 \end{cases} \qquad (3)$$

Due to equation (3) improvements are always accepted while the probability for a change to the worse depends on $\Delta L/T$. Generally all changes with $\Delta L >> T$ are forbidden but changes with $\Delta L <$ are possible. Doing such changes k times one obtains a chain of states (tours). It can be shown that in the limit $k \to \infty$ each tour occurs with probability $p(\{q_i\}) = const. * \exp(-\Delta L/T)$. In many cases the thermodynamical equilibrium will already be achieved after a finite number of changes. By this way a algorithm is given which simulates a certain system at temperature T. In the case of zero temperature the algorithm becomes extremely simple - only improvements are accepted. Actually it is the random gradient search described above. The problem of the gradient strategy is the existence of many local minima. Among these minima are tours with near optimal length but there are much more tours with relatively high lengths. Usually the algorithm stops in one of the bad minima because they are in majority. This difficulty can be overcame by starting the algorithm with none zero temperature. Until now it is a question of experience to find a suitable starting temperature. After a certain time of simulation the temperature can be reduced. Now the system is simulated at this lower temperature and so on until a (near) zero temperature is achieved. Usually the simulation is finished if no further changes occur. By the help of this simulated annealing algorithm it is possible to improve the results of optimization in comparison with a random gradient strategy. Actually the main problem of simulated annealing is the choose of an appropriate annealing schedule. Let us now explain the idea of the biological strategy.

4. The Biological Strategy

The starting point of the biological strategy is quite different from those of thermodynamic strategy. In thermodynamics one system is investigated. This system might have different states. During annealing the probability for the existence of states with low energy grows. The biologist is interested in states of different individuals. This individuals are more or less adapted; i. e. they have a certain fitness or optimality. In the course of biological evolution this fitness F was improved. But in biology the fitness of one individual depends on many factors, e. g. on the number of other individuals. It is possible to use this full analogy /7/. Here we will assume that F only depends on the state (the genetic code) of the individual itself. In the case of a tour F must be as higher as shorter its length is. Simply we assume the fitness F to be the negative length F=-L. In our simulation scheme the absolute value of F is unimportant. Let us now discuss the main elements of early biological evolution: Each individual produces successors. The number of successors is nonnegative and depends on its own fitness i. e. individuals with high fitness have a high number of successors. On the other hand each individual dies. The dying rate again depends on the fitness. Individuals with a higher fitness usually life longer. In the simulation we will assume that always a new individual is born an old one will die. Such combination of death and birth we will call a selection step. To obtain improvements there must be changes from generation to generation. These changes are usually called mutations. Here we will assume that a mutation might occur during life. That means it is not linked to the selection step. In the mutation step a random tour is changed without any interaction with other tours. By the help of this assumptions we can built up a simulation: The system contains N individuals (tours). The initial tours can be obtained by a greedy algorithm. Now selection and mutation steps occur with a certain probability. Later we will speak about the ratio between mutation and selection. In the selection step two tours are chosen randomly. The difference of the two tour lengths is computed. With the probability:

$$P(N_i - 1, N_j + 1 | N_i, N_j) = \alpha * |L_i - L_j| \qquad (4)$$

the longer tour is replaced by the shorter one; i. e. the probability for selection is as higher as greater the length difference of the tours is. α is only a normalization factor. It should be determined in such a way that no probability is greater than 1. In the mutation step one tour is chosen randomly from the ensemble of tours and afterwards changed by a mutation. For the TSP we have again

used the reversing a part of the tour mutation. By the help of the two basic steps selection and mutation one can built up a simple evolution algorithm. The corresponding master equation for the probability $P(N_1, \ldots, N_m)$ to have N_i individuals in state i has the following transition rates:

$$W(N_i - 1, N_j + 1 | N_i, N_j) = \alpha * N_i * N_j / N * |L_i - L_j| * \Theta(L_i - L_j) \qquad (5)$$

for selection and:

$$W(N_i - 1, N_j + 1 | N_i, N_j) = a_{ij} = \begin{cases} 1 \text{ if reversing is possible} \\ 0 \text{ if not} \end{cases} \qquad (6)$$

for mutation. The matrix elements must be chosen in such a way that only reversing a part of the tour mutations are possible. The algorithm described above is very similar to the evolution strategies developed by RECHENBERG and SCHWEFEL /2,3/. We have used the algorithm to optimize the two TSP introduced in chapter 2. But the results were not very encouraging. That depends on the fact that the mutations given by (6) are undirected. If a tour is already good the number of possible improvements is much more smaller than that of bad mutations. So it is necessary to increase the ratio of selection enormously. But this is very uneffective because of the relatively high computational effort which is connected with the reversing. In comparison it is much more faster first to test a mutation and than to carry it out as in the gradient strategy. But also the use of strictly directed mutations does not bring an improvement.

In this case the different tours find their minima very fast and selection has only a vanishing influence. This problems can be attacked by using more sophisticated biological strategies /5/. Here we will show that the use of thermodynamic elements can make this simple biological strategy workable.

5. Combined Strategies

Both strategies have their advantages and disadvantages /9/. From the computational point of view that are: The thermodynamic strategy is extremely simple to implement and gives a very powerfül method to leave local minima. But it is difficult to find a proper annealing schedule. The biological strategy works naturally parallel and explores a great area of state space. It is very easy to prevent that the best optimum will be forgotten. But the simple biological strategy described above is improper for frustrated landscapes with many local minima. Is it possible to combine these advantages? Formally this must be done by replacing the transition rate (6) with (3). That means the mutations must become directed like in the thermodynamic case. Now the chose of temperature remains an open question. In the most simplest way a slowly cooling like in usual simulated annealing is used. In that case the temperature strategy is the same for all individuals. Actually this brings a small improvement /8/. Here we want to discuss another possibility with different temperatures for different individuals /10/.

6. Life Cycle Strategy

If one starts with N tours in not necessarily different local minima and temperature T=0 no further improvements are possible, because a local minimum can not be left at zero temperature. On the other hand we want to prevent the present best optimum to be left. Selection steps may occur at least if the tour lengths are different from each other. The idea is to give a none zero temperature to the copies obtained by a selection step. By this way the new burn copy may leave their local minimum. If the temperature afterwards is reduced it falls into an other local minimum which might be of better quality. By this way improvements are possible. It must only be prevented that the new copy with high temperature can be selected out. By this way a algorithm is given which might be used to optimize the TSP. Following we want to explain the algorithm in more detail: The simulation works with N=10 individuals (tours). The initial tours are obtained by a greedy strategy with following random gradient search. So all tours are local optima. The simulation consists of selection and mutation steps. At the beginning for all tours T=0 yields. In the selection step two randomly chosen tours are compared. If the difference of their lengths is greater than a random number from the interval $0 \ldots \Delta L_{max}$ the longer tour is replaced by the shorter one. This new copy gets a temperature T>0. After some mutation steps the temperature is reduced. In the case of ROM-TSP it was sufficient to use only one temperature step (T=10.0). In the geometrical case it was better to use 3 temperature steps (T=0.5, 0.3, 0.1). In both cases the number of mutations during one life cycle was much more smaller than in the case of usual simulated annealing. The number of mutations per life cycle was about 200. So it was possible to simulated 100 life cycles in the same time like 1 usual annealing run. It is not only possible to use such short life cycles but even necessary. If the number of mutations is to high the new minimum is to far from the old. Of course it needs some experiments to find out a proper life cycle schedule. But we think this is easier than to get a proper annealing schedule. After one life cycle the next selection step will occur and so on. We have made our calculations on a sequential computer but it is easy to implement the algorithm on a parallel machine. In this case different life cycles will work on different processors. Communication between different processors is only necessary during a selection step. And selection steps take only a small amount of the computational effort. Let us now show the results of life cycle strategy in comparison with those of a gradient strategy and simulated annealing. Fig. 4 shows 50 lengths for the geometrical TSP obtained by random gradient search (a), by simulated annealing (b) and by the above described life cycle strategy (c). The number of life cycles was chosen in such a way that the computing time is equal for b and c.

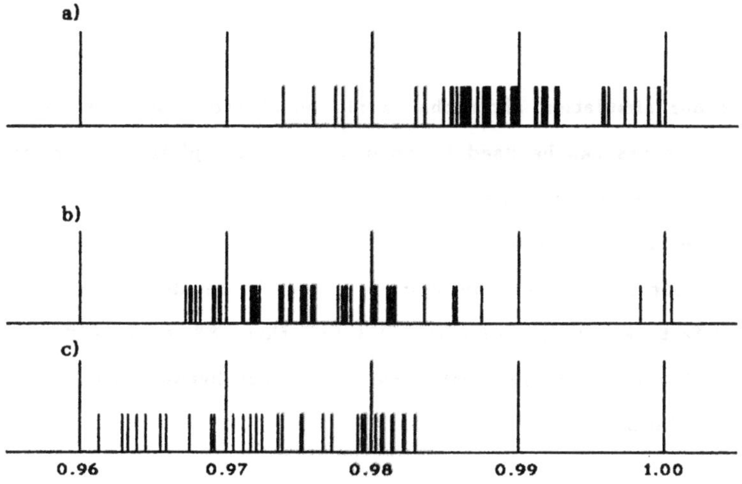

Fig. 4: Results for the geometric TSP
a)gradient b)annealing c)life cycle

The results for the ROM-TSP are given in Table 1.

Table 1: ROM-TSP

Results of 10 independent runs for the different strategies

	gradient	annealing	life cycle
	137	130	102
	137	129	98
	139	139	98
	137	113	102
	132	115	106
	137	127	102
	143	127	102
	138	109	107
	139	122	101
	147	115	91
⟨L⟩ =	138.6	122.6	100.9

Here it was necessary to give 10 results for each strategy; the improvements from strategy to strategy are evident. Again the computation time for simulated annealing and life cycle strategy is equal.

7. Conclusions

The results of our simulation show that a biological evolutionary strategy with thermodynamic elements can be used to optimize a NP-complete problem like the TSP. The life cycle strategy presented here is only one possibility for such a combination. Nevertheless it shows good results in comparison with other strategies. The question which is the better algorithm must of course be decided for each problem anew. The other fact we want to point at is the fact that TSP is not TSP. Our investigations have shown that there exist some differences between the geometrical problem and the ROM problem.

REFERENCES

/1/ M.R. Garey, D.S.Johnson: Computers and Intractability. (Freeman, San Francisco)

/2/ Rechenberg,I.:Evolutionsstrategie-Optimierung technischer Systeme nach Prinzipien der biologischen Information. Friedrich Fromman Verlag, Stuttgart 1977

/3/ Schwefel,H.P.:Numerical Optimization of Computer Models. Wiley New York 1981

/4/ S.Kirkpatrick, C.D.Gelatt,Jr. ,M.P.Vecchi: Science 220 (1983) 671

/5/ Mühlenbein,H.: Contribution in this volume

/6/ S.Kirkpatrick, G.Toulouse: J. Physique 46 (1985) 1277

/7/ Voigt,H.-M.: contribution in this volume

/8/ Boseniuk,T; Ebeling,W.; Engel,A.: Phys. Lett. A 125 (1987) 307

/9/ Ebeling,W.;Engel,A.: Syst.Anal.Model.Simul. 3 (1986) 377

/10/ Boseniuk,T;Ebeling,W.: Europhys.Lett. 6(1988)107

STOCHASTIC APPROXIMATION BASED ON SIMULATED ANNEALING

Christina Schiemangk

1. Introduction

Simulated Annealing is an approximativ, iterative and stochastic searching algorithm. It's motivation comes from the field of thermodynamics /Met53/. Kirkpatrick /Kir82/ and Cerny /Cer82/ applied this algorithm for the first time to solve NP-complete discrete optimization problems especially for optimal placement and optimal routing in connection with the circuit layout and for solving the Traveling Salesman problem.
The i-th step of Simulated Annealing looks at follows:

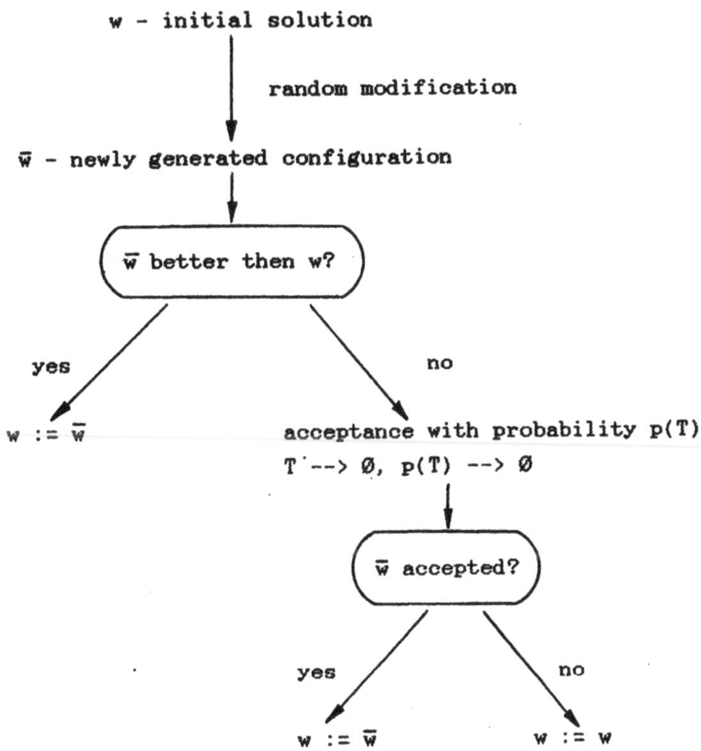

The speciality of Simulated Annealing compared with traditional searching algorithms, for example the local search consists in the acceptance of worsenings with a given probability p(T), depending on a so-called temperature parameter T. So it is possible to overcome local minima.

In the following the results of a mathematical analysis of the perform ance of Simulated Annealing are presented.

2. Simulated Annealing as a Markov-chain

This chapter presents the description of Simulated Annealing by means of Markov-chains, compare with Schiemangk /Sch88/.
Let be given any discrete optimization problem.
W denotes the state space room (number of solutions), $|W| = g_n$, $w \in W$.
$I = \{1,\ldots,g_n\}$ and $J = \{1,\ldots,\infty\}$ are index sets.
K: W --> R denotes a cost function, $K_i = K_i(w_i) \in R$.
Without loss of generality a solution $w \in W$ with minimal cost value is sought-after: $\min_{w \in W} K(w)$.
Simulated Annealing is based on a given system of <u>local random transformations</u>

$$TR = \{TR_i\}_{i=1}^{g_n} \quad \text{over } W, \text{ with}$$
$$T: w_i \dashrightarrow T(w_i) \in W, \ T \in TR .$$

The solution set $TR_i(w_i) \subset W$ is called <u>neighbourhood of w_i</u>.

The system <u>TR</u> is called <u>feasible</u>, if for each two solutions w_i and w_j there exists a finite sequence of transformations of TR which transform into each other.

Starting from any feasible initial solution the state of the system is changed by a successive random choice of exactly one transformation T of the partial set TR_i if in the N-th step the solution w_i is reached.

$P_{ij} = P(w_j/w_i)$ may denote the <u>one-step-transition probabilities</u>, $i, j \in I$:

$$P_{ij} \begin{cases} > \emptyset, & \text{if } w_j \in TR_i(w_i) \\ = \emptyset & \text{otherwise.} \end{cases}$$

The following assumptions must be fulfilled

(P_{ij}) - stochastic: $\sum_j P_{ij} = 1$

(P_{ij}) - irreducible (The irreducibility follows from a feasible system TR).

There exists a <u>sequence</u> $\{T_l\}_{l=0}^{\infty}$ of <u>parameters</u> with the following properties:

$$T_l > T_{l+1}, \quad \lim_{l \to \infty} T_l = \emptyset. \qquad (*)$$

The acceptance of a randomly transformed solution depends on <u>acceptance</u>

probabilties A_{ij} (T), $i, j \in I$.

$\Delta_{ij} = K_j - K_i$ denotes the cost value difference.

The following assumptions must be fulfilled

$$A_{ij}(T) = 1, \text{ if } \Delta_{ij} \leq \emptyset$$
$$A_{ij}(T) \in (\emptyset, 1), \text{ if } \Delta_{ij} > \emptyset$$
$$\lim_{T \to \infty} A_{ij}(T) = 1, \text{ if } \Delta_{ij} > \emptyset$$
$$\lim_{T \to 0} A_{ij}(T) = \emptyset, \text{ if } \Delta_{ij} > \emptyset$$
$$\forall i,j,k \text{ with } K_i \geq K_j \geq K_k$$
$$A_{ik}(T) = A_{ij}(T) \; A_{jk}(T).$$

Let be $K_1 \leq K_2 \leq \ldots \leq K_{g_n}$ without loss of generality. Then the transition probabilities p_{ij} (T) of Simulated Annealing look at follows:

$$p_{ij}(T) = P_{ij} \, A_{ij}(T), \; i \neq j$$

$$p_{ii}(T) = 1 - \sum_{i \neq j} P_{ij} = \sum_{k > i} [1 - A_{ki}(T)] \, P_{ik} + P_{ii}, \qquad i,k,j \in I.$$

A parameter sequence $\{T_l\}_{l=0}^{\infty}$ with the properties (*) and a function $N_l = f(l)$, which gives the dependence of the step number N from the temperature level l is called annealing schedule.

3. Convergence of Simulated Annealing

In the following some theorems for proving the convergence of Simulated Annealing to a global optimum are presented. The proofs can be found in /Sch85A/ and /Sch88/.

Opt denotes the optimal set and ANZ = |Opt|.

Theorem 1

Simulated Annealing is for each fixed $T(\emptyset < T < \infty)$ a finite homogenous Markov chain with the following properties:

1. $\sum_{j=1}^{g_n} p_{ij}(T) = 1$
2. It is irreducible
3. There exists at least one i with $p_{ii}(T) > \emptyset$.

Corollar

Simulated Annealing has an unique limit distribution (p_j) for each fixed T, $\emptyset < T < \infty$, independent from the initial distribution.

Theorem 2

For each fixed T Simulated Annealing converges to the limit distribution:

$$p_i^*(T) = S(T)\ A_{i_0}(T) \qquad i \in I,$$

$$W_{i_0} \in Opt$$

$$\text{if} \quad P_{ij} = P_{ji} \qquad i, j \in I.$$

S(T) denotes a scaling factor.

Special case

For the traditional acceptance probabilities

$$A_{ij}(T) = \exp(-\Delta_{ij}/T),$$

the limit distribution is equal to the Boltzmann distribution:

$$p_i^*(T) = S(T)\ \exp(K_i/T), \quad i \in I.$$

Theorem 3

For T --> Ø the sequence of limit distributions $(p_i^*(T))$ converges to the optimal distribution:

$$\lim_{T \to 0} p_i^*(T) = \begin{cases} \frac{1}{ANZ}, & \text{if } w_i \in Opt \\ \emptyset & \text{otherwise.} \end{cases}$$

Remarks

1. For T --> ∞ the sequence of limit distributions converges to the uniform distribution:

$$\lim_{T \to \infty} p_i^*(T) = \frac{1}{9n}, \quad i \in I.$$

2. The transition probabilities $p_{ij}(T)$ for the two extrem cases T --> ∞ and T --> Ø look at follows:

$$p_{ij}(\infty) = P_{ij}$$

$$p_{ij}(\emptyset) = \begin{cases} \emptyset, & \text{if } j > i \\ P_{ij}, & \text{if } j < i \end{cases}$$

$$\sum_{j \geq i} P_{ij} = 1 - \sum_{j<i} P_{ij}, \quad \text{if } i = j$$

If T = Ø the assumptions of the ergodic theorem are no longer fulfilled.

4. Stochastic Approximation based on Simulated Annealing

In the following a <u>probabilistic approximation schema</u> is presented. That means, for NP-hard optimization problems under certain assumptions for each problem instance I and for each $\varepsilon > \emptyset$ there exists an annealing schedule

$$\{T_l\}_{l=0}^{\infty}, \; N_l = f(l) \quad \text{with}$$
$$\max_i \mid p_i(N,,l) - p_i^0 \mid < \varepsilon .$$

<u>$p_i(N,,l)$</u> is the <u>probability for reaching the i-th solution after N steps and l temperature levels</u>.
<u>p_i^0</u> denotes the <u>limit probability</u> for Simulated Annealing.

Let us start with some remarks with respect to the limit distribution of Simulated Annealing on a fixed temperature level.

1. It is well known, that the eigenvalues of the stochastic matrix, which lie inside the unit circle of the complex plane, are responsible for the speed of convergence.
   For a special case the following hypothesis could be confirmed by calculating the upper bound of the second biggest eigenvalue. If the temperature T decreases, the goal-function value differences in crease and the one step transition probabilities P_{ij} increase, then the speed of convergence for reaching the Boltzmann-distribution becomes smaller, if $\exp(-\Delta_{ij}/T) < 1/2$ /Sch85/.

2. In the general case the number of steps N for reaching the limit distribution increases exponentially with $|W|$ /Sch88/.

3 Now let be $(p_i^*(T))$ the Boltzmann-Gibs-distribution.
  It can be proved:

3.1. $p_i^*(T)$ is a monotonic and decreasing function of T, $\emptyset < T < \infty$, if $w_i \in Opt$.

3.2. The limit distributions:

$$\lim_{T\to\infty} p_i^*(T) = 1/g_n, \; \lim_{T\to 0} p_i^*(T) = 1/ANZ \text{ if } w_i \in Opt, \quad \text{and}$$
$$\lim_{T\to 0} p_i^*(T) = \emptyset, \; \lim_{T\to\infty} p_i^*(T) = 1/g_n, \text{ if } w_i \notin Opt$$

are asymptotically reached:

$$\lim_{T\to 0} \frac{d_{p_i^*}(T)}{dT} = \emptyset, \quad \lim_{T\to\infty} \frac{d_{p_i^*}(T)}{d(T)} = \emptyset, \quad w_i \in W.$$

3.3. **There exists the following hypothesis:**

$p_i^*(T)$ is a monotonic and increasing function of T, $\emptyset < T < \infty$, if $w_i \in Opt$.

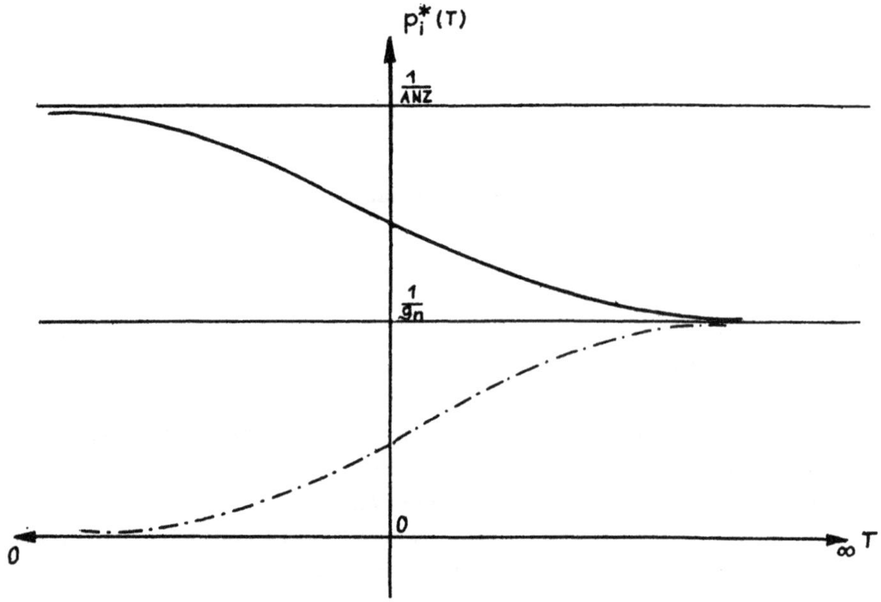

Picture: ._.: limit distribution $p_i^*(T)$, $w_i \notin Opt$

___: limit distribution $p_i^*(T)$, $w_i \in Opt$.

Both curves are drawn in a simplified manner.

In the following an annealing schedule is given in such a way, that the corresponding limit distributions for two successive temperature levels are closed together.

<u>Theorem 4</u>

An annealing schedule $\{T_l\}_{l=0}^{\infty}$, for which the limit distributions of corresponding homogeneous Markov chains are closed together

$$\frac{1}{1+\varepsilon} < \frac{p_i^*(T_l)}{p_i^*(T_{l+1})} < 1 + \varepsilon, \ \forall_i \qquad \text{looks at follows:}$$

$$\frac{T}{\{\ln(1+\varepsilon)T_l/C\} + 1} < T_{l+1} < T_l$$

with $C \geq \max_i \{K_i\}$ and ε a small positiv number.

Lemma

Let be given an annealing schedule $T_{l+1} = T_l/(1 + \alpha T_l)$, $l = 0, 1,$ with $\alpha = \ln(1 + \varepsilon)/C$, $C \geq \max_i \{K_i\}$. For the number l of steps the following unequation is fulfilled: $l < \frac{1}{\alpha T_l}$.

You can find the proofs in /Sch88/.

At least there is given a stochastic approximation procedure, based on Simulated Annealing.

Procedure Simulated Annealing

```
BEGIN
VAR T, ε, MAX, C: REAL
    FAK, K, N:    INTEGER
    CHANGE:       BOOLEAN
"Determination of initial conditions:
- Initial temperature T0 (T0 ≥MAX, MAX ≥{Δij })
- Initial chain length N0 (N0 = 100  T0)
- Parameters C, ε for the annealing schedule (C  ≥  max_i {Ki})
- Factor FAK(ε) > 1
  for chain lengthening (The smaller ε, the bigger FAK.)
- Acceptance probabilities Aij (T) (Aij (T) = 1^(-Δij/T))
- Stop criteria: Maximal number N of iterations without change
- Generation of an initial solution"
l := 0
  REPEAT
  CHANGE := FALSE;
  FOR J := 1 TO Nl  DO
     BEGIN
     Transformation of the actuel solution wi  (wi  --> wj );
     If Transformation is accepted then
          BEGIN
          wi  := wj ;
          CHANGE := TRUE;
          END
     END
                           T
          T      := -----------------;
                  ln(1 + ε)Tl/C + 1
          Nl+1 := Nl * FAK;
          l := l + 1;
  UNTIL NOT CHANGE
          T_END := Tl ;
END
```

6. Final remarks

Simulated Annealing was developed for several applications. It was tested with different annealing schedules for different examples. Specially, Simulated Annealing was implemented for the following graph optimization problems:

1. Solving of the Steiner-Tree-Problem on graphs /Sch85B/.
2. Optimization of stars on graphs with nonlinear cost function /Sch85B/.
3. Solving of some routing problems on graphs /Sch86/.

In connection with the placement of modules for flexible manufacturing systems, Simulated Annealing was developed for the optimal placement of rectangles with different sizes with respect to a minimal transportway length /Sch87/.

References

/Cer82/ V. Cerny, A Thermodynamically approach to the Travelling Salesman problem: an efficient simulation algorithm. Prep of the Inst. of Phys. and Biophhys., Comenius Univ. Bratislava.

/Kir82/ Kirkpatrick, S., C. D. Gelatt, Jr. M. P. Vecchi, Optimization by simulated Annealing. Research Report, RC 9355, 4/2/1982 Computer Science/Engen. Techn.

/Met53/ Metropolis, A., A. Rosenbluth, M. Rosenbluth, A. Teller, E. Teller, J. chem Phys. 21, 1087 (1953). For a review of recent work, see K. Binder, ed.: The Monte Carlo Method in Statistical Physics. Springer Verlag, New York, 1978.

/Sch85A/ Schiemangk, Ch., Remarks on the Performance Analysis of Thermodynamically Motivated Simulation. In: Optimization of Connection Structures in Graphs, ZKI, 1985, S. 74 - S. 90.

/Sch 85B/ Schiemangk, Ch., Thermodynamically Motivated Simulation for solving the Steiner Tree Problem and the Optimization of Interacting Path Systems. In: Optimization of Connection Structures in Graphs, ZKI, 1985, S. 91 - S. 120.

/Sch86/ Schiemangk, Ch., Routing and Simulated Annealing. Proceedings der internationalen Konferenz Mathematische Optimierung - Theorie und Anwendung, Nov. 10. - 14., 1986, Eisenach.

/Sch87/ Schiemangk, Ch., J. Hofmann, Design Optimization of FMS-Layout. Proceedings of the V. Bilateral Workshop GDR - Italy with International Participation Dresden, July 22 - 24, 1987, S. 321 - S. 335.

/Sch88/ Schiemangk, Ch., Simulierte Abkuehlung und deren Anwendung auf Graphenoptimierungsprobleme. Dissertation B, 1988.

Super-(Dinner)-Brain

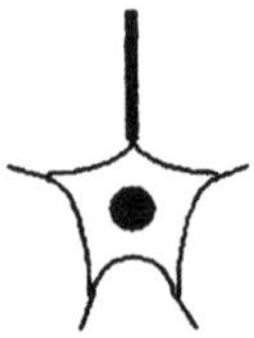

We came to Eisenach with train
and wanted to create a brain
with many neurons smart and clever
which cannot die and work for ever
to solve so many tasks, for us
that's very good and macht viel Spaß.

The problem was how to design
such wonderthing so nice and klein
so klug und freundlich, garnicht schwer
that you can take it everywhere.
This holy goal brought us together
the beer tastes well and pretty was the weather.

We put a lot of neurons in a bag
and take zunächst all the connections weg.
Then we should randomly them mischen,
the global goal was pattern recognition.
Now should we force the neuron's integration
by input pressure and synchronization.

We now apply all our mighty tools
at first the lovely neurons being stupid fools.
They have to learn how to recognize each other
as dominator or an equal brother
we imitate a little evolution
and sometimes organize chaotic revolution.

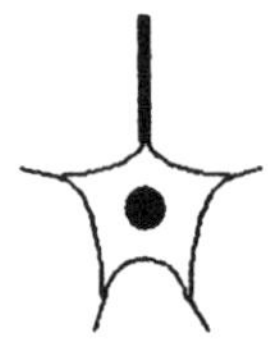

We also tried with random seeking steps,
some neurons using pseudochaotic maps,
we also need mutation and selection,
recombination and some term neglection.
We structurize with hard selection pressure
and formalize with Shashahani measure.
We need a mass of selfrefering loops
to stabilize the growing cluster groups.

With our instruments we break the symmetry,
build up some neurons layers in a hierarchy,
and having done some satisfying simulation
we can observe a funny integration.

A neuron network finally constructed
wird for the Abschlußchecking angetaktet
to recognize reliably a letter
or solve a TSP problem a little better
as could be done by children in the Kindergarten.
Doch for a long time muß man auf die Lösung warten

Nevertheless it was a good sucess.
About Neuronennetze we have learned a mess.
And when we afterwards should meet again
wir werden schon the biggest progress sehen.
The neuron-nets will then schon Zeitung lesen
instead of us as artificial Wesen.

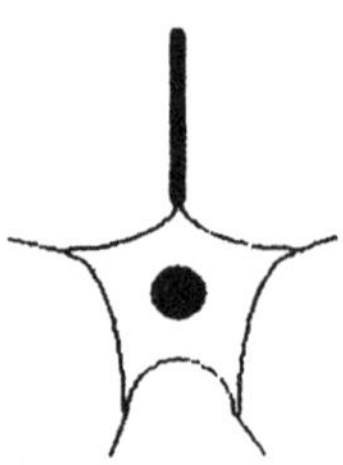

They will from boring thinking uns erlösen,
support us everywhere im Guten und im Bösen
and proudly we can then relax a bit
to plan in rest the allernächsten Schritt.
If we get out of our narrow holes
we can approach a lot of common goals.

March 1988, Eisenach

Yuri M. Svirezhev

Ecological and Demographic Consequences of a Nuclear War

1987. 112 pp – 17 cm x 24 cm – 45 tables
GDR 18,– M; abroad 18,– DM
ISBN 3-05-500193-1
Order number: 763 642 8
Order word: Svirezhev, Nuclear War 6975

The impact of a nuclear war upon ecological and demographic processes is estimated. The direct effect of nuclear detonations, the radioactive contamination of territories, the pollution by heavy metals and acid rain, as well as the effect of the sharp decline in temperature of the atmosphere ("nuclear winter") are taken into consideration. Estimated is the extent of destruction for the ecosystems of different types. The recovery of ecosystems is shown to be extremely slow or impossible. Demographic and genetic predictions for the nuclear war consequences are presented for various regions of the world. The book is intended for specialists in biology and applied mathematics, and for general scientific community as well.

Dynamical Systems and Environmental Models

Proceedings of an International Workshop cosponsored by IIASA and the Academy of Sciences of the GDR held on the Wartburg, Eisenach (GDR), March 17-21, 1986

Edited by Hans Günter Bothe, Werner Ebeling, Alexander B. Kurzhanski, Manfred Peschel

1987. 283 pp – 17 cm x 24 cm –
GDR 35,– M; abroad 38,– DM
ISBN 3-05-500334-9
Order number 763 719 9
Order word: Systems and Models 9044

The book contains the papers presented during the Workshop "Dynamical Systems and Environmental Models" which was organized by the Academy of Sciences of the GDR (Karl Weierstraß Institute for Mathematics) and the International Institute of Applied Systems Analysis. The aim of the workshop was the exchange of ideas between specialists in the theory of dynamical systems and experienced scientists working in the field of environmental models. Accordingly wide is the spectrum of the papers: It reaches from topics in theoretical dynamics which promise to become fruitful in application on the one end over general mathematical models for different kinds of evolutions to concrete dynamical models for environmental processes on the other end.

John S. Nicolis

Chaotic Dynamics Applied to Biological Information Processing

1987. 120 pp – 19 figures. – 17 cm x 24 cm
GDR 20,– M; abroad 20,– DM
ISBN 3-05-500377-2
Order Number 763 744 7
Order word: Nicolis, Dynamics 9067

Information processing aims at category formation in the (human) cognitive system or the classification of the external (and a good deal of the system's "internal") world in an hierarchy or abstract patterns. These patterns in turn may be used as algorithms for simulating observed physical processes.
In this paper we examine how this abstraction process may be dynamically implemented using the concepts of "Chaotic strange attractors".

Friedrich Recknagel

Applied Systems Ecology

Approach and Case Studies in the Aquatic Ecology

1988. approx. 130 pp – 56 figures – 6 tables – 17 cm x 24 cm –
GDR approx. 25,– M; abroad approx. 25,– DM
ISBN 3-05-500475-2
Order number 763 813 2
Order word: Recknagel, Ecology 9110

In the context of this book systems ecology will be comprehended as a connecting link between ecological phenomena, their scientific formalization, and their anthropogenous control on objectified fundamentals. The general approach suggested refers to the elements: real system, model, computer, and decision maker, for which adequate concepts are proposed. Within the framework of case studies the approach will be applied to different aquatic ecosystems such as waste stabilization ponds, lakes, and reservoirs. Great importance is attached to a wide spectrum of water quality management problems under consideration, thus checking soundness of the approach, particularly of the model concepts proposed.
To successively overcome contraints in handling uncertainties of ecosystems by simulation methods, new perspectives by using of AI-methods are pointed out by the hand of a deep expert system for water quality control of lakes and reservoirs.

Hans-Michael Voigt

Evolution and Optimization

An Introduction to Solving Complex Problems by Replicator Networks

1989. 236 pp – 83 figures – 17 cm x 24 cm
GDR approx. 40,– M; abroad approx. 48,– DM
ISBN 3-05-500617-8
Order Number 763 927 4
Order word: Voigt, Optimization 9177

The primary goal of this book is to present an introduction to solving complex problems by selection pressure controlled replicator networks.
The application is demonstrated by some combinatorial optimization problems (graph partitioning, modul placement, travelling salesman problem). Solution proposals for the layout design of integrated circuits and strategies for a mapping of process nets to processor networks for multiprocessor computer systems are included.

In preparation:

M. V. Galperin
The Applied Aspects of Marine Ecosystem Simulation

M. Peschel / F. Breitenecker
Evolution and Recursion

N. V. Stepanova / T. A. Petrova / O. A. Smirnova
Dynamical Models of Continuous Cell Populations

V. A. Vavilin
Biomass Turn-Over Time and Organic Matter Destruction